the calling card script

A WRITER'S TOOLBOX
FOR STAGE, SCREEN AND RADIO

the calling card script

the calling card script

A WRITER'S TOOLBOX
FOR STAGE, SCREEN AND RADIO

PAUL ASHTON

A & C Black • London

A & C Black Publishers Ltd

1 3 5 7 9 10 8 6 4 2

First published in 2011

A & C Black Publishers Limited
36 Soho Square
London W1D 3QY
www.acblack.com

A CIP catalogue record for this book is available from the British Library

ISBN 978 1 408 11017 1

Available in the USA from Bloomsbury Academic & Professional,
175 Fifth Avenue/3rd Floor, New York, NY 10010
www.BloomsburyAcademicUSA.com

Typeset by Country Setting, Kingsdown, Kent CT14 8ES

Printed and bound in Great Britain by Martins The Printers,
Berwick-upon-Tweed

FOR SUSIE, NIAMH, EMRYS
AND THE LITTLEST ONE TO COME . . .

CONTENTS

ACKNOWLEDGEMENTS

To my family for always supporting my work – taking me to the theatre, showing me great films, and having books around the house.

To Jenny Ridout for commissioning this book. To Julian Friedmann for selling it to Jenny. To Celia Brayfield for suggesting I talk to Julian. It was a serendipitous chain of events. To all at A&C Black and Blake Friedmann who helped this along the way behind the scenes. To the writers who so generously contributed their thoughts in quotable form – Jack Thorne, Joe Penhall, Toby Whithouse, Peter Moffat, Ashley Pharaoh, Matthew Graham, Sarah Daniels and Katie Hims.

To Kate Rowland and all the brilliant people I have worked with through BBC Writersroom – within the corporation and outside it – with a special mention for the dedicated script readers who are a mostly unsung and sometimes unfairly maligned team of talent-spotters. There are too many BBC people to mention individually – but thanks to anyone who ever agreed to read a script and consider a writer I recommended to them and then had the desire and confidence to commission and produce them. Also to the agents, literary managers and development people across the industry who ever gave me a good steer on new writers (Abigail Gonda is a particularly guilty party in this regard).

To the various (non-BBC) people and places that helped me hone my instincts with writers and new writing – the Arts Council, Spice Factory, Liverpool Everyman, Paines Plough, New Writing South, Theatre and Beyond, University of Sussex, NAW and the many theatre companies, universities, writers' networks and festivals that have provided me with willing audiences and sometimes difficult cues.

To those who have written about scriptwriting before me, in particular people cited in the Appendix. Anyone who claims to offer a complete swathe of utterly original, never-before-seen hints, tips, ideas and information for scriptwriters must surely be lying – or fooling themselves. Most of this stuff has probably been said before by someone else in some way, shape or form;

the job of any new book is to find a new perspective on it, a new way of organising it, and a new way of focusing and expressing it. And if you are lucky (or brilliant – or both) you will find yourself saying a few things that nobody else has thought to say. When I set out to write this book, I very deliberately avoided rereading scriptwriting books I had already read or seeking out ones I had not previously read because I wanted to feel sure that if I was going to come up with similar ideas (which I inevitably would at some point) then at least it would be a meeting of minds or a latent influence rather than a shameless regurgitation from a recent brush-up. That said, if I do accidentally borrow unacknowledged from anybody else, I feel reassured in the knowledge that they too will have borrowed.

To the thousands of writers whose work I have ultimately been responsible for rejecting along the way. It might seem strange and this may be little consolation to you, but the vast amounts of time spent trying to decide and express quite why your script didn't work has undoubtedly sharpened all my instincts and I am genuinely grateful for that.

To the many established writers (and other industry professionals) who have had the generosity of time and spirit to help inspire the emerging writers who I have spent so much time trying to bring through at the BBC.

Finally, to all the fantastic writers whose work I have had the fortune (and I hope insight) to spot and the desire to help. Again, there are too many to detail. But some of you I have referred to along the way in this book, so please do take that as the ultimate acknowledgment.

INTRODUCTION

Today, many professional writers are chameleons at some point in their career and work across mediums, formats and genres in order to survive, thrive and stay fresh. The climate at the time of writing this book (worldwide recession and a tightening of opportunities for scriptwriters) means that it's even more pertinent for writers to stay flexible and not be solely defined by only one medium or format. This book takes a uniquely broad perspective across all dramatic media, exploring the crucial differences and drawing together the universal similarities in writing drama for stage, radio and screen.

The 'how to' of writing scripts always has and always will divide opinion. Probably the only certainty is there are no hard and fast rules, only an ever-varying combination of talent, craft, technique, practice, effort and luck. Script development is an imperfect science, but many elements of the writing process are not a mystery. And while talent can't be taught in a classroom or acquired through reading a book, the application of understanding, craft, technique and approach can. It would take a pretty big ego to claim I have answers that nobody else has. But what you get here is a particular way of asking the questions that need to be asked by scriptwriters who are serious about their craft.

AN ACT OF FAITH

In drama commissioning, development and production across mediums and forms there are no secrets, no hidden agendas, no absolute rights, no absolute wrongs, and there is a huge range of disagreement about what is and is not good quality, worthwhile, entertaining, original or satisfying. Every decision, commission, green light and production is an act of faith in a writer's idea in some way, shape or form. Many resulting productions turn out to be something other or less than what was intended. But this doesn't render the decision-maker a fool or the producer a failure; it simply underlines not only the inescapable sense of risk in the industry, but also that essential act of faith.

It takes a brave person to put their head above the parapet to make top-line editorial, commissioning and production decisions. It's easy for un-produced aspiring writers to criticise things; it's much harder to improve on them. The only way to do so is by writing the kind of script that demands attention. Such scripts don't turn up very often and they don't appear out of thin air; they are a rare spark of idea and insight given form through craft and technique, fuelled by energy, sweat, distraction, despair, hope. They too are an act of faith.

THE 'TOOLBOX'

This book is a metaphorical box of tools to aid the inspired craftsman – whether you are a first-timer, or new to a specific medium, or experienced and looking to refresh what you do. It assumes that you truly believe you have a talent and an instinct for scripting drama, and that you are a writer with something to say. It can't and won't teach you how to acquire that intrinsic, inherent, inimitable talent; but it will help you build on it in order to write a script that the right people will enjoy enough to want to talk to you.

'Toolbox' denotes a very specific image – a collection of tools, each of which serves a very particular purpose in the daily work of the craftsman. I won't pretend that you can ever have a true scriptwriting toolbox from which you simply apply a tool to a problem and fix it. The tools of the script-writer's trade are strangely shaped, they do not apply to inanimate objects but to people, ideas, journeys, conflicts, resolutions, experiences, actions, events, desire, love, hope, need, anger, despair, empathy, insight, instinct. This book explores these strangely shaped tools of the storytelling trade.

If you think that simply kitting yourself out will solve every problem, think again; a craftsman's tools in the hands of a DIY disaster do not fix the problem, they exacerbate it or leave it looking like shoddy workmanship. This book is not just about using the tools, it is about acquiring the skill to use them, learning the trade, thinking like a craftsman. Thinking like a writer.

This book is not meant to be fully comprehensive – but essential. It is designed to be useful, usable, readable, with information broken down into bite-sized chunks. But it's not a crib or an easy way out. There are no easy ways out. It's not 'for dummies' or 'made easy'. Writing great scripts is always extremely hard. It is meant to be hard, otherwise it would not be a vocation so coveted or so worth pursuing. And while this book is designed to be user-friendly and not too dense, the material and ideas are complex, and it is intended to be rigorous because nothing to do with the scriptwriting process is easy. Everything that I expect you to ask of yourself is extremely demanding. No cribs. No easy ways out.

Also, this book is about the script as a blueprint because writers write scripts in order for them to be made; they are 'literature' in so far as we read them in order to produce them. Scripts are a stage in a process. Every dramatic medium is collaborative to a greater or lesser degree. Unless, that is, you plan on directing, producing, editing, acting and writing the score too. But we can't all be Vincent Gallo. And most professional writers write a script that other people will realise.

THE FORM OF THIS BOOK

The book is largely structured around the idea of beginnings, middles and endings – both in the story itself and the process of developing and writing it. But that shape is loose, not prescriptive. It's a way of organising the material, but it's not the only way of reading it and using it. If you have an idea and want to develop it into a script, the book will help you do that. If you want to dip into sections about, say, the medium of radio or writing scenes, you can do that too.

I offer no specific, overarching, all-encompassing or deceptively comforting theories. The problem with totalitarian theories is that if something doesn't fit then it either must be decried or ignored otherwise it is in danger of corrupting the theory. In this book, there may well be parts that conflict with one another and that's (hopefully) not because I'm incoherent and hypocritical but because they just do conflict – because things disagree, because nobody knows everything, because minds can be changed and developed and work in different ways to tackle the different problems that arise at different times. Like I say, it's an imperfect science. In fact, it isn't science at all.

WHAT THIS BOOK DOES NOT DO

This book is not about creative writing tips or exercises, nor about sitcoms, sketches, pitches, detailed treatments, the finer technicalities of script formatting, how to sell your idea, who to contact, how to get an agent, what it's like to work on a particular soap opera. There are plenty of other books and websites that can steer writers seeking out such information (see the Appendix); this one concentrates on writing the original script that tells a dramatic story and gets you noticed.

AN INDUSTRY PERSPECTIVE

This book is to a degree born out of my own experience as a (modestly) produced writer for stage and screen. But primarily it is born out of much greater experience of reading scripts, working with writers, developing ideas and voices, lecturing, workshopping, tutoring, and being one of those people who writers seek to impress by virtue of being a 'gatekeeper' in the industry. I ask questions of the writer in this book in the same way that I ask questions of the thousands of scripts that I have read across theatre, radio, film and television. When I say thousands, I really do mean thousands.

If you were to ask me what were the common or recurring problems with the majority of these scripts, my answer would be something along these lines:

> ➤ The writer isn't in control of the medium, often making fundamental mistakes and forcing basic errors regarding the form of their story.
> ➤ The writer isn't thinking clearly enough about who might want to produce their work and who the audience might be.
> ➤ Or: they are thinking far too hard about a potential commission and trying desperately (and pointlessly) to second guess what people want.
> ➤ The writer's individual voice doesn't shine through – the story isn't passionately told from a unique perspective.
> ➤ The writer isn't thinking hard enough about genre, tone and the kind of story they are telling.
> ➤ Or: they are thinking far too obviously about genre and slavishly applying a generic shape and form to an idea.

> ➢ The writer hasn't really clarified their idea and premise, what is distinct about them, what it is they fundamentally have to say about them.
> ➢ The writer hasn't got the story straight – they don't know where they are going and so begin and end in the wrong place and the wrong way.
> ➢ The characters are not strong, engaging, distinct, active, complex or vulnerable enough and I don't connect with them emotionally.
> ➢ The script does not hit the ground running and hook my attention.
> ➢ The story does not have a necessary shape and structure – a beginning, middle and end that really cohere and satisfy.
> ➢ The writer has begun writing the actual script too soon – before they have really thought about and gestated most of the above.
> ➢ The story gets lost in the middle – the direction confused, the momentum lost, the progress mired in quicksand.
> ➢ The characters do not grow and develop as the script develops.
> ➢ The story is not surprising as it progresses.
> ➢ The writer has a story and narrative but struggles to bring scenes to dramatic life.
> ➢ The writer does not voice the characters convincingly and authentically – the dialogue is awkward, on the nose, overly expository.
> ➢ The story does not reach a necessary, satisfying ending.
> ➢ The writer has not forced themselves to go back, look again and rewrite – they have not given themselves the space to get their script as right as they can before sending it out.
> ➢ Or: the writer has over-developed their script to death and rewritten all the personality out of it.

And finally, the thing that I find is increasingly common and perhaps the most demoralising of the lot:

> ➢ The writer has churned out a script (particularly for film) that looks like the real thing, that is polished and slick, that has probably benefited from workshops, courses and every structure book going – but that has no personality, no voice, no charm, no edge, no surprises, nothing original or distinct or unusual about it.

What you see here is an attempt to explore all these questions. This book is not about writing the kind of slick, polished article that looks like the kind of thing that could get made. Nobody really expects your signature script to be perfect, but they do want to be picked up at the beginning and swept on to the end. I have wasted far, far too much of my professional life reading meticulously formatted and utterly soulless scripts – there are too many of them swimming around. This book is about telling a great story in script form, not about somehow hoodwinking the script reader. There is no point mastering scriptwriting software or script formats until you've really started to think hard about what the story is and what you have to say for yourself.

POINTS OF REFERENCE

My primary field of reference is British stage, radio, film and television scripts – because it's where I work, it's what I know best, it's an industry that offers the possibility to work in all four mediums. It's also because contrary to the belief of a vocal few, British drama always has been just as brilliant and ambitious and original as anything else from anywhere else; the pedigree of the best of contemporary British theatre is rarely in doubt but, for example, television drama is often unfairly maligned for not being *The Wire* as if that is the only benchmark of quality (brilliant though it is).

But this field is also not narrow; it is eclectic and I would happily take in a Greek epic and a contemporary returning series drama for TV in the same breath because in the end they are both stories. The exception is that I refer somewhat less to produced radio dramas for the sole and simple reason that they are not easy to get hold of, either as published scripts or transmitted dramas, and therefore are not easy for the writer to refer back to. There is a reading list in the Appendix of the works I refer to most, and in the greatest detail.

THE 'CALLING CARD' SCRIPT

I focus on writing the original 'calling card' script that expresses your voice and gets you noticed; even if it is never produced, it can be the crucial thing that starts your conversation with people who make drama. The book is also designed to be useful on any script at any time because it seeks to raise the fundamental questions rather than prescribe narrowly defined templates or practice.

But what is a 'calling card'? When it is written well, it is a script that simply speaks your voice: it is interesting and engaging and intriguing and in some way unusual; it shows what you can do; it is an opportunity to be truly original; it shows the choices you make when you are not writing to a strict brief or commission; it demonstrates your skill and hints at your potential; it opens doors and starts a dialogue; it is the start of a writer's journey, not the final goal or end point of it; it is a means to any number of ends yet must not feel like it's been written solely to be expedient.

> *I actually wrote a number of scripts I thought were 'calling cards' –*
> *ones that I thought had depth and intrigue and were what people*
> *wanted to read. Turned out all were quite shit.*
>
> Jack Thorne

> *I just went for it, I didn't care how authored or mannered it*
> *sounded, if people liked it then they'd go for it. It made me confident.*
> *Find that place to be yourself.*
>
> Peter Moffat

A calling card script is not necessarily the first script you write. You must apply the same rigour to every script until you complete one that you feel speaks your voice. (And then you must apply the same rigour to everything you write thereafter too.) If you really want to write, then the calling card script must not be the only script you write. If all you have is one story – your story, or a 'passion piece' – then you are not really a writer, you are someone with one story.

You can write whatever kind of script you wish to write, but in practice some things will work better for you than others:

➢ For theatre, I think you can write with fewer restrictions – but much less than an hour and much more than two hours smacks of either lack of substance or lack of focus respectively.

➢ For radio, aim for a 45-minute single drama but don't fret if it ends up nearer 60; the Radio 4 'Afternoon Play' is by far the biggest window of opportunity, for which you can write all kinds of stories, though there are other slots.

➤ For film, much less than 80-minutes and much more than 120 again smacks of either not enough story or not enough control over the story – as well as a lack of understanding about the length of films that tend to be made and distributed.

➤ For TV, the hour-long episode is the ideal format; the ubiquitous soaps are in half-hours but writing the pilot episode of your own original soap is pretty suicidal in a calling card script and you're better off thinking about a returning series. The commercial broadcasters' hour-long slot is nearer to 45/50-minutes when the ad-breaks are factored in but don't write in ad-breaks, just write an hour's worth of TV story.

The script that got me noticed was a movie about a dragon egg hatching in Victorian London. It was outrageously big and expensive but it had a movie sensibility and it wasn't Letter to Brezhnev, *so at that time it was different.*

Matthew Graham

A BASIC DEFINITION

Before we go any further, I want to state a fundamental, essential, inescapable definition that should never be forgotten. The word 'drama' derives from the ancient Greek term 'δρᾶν', which means 'to do' or 'to act'. Drama quite literally is 'action'. The ramifications of this should become evident as we go. But understanding it at the start will set you off on the front foot.

THE WRITER'S EGO VERSUS THE WRITER'S JOURNEY

This book is for not for people who just want to 'be a writer'; it is for people who want to write better. It will not massage your creative ego; it will make you use your brain and flex your writing muscle. It is not a smooth path but a rocky road. It is not for those who simply want to know the fastest, easiest possible route to get them a commission, money, admiration and award nominations. It is for those who are ready and willing to go on a difficult journey every time they sit down to write. This thing is meant to be difficult. And as Matthew Graham so succinctly put it to me:

'You're always a hair's-breadth away from being shit.'

1
The Medium

THE WRITER AS MEDIUM

Many scriptwriters will in their career write for more than one dramatic medium. Therefore many will need to try to master various mediums – and not simply to be able to write competently for them but to write brilliantly for them, because the competition in each given medium is so utterly intense and dauntingly relentless.

'MEDIUM'

What is 'medium'? It is the place, person or means through which information is related – through which story is expressed.

What is 'a medium'? In one guise, it is the receptacle – a person – through which a spiritual world communicates with a corporal world.

So is a writer a medium? The means through which imagination (idea) is communicated in tangible form (text)? Maybe. Maybe not. It's not a clear and coherent metaphor, because 'medium' implies a passive receptacle and we expect writers to create and invent in proactive ways. But it does raise questions about what it is to be a writer and an author.

ONE MAN AND EVERY MAN

An author is a singular, distinct voice, with things to say and an identifiable way of saying things. Yet a dramatist must literally give voice to characters that are fictional personalities and creations to be played by actors. An original dramatic writer must in every way express themselves through other 'people'.

A great dramatic writer is, I think, a combination of both these things – or somewhere between the two. They are a person with something unique and engaging to say. They are also puppet-master who fabricates a dramatic reality. And the two are in friction, since writers must somehow fictionalise convincingly while retaining their own sense of voice and perspective.

WHAT WRITERS DO

Writers think about stories and writing all the time. They struggle to turn off. Writers *write*. They can't *not* write. (Yes, that is indeed stating the obvious. But it's amazing how many aspiring writers don't actually write very much, very regularly.)

Great dramatic writers write from the heart – but they remember that the audience is other people. Great writers write with a passion – stories keep them up at night, get under their skin. Great writers don't write to be expedient, but because they have great stories that must be told, heard, seen. Great writers have an instinct to tell stories that can't be taught, learned, begged, borrowed, bought, stolen or gleaned from a book like this. But they are also masters of craft in a process that never really ends, that they never wholly master, because for great writers there is always a new story, and every story means a new challenge. For great writers, it is an on-going occupation and vocation – a never ending climb up a steep mountain face towards a summit that is never quite reached.

INSTINCT AND CRAFT

If you don't have the instinct, the passion, the urge, then I don't think you can simply acquire it. You should never aspire to 'be a writer'. You should want to write, again and again and again – and therefore by dint of your storytelling instinct you become a writer. People disagree about what, in practice, is an accurate ratio of talent to craft, or talent to effort, or talent to luck. But talent is always going to be a small percentage. You can't be a great dramatist through talent alone.

Craft can be honed. Skills and resources can be taught, learned and developed. A toolbox can be filled, and be endlessly useful. There are some things that can't be acquired: the instinct and urge; the ability to 'hear' character voices; the ability to have an inspirational idea; and that thing people call 'a voice'. But the rest can be developed.

IS THE WRITER A MEDIUM?

Many will disagree with me, but I think the instincts and innate abilities des-cribed above are in some strange sense supernatural, beyond the ordinary –

a kind of communion with a kind of spirit world. Indefinable. Unquantifiable. Immeasurable. Fallible too. And reliant on a faith in storytelling and a faith in yourself as a storyteller. But in being a medium of story and stories, only so much is supernatural. The rest is honing craft, sharpening technique, developing an understanding, practising and practising again, writing and rewriting again, becoming self-conscious and self-aware, then making that reflexivity second nature through application.

Another way of phrasing it is: a great writer is a medium of storytelling magic who perfects their instinct through the practice of craft. As Marshall McLuhan's infamous phrase goes, 'the medium is the message'. Everything has form. Everything is mediated through form. There is no such thing as free-form drama.

USING MEDIUM

Writers who work across various forms and mediums can write for them in extremely different ways. They recognise that different mediums allow them to do different things in very different ways and utilise that difference to tell their stories. The best writers will also challenge and develop the medium because they have understood it and are mastering their craft to manipulate it. But to reinvent a medium or form you must first master its received conventions – and you should respect them, even if you don't necessarily like, agree with or apply them.

THE THEATRICAL SPACE

WHAT IS THEATRE?

The term 'theatre' derives from the ancient Greek word, Θέατρον, literally meaning a 'place for viewing'. Which tells us everything – and nothing.

I'm going to state the obvious – in a roundabout way. You pick up a theatre brochure, spot a show that looks interesting. You buy tickets, book a babysitter, eat out before the performance. At the theatre you buy a drink, read the programme, perhaps buy a copy of the script/text. You take your seat, turn your mobile phone off, get comfortable. You're in a room full of people (who you most likely won't know), all waiting. Lights fade to black.

You look at the stage, expectant. The play starts. You see actors pretending to be people in places that are represented by scenery and props. There's an interval, you get another drink, chat about what you've seen, nip to the loo, rush back to your seat, watch the second half. At the end, you (probably) join the audience in applauding the actors and performance. And (hopefully) satisfied, you go home.

Everything about this experience is a self-conscious artifice. It is clear that a fiction is being engineered and experienced by all involved. That fiction and artifice is immediate, right in front of your eyes. This is what theatre is.

All fiction is artifice, but none so much, so immediately, so self-consciously so as theatre. As a writer, you shouldn't be afraid of this – you can embrace it and use it. It's your job (and that of the whole company) to inspire the willing suspension of disbelief in your audience, even though everything around them screams 'pretence'.

MAGIC, RITUAL AND SPECTACLE

Theatre is the oldest, most venerable dramatic medium. Looking at our current picture of West End smashes / flops, national theatres, new writing theatres, regional reps, fringe pub theatres, public subsidies and commercial operations, it's easy to forget what theatre was before it became an 'industry'.

Theatre derived and developed out of the need of societies and communities to hold a mirror up to their experience, to commune with a higher sense of being and spirituality, to create magic and delight, to participate in a ritualised event in which the audience – and their society/community – would undergo some form of catharsis, of purging and purification – where an audience could laugh, cry, gasp, cower and sing together.

Modern theatre has developed on a long way from this. But the best writers will understand that there is something magical, spectacular and ritualistic about the bringing together of an audience to see a play. Not all great plays will necessarily express or explore this dynamic in a conscious way. However, as a writer, never forget the power of magic, ritual and spectacle.

SPECTATOR AND AUDIENCE

Spectacle is about what can be seen. The audience is the spectator. Though perhaps a better term than 'spectacle' is 'experience' (theatre is no less of a spectacle to the blind or partially sighted). Theatre means creating a 'show' – an event. Spectating means experiencing a show in the here-and-now – live – with a specific group of other people, never to be replicated, never to be exactly the same again. Theatre is not a static medium. It is fluid, plastic. The show you see will be unlike every other, even if in only one small detail. The 'mood' in the room can change the experience.

It is crucial for the writer to remember what being an audience in theatre means: real, present, uncontrollable but malleable, willing to be transported but hard to please. The audience can change a performance. The success of the play is reliant on the audience's engagement and compliance; their collusion is a kind of contract you enter into at every performance. At its best the atmosphere in the auditorium can crackle with excitement and anticipation; at its worst, it is utterly deadening. The writer can't control it. But in your play, you can engage with it – and you can manipulate it.

Complicity is crucial, because it takes us back to the early religious, spiritual, ritual significance of theatre. For the collective catharsis in the ritual to occur, the audience must give themselves up to the experience. Without this, it is just people watching performers pretending to be other people.

AUDITORIA

The relationship between audience and performance very much depends on the kind, size and layout of the theatrical space. You can find extreme intimacy in a small studio, spectacular grandeur in a Greek amphitheatre, and everything else in every other space in between – encapsulation in-the-round, the framed picture of a proscenium arch, the alternative relationship in a site-specific show, even the feel of being within the action of a promenade piece. Think about what your story is, what its physical and emotional scale is, and where it would best connect with an audience. I've seen a monologue that worked beautifully in a studio turn to dust on a big stage – equally, a big show strangled to death when squeezed into a small playing space.

THE COMPLEXITY OF SPACE

Space isn't just about the physical relationship between character and character, character and set, play and audience – it is also about the emotional and imaginative experience of the audience. In theatre, you are given a space in which to conjure up an experience that moves, inspires and challenges the spectators. You're not simply blocking out movement and action – this is what a mediocre director will do. Rather, you are creating a world. It's easy to be constricted by physical space and logistics – but when your emotional and imaginative boldness is constricted, you stop being a writer and you become a stage manager of words. Be a writer. Be bold.

THE COMPLEXITY OF FORM

This is the tension, perhaps contradiction, at the heart of theatre. Theatre can be the most physically delineated, confined and restricted of storytelling arenas, yet it can also be the most free, fluid and mutable of forms, offering the most imaginative and emotional potential available to a writer. If you can embrace the contradiction and keep writing, then you can become a true dramatist for the stage.

THE EMPTY SPACE

In modern Western theatre there are two views at seemingly opposing ends of the spectrum of what theatre can and should be. One of them, the 'empty space', finds its chief advocate in director Peter Brook, and asserts that the power in theatre comes not from a space filled with noisy, bright, busy spectacle but from one which may be filled simply by the presence of actor, moment, emotion and a minimum of physical props; where a chair can be made to represent anything the director, company and audience wishes it to represent; where technology can be a seductive smokescreen that masks the inefficacy of idea, story, character, relationship, drama and theatrical experience.

It is a powerful thesis in that it perhaps purports the ultimate willing suspension of disbelief. I have seen brilliant theatre that has kept to a beautiful minimalism and purity of space. And not just small-scale work for a small cast – a fantastic production of *King Lear* by Kit and Kaboodle

Theatre Company squeezed into the tiny Unity Theatre in Liverpool with few props and a powerful ensemble performance. Because of the nature of the playing space, many productions in the RSC's Swan Theatre tend to go light on design, props and technology. Shakespeare's Globe, in its replication of the Elizabethan playhouse experience, makes a virtue of eschewing complexity of design. These are not quite what Brook means by the empty space, though, because he is also concerned with the kind of story and play, the kind of theatrical and emotional experience, and not simply a clearing out of design, set, technology and elaborate props.

THE TECHNOLOGICAL SPACE

At the opposite end of the spectrum is theatre that takes spectacle and theatricality to a new, other level. Canadian director Robert Lepage is perhaps the most obvious advocate and his too can be a powerful thesis. The epic *Seven Streams of the River Ota* wove an intricate tapestry through glimpses into an array of lives somehow connected by the River Ota as a symbol of fertility. It was a stupendously imaginative show, from its Noh Theatre shadow puppetry, to the backstage chaos of a French farce being played before a Japanese audience, to a literal cross section of a New York apartment building, to a heartbreakingly simple scene of euthanasia played out behind glass screens through which the audience could barely hear the dialogue.

When the curtain call came at the end, I was amazed that the cast and crew was so small for a show that was so big; I simply didn't believe it could be possible. Lepage also performed a one-man version of *Hamlet* that mostly took place inside a revolving cubic structure; it was a brilliantly strange and original experience (though the opening performance, the first event of that year's Edinburgh International Festival, was a celebrated disaster when the cube failed to revolve).

Lepage will use technology and design that he feels can bring either a fresh insight to old material or a fresh take on theatre itself. And he's not alone. In a technologically advanced world, it somehow seems a little perverse to wilfully ignore what technology can bring to story.

THE CLARITY OF SPACE

They are not really utterly opposed camps. Rather, they are just extreme modes of practice, two choices about what will work, what will engage an audience, what will affect an audience. The point for the writer is that while you may aspire to create theatrical magic, complexity and wonder, your script should aspire to set forth clarity and perhaps simplicity, not obfuscation and complication.

My own play *Cued Up* played to a teenage audience (the hardest kind, believe me – though also the best). When it was commissioned and developed, the producer/director asked me to be bold with space. I was given one major restriction – ideally there were to be no more than three actors. And also the restriction of an easily installable set which could be taken on tour. The play I wrote moved swiftly between locations that included the Notting Hill Carnival, a dilapidated East End house, a residential hostel, a stolen car and a deserted beach. The designer achieved this metaphorically with a simple, non-realistic structure that represented these settings. And so rather than being stuck in one realistically dressed room/set, the audience was taken on a physical, even slightly filmic journey with the characters.

When I asked the director how specific I should be when describing the setting and action, he said keep it simple – he usually ditches all the stage directions anyway when he gets into the rehearsal room with the actors. He did rightly promise, however, not to change any dialogue without my express permission. As a writer, this was all both scary and liberating. Scary in that I couldn't hide behind lots of words and dramaturgical detail; liberating in that I could write what I wanted within a few defined limits and we would then work out how to make it happen.

MONEY, MONSTERISM AND MINIATURISM

In your calling card script there is no budget and no brief, no restrictions on cast size, set, or technological requirements. However, if you really want this to get made and are even willing to try to mount a production on a small scale yourself, then realities, restraints, practicalities and logistics come very much into play.

There is a recent movement and collective of 'Monsterist' playwrights who are sick of making small choices and instead want to make bold ones, leading to plays on a grand scale such as Rebecca Lenkiewicz's exploration of suffragism in *Her Naked Skin* at the National, or Richard Bean's family saga spanning a century on an East Yorkshire farm in *Harvest* at the Royal Court.

Yet there is also an increasing 'miniaturism' in the form of writers, directors and actors with no money putting on readings, showings and productions with a minimum of scale, or writers delving into short-form theatre.

This is the hard choice for the early stage playwright. Be big and bold or be focused and doable? Well, it is possible to do both. You can be bold within severe limitations. And no amount of screen projection, holographs, VJs, DJs, flashing lights and hydraulic sets will compensate for characters and story that do not engage. The reason *Seven Streams* worked was due to the intense, focused attention to character amidst the ambition of scale and design. And a lot of small studio-space plays are barely worth seeing because the characters are not worth spending the time with. (But then neither are they in many a big, brash West End production.)

Fundamentally, you don't have to worry about whether your script will get made at this point. I always say to write the play you want to write and to hell with the realities, the theatrical politics and the chances of it getting made. You won't get commissioned later for having played it safe in the beginning, when the only person reining you in was yourself.

THE DIRECTOR

The director can be your greatest challenge, your biggest headache, and yet your most valuable asset (and friend). In some ways, especially in dedicated new writing companies, theatre is the writer's medium. But in more recent history, it has become as much a director's medium. If the playwright is dead, this is less of a problem. But if the writer is, like you, alive and well then it's a more complex relationship. Every writer's style will differ, but it's worth remembering that directors can and will feel restricted by lengthy, unnecessarily detailed stage directions; they enjoy the scope to bring their own vision and mercurial touch to your play. When it works, it's magical. When it doesn't, it's despairing – and invariably it's the writer and play that will come away feeling and looking worst off for the experience. The more open you are to the potential in the collaborative medium, perhaps the less likely it is that you will write yourself into a corner.

Whether apocryphal or not, the story goes that when Harold Pinter directed his own plays he drew a sharp distinction between the two roles of writer and director, and in rehearsal referred to 'what the writer might intend' rather than 'what I mean'. Not many writers are capable of successfully, objectively directing their own writing. Do yourself a favour: think like a writer, not a director. And if you do want to direct your own work, then you need to learn to be a director – and this is most usefully done by first directing other writers' plays rather than your own.

THE ACTOR

We've always needed great actors (obviously). They aren't always easy to control or keep consistent. I had to discipline a very experienced actor for messing around on stage – but the night he brilliantly ad-libbed his way out of a big hole dug by a forgetful stage manager was the moment I realised how indispensable he was. In theatre, you are reliant on actors in a way alien to radio, film or TV, because once the play starts there is little you can do from the comfort of your seat. But if you create characters that actors can really sink their teeth into, they'll probably love you for it and veer less from what you have actually written than they otherwise might.

DIRECTING THE ACTION

As a writer, you direct the action rather than direct the play or direct the director. Stage directions in ancient theatre and classical English theatre were traditionally sparing, simple, affecting the action rather than describing the set. And this is because an elaborate 'set' is a relatively modern phenomenon.

Extremely detailed description came to the fore in the realist works of Ibsen, Strindberg and Shaw, though this was more to do with setting the scene rather than a continuously dense dramaturgy throughout the play. I'm not sure stage writing has quite recovered from this – at least not in the work of anxious, aspiring, precious, protective writers who have not practically engaged with the production process. The simple fact is that dense stage directions are usually not good to read; they are somehow alien to the usual purpose of a stage script, which is to show the action. Directors hate them, actors hate them, designers hate them.

Thankfully experienced dramatists tend to know better and to have more faith in what they do with character, story and space, so that they do not need to rely on overwriting the stage directions.

Read Gary Owen's *Shadow of a Boy* and you will see spare, minimal stagecraft in all its pregnant glory. The point is that plays are written to be played. It's not the playwright's job to weigh the script down with unnecessary words. It's the playwright's job to craft a play that will *play*.

THEATRE AND METAPHOR

Theatre is also the place where metaphor can inhabit a space and grow. In film, if you point a camera at a dead bird then it remains a dead bird and no amount of pointing will really change that. In theatre, a dead bird can become a symbol, a metaphor that grows and develops and deepens by its continued presence. Chekhov's *The Seagull* is not about a seagull, even though there is an eponymous dead seagull in it. *The Seagull* is about the death of dreams, ideals, ideas and aspirations in both the asphyxiating boredom of a provincial town and the destructive anonymity of a big city. This only works in theatre because only in theatre does the metaphor grow and linger in the physical and theatrical space.

RADIO AND THE ACOUSTIC ENVIRONMENT

'THEATRE OF THE AIRWAVES'

If you ever hear anyone suggest that radio drama is the 'theatre of the airwaves', strike it from your memory and consign it to the dustbin of poor understanding in which it deserves to remain. Quite how the form, medium and experience of theatre might translate and transpose to audio broadcast, I'm not exactly sure. Many (though not all) writers are able to write well for both forms. Beyond this, the main similarity between the two is that it's much more likely that a writer will get an original idea before an audience in theatre and radio than in film or TV.

CINEMA OF THE AIRWAVES

This is also an imperfect way of simplifying the form and medium – but I think it's much closer to what you as a writer could be thinking. The most powerful radio has the ability to provoke lasting images in the mind, and this is akin to the visual scope of cinema. If you can apply the potential fluidity, scale, scope, visual imagination and ambition in the best cinema to your radio writing, then you will be setting off on the front foot rather than finding yourself sinking in a quicksand of words, words and more words.

THE CONTRADICTION

There is an inherent contradiction in scriptwriting for radio: you are utterly reliant on the effect and power of words, in particular dialogue/monologue writing, but story and drama can quickly be smothered and weighed down by too many words, too much dialogue – heavy blocks of monologue and 'speeches'. The reason for the reliance is because you only have the sense of hearing and the medium of sound through which to tell your story. You can't use literal visual images and physical relationships as you can in theatre, film and TV. Radio is purely acoustic, purely audio, and sets a constant challenge.

AUDITORIUM

The radio audience's auditorium can be any number of places on the surface – anywhere you can receive and amplify a signal, or listen again online. But actually, the true auditorium of radio is in the head and in the mind – the space into which the ears channel the sound. For radio more than any other medium the success of the play depends utterly on its ability to stimulate the private auditorium that each listener individually possesses. When you become a passive, casual listener of radio drama, you are essentially not hearing, not listening, not in the auditorium, and it will wash over you, as soon forgotten as it is heard.

THE PUREST FORM

Perhaps there's no such thing as a pure or purest form. But for the scriptwriter, radio is certainly the most naked dramatic form – the one in which your words either stand up and carry the whole production, or buckle under their own dead weight. There are few other distractions, no places to hide, and only so much that a director, producer or engineer can do to mask a poor or workmanlike script. So if it isn't the purest form, then perhaps it is the one in which the purities and impurities are most starkly and candidly on display. Brilliant when it works, leaden when it doesn't.

THE AUDIENCE

Another reason why it is the most naked form is because the medium tends to define the audience experience narrowly. In the past, before the ubiquity of TV, families did listen to radio together. A testament to the power of that experience is the story of the Orson Welles radio production of *War of the Worlds*, which when it began wasn't framed as a fiction and so set off a panic in many a listener (as recaptured in Woody Allen's film *Radio Days*). But increasingly radio drama is something people tend to listen to alone.

Here lies another contradiction. It is the most intimate, direct and therefore naked of mediums, and yet because it is unusual for it to be experienced in group settings, it is almost impossible to measure how affecting that intimacy is, because it's more difficult than with other mediums to observe, feed off, share with, experience with. As a writer, you can get deep into the audience's head – yet you will never really get to see them being an audience. This isn't as true of radio comedy, which is frequently recorded before a live audience; but radio drama will tend to remain a leap into the unknown, measurable only by listening figures or letters, calls and emails of praise or complaint.

ONLY FOR RADIO

You should always ask yourself if your idea is something that would only really work on radio – or would work best and most powerfully on radio. What if your story is set on a chaotic battlefield in the middle of a dense fog? Or in the Gobi desert in a sandstorm? Or a black hole in outer space? What if? It may be you would never get the money to shoot these settings with a camera crew. It may be that the listener's mind is the ideal canvas on which to project them. The radio version of *The Hitchhiker's Guide to the Galaxy* will in my opinion always be the best – nothing looked cheap, nothing was cut due to excessive expense, the characters and settings always 'looked' like you expected them to in your head, and anything was possible, no matter how weird.

ACOUSTIC ENVIRONMENT

Radio isn't about sounds and SFX (sound effects) so much as it is about significant sound and acoustic environment. Here's an example of SFX:

> *The sound of a car engine rumbling away. The car slows and stops.*
> *Handbrake on, engine off. Door opens, then closes. Door locked.*
> *Footsteps. Gate creaks open and shut. Footsteps down garden path.*
> *Key in door lock, door opens, then clicks shut. Footsteps down corridor.*
> *Kettle switched on and kettle boils. A tinny radio is turned on.*
> *A mobile phone rings.*

So, a lot of SFX. But really, nothing at all of significance has happened – except perhaps, potentially, the mobile phone ringing. Every other sound signifies nothing of meaning – no story. They are just noises. It is amazing how much time and energy new writers can waste on meticulous detailing of SFX to no dramatic end. It is usually more powerful to simply state the acoustic environment, get on with the scene and story, and allow the producer and sound engineer to do the rest.

SCOPE

On radio, you can be fantastically bold with ideas. You can literally do things and go places that would be impossible or expensive in another medium. And not just physical things and places. You can go into the womb with an unborn baby. Into the conscious head of a physically inert 'coma' patient (though this has been done a great deal now). To the centre of the earth. Into the guilty part of a character's conscience. In radio, there is unique imaginative scope and potential. In any other medium, such things might appear very odd – yet in radio, they don't appear half so strange.

You can work on the grandest scale imaginable or go direct to the most intimate part of a character and audience's mind. You can be ambitious. You can be fluid in the storytelling and challenge the audience's sense of disorientation because they only have one sense with which to orient themselves.

You can explore the physical and subtextual space between words. You can make silence truly silent. You can't read a character's facial expression – but you can play with the intrigue around what they mean by what they say. You can help the audience create their own unique personal visualisations rather than simply laying it out on a plate for them. The acoustic environment is a unique storytelling arena.

VOICE

Some assume that words and dialogue are the most crucial thing in radio. I would say, rather, that it is voice. The character's voice is truly crucial. It is what we use to filter their personality, the drama and much of the action. How the voice communicates with us will set the tone, feel, pace, rhythm, experience of the play.

Many plays are, like much theatre, film and TV, made of realistic 'exterior' action and dialogue, where characters interact and the drama is in the tangible external world. But you need not be limited by this.

Voice over (VO) is very hard to achieve because action on radio barely exists without voices of some kind, therefore it will be a 'voice over voices', and that way potential confusion lies. But you can go 'close', rather like in a theatrical soliloquy, where you can hear what other characters can't, where you are privy to a direct line into a character's head, thoughts, feelings, opinions, point of view.

You can write monologue, where everything we hear is from one voice. This is extremely hard to do well and needs to be dramatic – not simply to relate or explain the story, but to live and breathe the story in the moment. You can write 'narration' – but again be careful. Don't write a blank, expository narration: great narrators are subjective, have voices, opinions and are not necessarily trustworthy. You can use voiced epistles – letters. You can use voiced diary.

Language is crucial. Not just words, but how a voice is characterised and expressed – as in Lee Hall's *Spoonface Steinberg*, in which a young girl who is dying has a language that is poignantly all her own.

Language is everything. And you can interplay between any and every different form if that is the most effective way to tell your story and voice your characters. As Katie Hims says, 'A voice can inspire a story in the same way that a face can.'

MUSIC

Don't underestimate the power of music to express, underscore, underline, counterpoint, contradict and undercut your story and characters. A well-chosen movement, aria, song, refrain, beat and rhythm can tell the story of a thousand words and express a gamut of emotions. But again, keep it simple, clear, specific and meaningful. Think hard about what the music is saying, because on radio music says a great deal. It isn't just background – it's as powerful as a broad vista of landscape is on the big screen.

SOUND

Radio isn't just about sound. It is about significant sound. Sound that is intrinsic. Story driven sound. Part of the texture and fabric of your world rather than just a bunch of SFX. Sound that means something, that says something, that tells the story – that resonates uniquely in each listener's head.

FILM AND THE CINEMATIC CANVAS

THE BIG PICTURE

The arrival of the movies marked a revolution in dramatic storytelling. When the Lumière brothers publicly screened their first films in the late nineteenth century, one in particular caused havoc. A short film of a steam train arriving at a station – and seemingly heading towards the camera – convinced the audience that it was about to burst through the screen, and they fled in panic. Whether true or apocryphal, this brilliant moment tells us two things: a live audience, as in theatre, is a fundamental part of the cinematic experience; and cinema has the curious, perhaps magical potential to make us believe that what we are seeing on the screen is quite literally real.

'Cinema' is an abbreviation of *cinematographe*, the term coined by the Lumière brothers which in turn derives from the ancient Greek, μετακίνηση, and means 'movement'. Cinema is all about movement and action, from the film running through the projector to the momentum of the story.

THE THEATRICAL RELEASE

Film, like theatre, is designed to play before a live audience. In cinema, you can't change the performance on celluloid, but the audience can dictate the mood in the room and there are films that truly bring an auditorium to life: singing the theme tune to *Ghostbusters*, holding back that teary gulp in *E.T.*, collective shock in a horror film, infectious belly laughter in a comedy. It's not just that the song is fun, the scene sad, the horror terrifying or the comedy hilarious; the audience takes it to a whole other level. So make the most of the potentially full screening-room. The movies can in their own way be as much a ritual experience as theatre; the audience can seek the same level of 'catharsis', of relief and release.

CINEMA SCOPE

Technically, in CinemaScope, new lenses were developed to expand the wide-screen image in projection. Cinema is essentially designed to fill the frame, to occupy your field of vision. Cinema should wash over you. Theatre has an inherent flexibility; an audience can be seated and moved around so that spectators are self-consciously aware of one another, and differently aware of the play before them. But the flat screen and the rows of audience seating in cinema are designed so that approximately the same view washes over all of us as we collectively stare up at it.

The writer and director must frame the action for us – that frame, and the canvas within it, is potentially huge. The scale of ideas, visuals and emotions is potentially limitless. Moreover, special effects and CGI technology mean the screen can still represent what a camera cannot literally capture. So be bold. Don't write glorified TV for a big screen. Write big ideas and big themes. Fill the frame – dramatically, visually and emotionally.

'I learned a lot from writing The Road. *I finally understood a few things about scope and scale. The cinema screen is sixty foot wide . . . You need to fill that with something worth seeing. You do need to think big. I was raised on small talkie indie films – which I still love. But I can't help thinking now that film is a huge, broad canvas – and its wasted if you think small.'*

Joe Penhall

KNOWING YOUR PLACE

It's fair to say that cinema is a director's medium. Writers generally speaking have less ultimate influence, control and say in the production and post-production process (unless, that is, you are a writer-director – although many directors will have to defer to studio executives). But it's also fair to say that the more brilliant and compelling your script is, the less need there might be to interfere with what you have created.

Film scripts, along with TV scripts, require a level of acquired technical skill and craft that tends not to come naturally to anyone. Put two characters together in a moment of conflict or tension, and you have a dramatic scene. But for the screen, you need to clearly specify interior/exterior, place, time and employ a range of standard and required format shorthands that are there not simply to tell the story but to tell a production team how to cost, schedule, prepare and set a film shoot in order that it runs as smoothly and therefore as economically as possible.

The challenge you face is to make this strange format language as absorbed and second nature as possible, without your script 'directing' from the page with interminable over-writing of scenes and jargon (CU, ECU, SMASH CUT, TRACKING SHOT, DOLLY SHOT, PAN, LONGSHOT, CRANE SHOT, PULL BACK ad infinitum). Don't direct the camera angles from the page – that is the preserve of director and cinematographer. Direct the action – tell the character story, show us what the drama is, present what is done and said.

'SHOW DON'T TELL'

Everybody will tell you this. And that's because they are right. Although it's a mantra more easily trotted out than put into practice – or done well. It's all about remembering that film is a visual form and medium. As they say, a picture can tell the story of a thousand words. Don't explain the drama, story, action, plot, emotions and themes through expository, explanatory dialogue that is employed solely for that purpose. Show it through visual storytelling. This basic principle is fundamental in great cinema.

Nicolas Roeg's *Walkabout* is a brilliant piece of cinema with little dialogue and two central characters who are simply unable to communicate with words. Look also at the bulk of Spielberg's *Castaway*, where a man is stranded alone on a desert island, with nobody to speak to and therefore little reason to say anything.

SIGN LANGUAGE

Cinema is the medium in which image can have a particularly resonant meaning and effect. A pram tumbling down steps in *Battleship Potemkin*; the shimmering speck on the horizon of *Lawrence of Arabia*; the dancing brown-paper bag in *American Beauty*; the fertility patterning in *Alien*; the red coat in *Schindler's List*; the shower of frogs in *Magnolia*; even the train as it enters the tunnel at the end of *North by Northwest*. You have the potential to fix a meaningful image (or symbol) in an audience's vision, understanding and memory. It takes a smart writer to make image, idea and story cohere. Is there a visual code that unifies and expresses meaning in your story without being clunky and clumsy.

UP CLOSE

In close-up on a big screen you are able to see, dissect and reach behind an image. On a big screen you can see every crease and wrinkle that time, experience and stress have etched into an old face, and you can see the beautiful unblemished purity of a young face as yet unspoiled by life. You will see this in much greater detail in film than in any other medium. You will also see the minutiae and tiny nuances of expressions that tell a story and express a character without a word being said. But, such things are extraordinarily difficult to write – there needs to be an action preceding, following, surrounding, contextualising it. Remember to only write what an actor can play and show. Asking them to somehow chart the progress of shock to horror then despair and finally resignation in a single moment/ expression is nonsense (believe me, I have read exactly such 'action' in screenplays). Giving them a small, simple action through which to filter that progress will give their physical expression an emotional meaning.

In *Fargo*, Jerry takes a deal to his father-in-law that he believes will solve all the money troubles he is keeping secret; but Wade won't just give Jerry the money he so desperately needs and so he is cut out of the deal. Jerry walks back to his iced-up car, which sits alone in the middle of a deserted car park, and begins methodically scraping the ice away from the windscreen. As he scrapes, he just cannot control his frustration any more and takes it out with the scraper on the car in a childish fit of impotent temper. Once the tantrum has passed, he goes back to his methodical scraping. In that simple act and moment, we see a whole married lifetime of the frustrations that have left him in a position where his only option now is a wild, crazy plan that will end very badly indeed.

MONTAGE

A montage isn't really something you write, it's what a director and editor do – a stringing together of shots, moments, pictures, images, symbols, actions that sum up a section of story or passage of time. It's narrative shorthand. What's important for the writer is the ability in film to leap forward and get to the next significant scene. Writers normally overestimate how much they need to explain and show in order to orient their audience. Don't montage your way out of a hole in the plot or lack of substance in the story. In fact, you should never need to 'write' a montage at all. But remember how fast, fluid and free you can be in moving your story forward. Show, don't tell; but don't show everything.

THE WHOLE STORY

Fundamentally, cinema works best for the one-off telling of a single story. Even if it is part of a sequence – *The Godfather, Star Wars, Lord of the Rings* – each should stand up in its own right as a satisfying experience. Therefore the skill you must master is that of crafting the single, closed, complete, coherent, satisfying narrative. There is a big industry around sequels, prequels, 'the early years' and spin-offs because when an idea and characters work, the audience want to see more and the industry wants to make a sure bet profit out of it. But the screenwriter doesn't really master the art of writing a sequel – only that of a single story (with perhaps the added bonus of a cheeky open ending). This is why the 'hero's journey' from Western epic poetry has become the mainstay of film story structure.

THE COMPLEX SINGULARITY

While the hero's journey is a universal story shape, it can be played in an infinite number of ways, and cinema embraces complexity and sophistication of narrative structure more than any other medium – whether it's the playfulness of *Fargo*, the simultaneously reverse/forward structure of *Memento*, the broken flashbacks of *Reservoir Dogs*, the Act One swerve in *Psycho*, the expansive flashback of *The Godfather II*, the repetition of *Groundhog Day*, the fluidity of *Eternal Sunshine of the Spotless Mind*, the tripartite form of *Amores Perros*, the wholly non-linear structure of *21 Grams* or the multi-stranded worlds of *Short Cuts*, *Magnolia* and *Crash*. There's never a need to be complicated for the sake of it, but if it's intrinsic to your idea and story, then the big screen is the most exhilarating place to challenge the audience with narrative, structural and temporal complexity.

THE KIND OF STORY

Most of the films above are instances of a genre given a fresh take or spin. *Fargo* is set up as a 'thriller' and 'true story' but is neither; *Psycho* a thriller in which the apparent heroine is killed off before the halfway point; *Groundhog Day* a romantic comedy in which the first date happens again and again and again; *Reservoir Dogs* a heist movie in which we never actually witness the heist; *Memento* a detective story in which the detective can't remember the information he has just uncovered.

It's fair to say that film, the audience's understanding of it and the producer's ability to sell it, has a fundamental relationship with genre. It is often the mark of a strong writer that they understand, embrace and then challenge genre; it is as often the mark of an inexperienced one that they resist, fail to understand and fail to master or challenge genre (often, ironically, while they claim to be reinventing it). Don't see genre as a reduction or belittling of your ideas – see it as a way of defining your story and reaching an audience. The films above are so good that they reinvent genre while embracing it wholeheartedly. In film, you need to be able to think in genre terms – otherwise you are unlikely to get your script developed seriously, never mind produced, distributed and seen by an audience likely to engage with it. Genre is of course important for every medium – but it's especially important when attracting an audience into cinemas.

UNIVERSAL

Great film stories can appeal, travel and translate across languages, cultures, countries, territories and continents. Again, it's about an audience being able to understand what kind of story you are telling and quite how it might connect and relate to their own life and experience. Think about whether your story, no matter how particular the cultural specifics, has the potential to reach, touch, engage and speak to an audience anywhere in the world. Film is absolutely the most universal form – when, that is, the storytelling is as visual as the story is universal.

> *'It's a weird medium. High art and bubblegum together. Church and whorehouse all rolled into one. It's hard to know just how seriously to take it. If politics is showbiz for ugly people, then film is art for crazy people.'*
>
> Joe Penhall

TELEVISION AND THE RELENTLESS FORMAT

There are two key elements to contemporary TV drama writing: the relentlessness of the storytelling and the format in which the story is presented. The two are inextricably linked and pretty much unavoidable.

Why relentless? Because the way we watch, experience, consume TV drama tends to dictate the constant need to keep us, the audience, hooked.

Why format? Because all TV is format. No TV programme exists that doesn't also set forth a format. Soap, classic adaptation, docu-drama, news, weather update, game show, chat show, documentary, consumer show, sports coverage, magazine show and every variation in between is a format or sub-format, a genre or sub-genre, of TV programming.

DISTRACTIONS

In theatre and film we make a date with a story. In radio, the ubiquity of the BBC means there is little other radio drama to choose from. In TV, stories constantly vie with one another to grab our attention, each under constant threat of being turned over, turned off or stored for viewing later.

In the ritual experience of an auditorium there is normally a collective focus. In the ritual experience of TV viewing, potential distractions are legion – the people you watch it with, the people who are doing other things while you watch, the people who phone you halfway through a programme, the meal you are simultaneously eating, the ad break, the cup of tea you plan to make during the ad break, the text message from the friend who is watching the same show in their home, the text message from the friend who is telling you there is something much better on another channel, the websites you are simultaneously surfing.

The possible and probable barrage of distractions varies from channel to channel, slot to slot, demographic to demographic, household to household, but it never really goes away. And as the volume and intensity of distractions have increased over time, so too has grown the volume of story required to keep an audience's attention above them.

THE MORNING AFTER

It's not just about the audience and experience on the night. TV broadcasters and producers examine the overnight audience figures published the next day. Audience figures are something of a dark art. They comprise data derived from around 5,000 random homes extrapolated to represent the range of the 25 million-plus TV households in the UK. Some mistrust them, but there is little else to utilise, so they are a necessity. They are not simply a measure of how many people watched a programme, they are also used to examine the proportion of different demographics watching it, how the figure rose or fell as compared with the last or a comparable instalment, and how it compares to what the broadcaster expected and hoped for.

Set against this is the AI – the Appreciation Index. This explains how much the audience that watched a programme actually enjoyed it. Disappointing viewing figures can be assuaged by a higher AI – and vice versa. For some, the AI is as important (if not more so) than simple audience numbers.

The truth is that the future of, for example, a series that has returnable potential may be decided early on in the season. Commissioner and network controllers don't necessarily wait until the end of the series to book the next season if the figures are chiming in with their own feelings about a show.

Commissioner and controllers want programmes that 'punch through' the schedule, that might have 'staying power', and that can become a 'brand'. Let's say that again without the jargon. They want programmes that truly stand out in a crowded array of channel schedules as *the* thing to watch, that might have the potential to return or spin-off (as *Torchwood* and the *Sarah-Jane Adventures* did from *Doctor Who*), and that will become more important in their own right and in the mind of their audience than the broadcaster that makes them (increasingly, younger audiences don't necessarily make as much connection between brand – say, *EastEnders* – and the channel it is on – BBC1).

The other thing to remember about shows deemed not to be performing in the overnights is that they can be shifted to another slot and effectively buried in the schedule. So even eventual transmission isn't a guarantee that your show will reach an audience in the way that it might or should.

THE COLD LIGHT OF DAY

The reality is that TV drama generally needs to perform instantly. The idea of a slow-burner that garners an audience through word of mouth is a retreating memory. Gone are the days when broadcasters would make a programme primarily because an in-house producer believed in it – now, their belief must have a demonstrable demand from an audience.

This doesn't mean that risks aren't taken. Every commission, green light and transmission is potentially an extremely expensive risk. But if your idea and writing is extremely ponderous, extremely niche, extremely expensive, extremely dense or extremely disrespectful of an audience's desire to be engaged and entertained then the chances of it being developed (never mind made) are extremely slim.

Why should anyone take a risk on you if your idea disregards what's essential about the medium? TV storytelling is more relentless than it's ever been. TV is not the place to indulge your creative peccadilloes. It is the place where you either engage an audience, or you fail.

Again, this doesn't mean inspired risks aren't being taken all the time and especially in the first series of a show: the manic world of *Shameless*; the youthful POV of *Skins*; the genre-bending of *Being Human*; the dark grubbiness of *Funland*; the scheduling over five consecutive nights of *Criminal Justice*; a soap-structured adaptation of *Bleak House*; the intense glare on the 'womb' of a hospital in *Bodies*; the unadulterated truth of *Sex Traffic*; the anthologised storytelling of *The Street* – each and every one a brave leap forward. Each relentless in the storytelling. Each clearly, brilliantly formatted.

THE SCHEDULE

In this dawning age of online viewing and TV on demand, the question being asked is: will the traditional schedule disappear altogether? Reports of its demise are perhaps exaggerated. Times are indeed changing, technology has advanced rapidly, and the habits of newer audiences are emerging. But it will take some time yet before the experience of selecting a channel to watch a programme dies out – not least because the older audience that tends to watch TV in the traditional manner is living longer.

New habits always emerge with new technology. With the growth of digital TV storage comes the problem of 'entertainment debt' – of deferring watching by storing episodes or programmes for later. The more you store, the greater the debt, and the less likely it is that you can find the time for everything you think you want to watch. So the technology of 'convenience' doesn't always make life easier.

People will increasingly catch what they miss online or 'stack' it for later, and some will do this much more than others. But I don't see the schedules dying out for some time yet, because when they do the whole industry and medium will need to reinvent itself – and I question how ready we all are to stomach this level of change.

AUDIENCE IS GOD

A lot of time is spent measuring, analysing, understanding, serving, manipulating and second-guessing the audience's habits. The audience is god in every medium – without it, the story means nothing. But in TV, it is not just audience figures that rule. The audience has become extremely knowledgeable and savvy about the formats, genres, styles and techniques of TV storytelling (for example, thriller, detective and forensic drama). Surprising a TV audience convincingly gets harder and harder. It's also sometimes true that a hard core of the audience may know a long-running soap and its history even better than the people making it.

THE PHENOMENON

TV has the unique ability to seemingly hook a whole nation with its storylines – from 'Who shot JR?' in *Dallas* to 'Who is the father of Michelle Fowler's baby?' in *EastEnders*. Every now and then a storyline becomes a phenomenon. In no other medium will such a volume of people simultaneously watch the same story. With so many channels available and different ways of watching emerging, that volume is reducing considerably over time – but it's still the mass medium for the mass audience. *EastEnders* can regularly pull in 8 million viewers on the first airing. That is a meaningful proportion of a nation of 65 million people. And fittingly, you tend to need big storylines and big hooks to grab them.

JUMPING THE SHARK

The big danger of this big need is when a show runs out of ideas and all there is left to do is 'jump the shark'. When *Happy Days* really had exhausted the format, all they could think of to up the ante was for the Fonz to literally make a water-ski jump over a shark to safety (or, God forbid, to certain death – which, in a way, it ultimately was for the show). It wasn't a story line driven by the show, by character, by relationship, by situation, by format – by anything other than sensation. The greatest danger in TV drama, especially soaps, is the sensation. The shark. The siege. The flood. The serial killer. The mockney gangster. The plane crash. Some would say *Brookside* simply went through one too many sensational happenings for such a small, new-build cul-de-sac in suburban Liverpool.

At its best *Dallas* kept the audience hooked by waiting to reveal the identity of the person who shot the show's charming but ruthless villain J.R. Ewing. At its worst, Bobby Ewing stepped out of the shower and we were asked to believe that everything we'd seen since his apparent death was all a dream. It was the death of the show. Ask yourself this: does my idea/world really have a long enough potential life on TV? If it does, how long might it be? There's nothing worse than a melodramatic, unbelievable, dragged-out death rattle from an idea desperately clinging on to a life that is barely worth living any more.

THE SINGLE EXCEPTION

The one exception to much of what I have said (and will go on to say) about format is the single drama. The single remains, as a form, pretty much the same as films for the big screen. Singles for TV are not usually cinematic or filmic in visual scope and storytelling; they are still commissioned because it is believed an idea is bold enough or explored interestingly enough to punch through the schedule. It is a dwindling form – there will never again be as many TV singles as there once were, a fact bemoaned by some. The reason being that it is expensive to make any TV drama, so the potential 'return' on an investment in an idea, world, characters will be greater the more long-running it is. It is also felt that the audience for one-offs is dwindling (which it is) because TV audiences want a brand to which they can continue to relate and return. It's normally only a very big-name writer who will get a TV single commissioned.

Some celebrated examples from the annals include *Cathy Come Home*, *Culloden*, *The Naked Civil Servant*, *Abigail's Party*, *Scum*, *Made in Britain*, *The War Game*, *Tumbledown*, *Hillsborough*, *Blue Remembered Hills*, *My Beautiful Launderette*. Some recent examples include stories about soldier abuse in the Iraq war (*The Mark of Cain*); a young girl's faith in a ghetto-ised community (*White Girl*); the rehabilitation of child killer who is now a young adult (*Boy A*); a black man deciding he hates black people (*Shoot the Messenger*); Churchill's convictions about the danger of fascism (*The Gathering Storm*); and a range of small but thematically linked pieces about TV celebrities (*Fear of Fanny*, *The Curse of Steptoe*). They all say something big or explore something in the popular consciousness. Probably the only exception to the rule – cinematic scope on the small screen – is the recent work of Stephen Poliakoff. We can all aspire to this freedom. But don't be fooled that it might actually happen. Because it simply won't.

FORMAT NOT FORMULA

A format is a recognisable place in TV scheduling from which and through which the best writers can tell stories that engage, delight and challenge an audience. A formula is a closed, unbending and usually simplistic shape into which stories are forced and through which the audience is served up the same old fodder they've seen a million times before. A format has infinite potential; a formula has only limits. Don't mistake the one for the other. You need to master format – and avoid formula.

BASIC DISTINCTIONS

A series is a run of episodes that have the ability either to continue ad infinitum or to return for a new season, with the primary focus on telling episode stories that have varying degrees of serialisation from what precedes and into what follows.

A serial is a run of episodes that has a definite, finite ending, with the primary episode focus being a serialisation of events, with varying levels of completeness for episode story.

It's an obvious distinction, but one that very often gets very muddied in the minds of inexperienced writers.

The more sophisticated TV writers become in their craft, the more the basic format can be challenged. In the BBC's most recent version of *Bleak House* – adapted from Dickens by Andrew Davies, and told in twice-weekly half-hour episodes – the serial took on the feel of a soap, or rather, the feel of a major storyline in a soap that culminates in a major climax. Series one of *Shameless* could conceivably have ended in the final episode and remained in our minds as a one-off serial, such was the exquisite structure of the show. *Five Days* was absolutely a finite serial, uniquely structured – but the central police detectives earned themselves a new life in a very different spin-off drama later.

These are examples where format is developed, manipulated, subverted, challenged – yet where format essentially remains recognisable and firm.

SERIAL

A serial has a finite ending and each episode (and everything therein) should be key in reaching that ending. As a format, therefore, there is a reliance on an audience's ability and willingness to tune in for each episode, lest they miss what should be crucial stages of the journey. The drive and need, then, is for a powerful ending and powerful hooks at the beginning and end of each episode to keep the audience constantly engaged. The mysteries deepen, the drama develops, the characters continue to journey and the surprises keep on coming.

Serial is a word with conflicting connotations. We expect a serial killer to keep on killing, a serial offender to keep offending – unless or until, of course, something stops them. In drama, a serial is reliant on the momentum reaching a powerful climax. Without that climax to work towards, your serial is already failing.

Adaptations of classic (and modern classic) novels form a large proportion of TV serials, from Defoe to Jane Austen, the Brontes, Dickens, Hardy, right through to Tom Sharpe, Zadie Smith et al. Original serials tend to be either uniquely imagined and/or big, state of the nation pieces that often capture a particular world and place in time – *The Singing Detective*, *The Lost Prince*, *The Edge of Darkness*, *Boys from the Blackstuff*, *Our Friends in the North*, *State of Play*. Recently, some serials have had a more distinct feeling of an 'event' about them – for example, *Criminal Justice* and *Five Days* stripping across five consecutive nights, or *Bleak House* adapted into bi-weekly half-hour instalments.

The serial format is usually very much about and dependent on the scale, ambition, boldness, imagination, politics and scope of an idea. Think small, safe and 'soapy' and you misunderstand this format for the medium.

CONTINUING SERIES

Continuing drama series (CDS), otherwise known somewhat disparagingly as 'soaps', do exactly what it says on the tin. A CDS show can run and run and run. As time has gone on, the big shows – *EastEnders*, *Coronation Street*, *Emmerdale* – now transmit more frequently. The volume of story and stories needed is mind-boggling. These shows are truly for the mass, loyal audience who structure their evening around them on a regular basis. These shows are part of the fabric and tapestry of millions of TV viewers' lives. This format is utterly, intrinsically relentless. These shows and the infrastructures that keep them going must be well-oiled machines to continue so unstoppably.

The world of a soap loosely mirrors that of an 'average' audience in that they are usually a combination of residential, work and communal settings – a square, street or village where characters' lives can interact, overlap, intersect, but also find a private space.

For the writer, this means the complex art of multi-stranded storytelling. Episode by episode, you usually balance between three A, B and C strands. It won't look as neat and tidy as the diagram below and the best episodes tend to overlap and combine the three strands towards a climax that impacts all of them, rather than simply interweaving them. But they might look something like this:

$$A \rightarrow A \rightarrow A \rightarrow A \rightarrow A \rightarrow A$$
$$B \rightarrow B \rightarrow B \rightarrow B \rightarrow B$$
$$C \rightarrow C \rightarrow C \rightarrow C$$

You will need to tell an episode story while developing the longer-term serial arcs of characters and strands, which in turn will serve the super-serial arcs that span over months. You also need to set up and hook the audience for the coming episodes that you don't necessarily write. Each episode will build to a main climax. Each weekly block of episodes will build towards a weekly climax (watch the omnibus and you'll see this in action). And months' worth of weekly blocks will constitute overlapping major story lines and arcs.

At its best this will feel like ever-arriving waves. As one wave breaks and climaxes a major strand, below it will be other waves at varying stages of build towards their own staggered breakers. Sometimes you will get a huge wave – a rip curl, a 'Who shot JR?' – that builds so long and crashes so hard that it becomes a phenomenon and sends out story ripples into subsequent strands for a time to come. Or you will get the two-hander climax episode that doesn't necessarily have a huge aftershock but that has a total focus on a couple of characters. In 2008, Tony Jordan even managed to work towards a one-hander in *EastEnders* – a monologue of Dot Cotton's message for her sick husband.

Soaps are wholly storylined for a core cast with no 'guest' characters or strands for the jobbing writer to sneak in. There are some general received conventions. Episodes represent up to one day and night in time frame. They are linear, with no flashbacks or forward cuts, leaps or montages within any given scene or setting; scene time is real time. The feel is essentially naturalistic, realistic, believable – possible and plausible (if not necessarily probable). The setting is contemporary – the same date as that on which it first transmits on air.

At the structural heart of the soap format is the ongoing need to create hooks, build suspense, play with expectations and climb from cliff-hanger to cliffhanger. The multi-stranding between numerous storylines means each scene will need a hook at the beginning (why we need to see it) and a hanger at the end (why we need to pick the strand up again later). Episodes generally have varying degrees of hook at the start (whose story the episode primarily is) and hanger at the end (how it feeds into the next episode). If each episode in a weekly block is building towards a weekly climax, then each needs a strong hook of a cliffhanger at the end to maintain momentum across the week. The hook should be character/emotion driven; the hanger might be suspense (how do they get out of that mess?) or mystery (what the hell is going on?) What they must do is propel us from scene to scene, strand to strand, beginning to end, episode to episode – and ultimately block to block over the serial arcs. The format must be relentless.

PRECINCT

A precinct show takes a very specific place, setting, environment – a workplace of some form – as its lynchpin. For example, a hospital precinct might be an A&E unit (*Casualty*), a hospital ward (*Holby*) or a period setting (*The Royal*). Through the work-based setting, the core characters interact with the 'general public' of 'guest' characters. The precincts that have remained truly continuing – hospital, doctor's surgery, police station – are arenas with which the general public from just about any walk of life, background and outlook might easily or conceivably connect. (Even a member of the royal family might attend the opening ceremony of a new hospital wing.) It is this fundamental quality that gives them their ever-renewable subsidiary cast, a never-ending treasure trove of lives and stories, and the potential to remain relentless.

You are likely to have one episode a week at a longer format (50–60 minutes). The difference between shows will be not only their specific precinct or variation on it, but also the balance between serial strands for the core cast of continuing characters and the guest-episode story bringing a new character into the precinct. This balance can also shift and change within a show and over time.

What tends to characterise these precincts is that they are arenas in which core and guest characters have the potential to be everyday heroes (and villains). Many new writers have naively tried to pitch a new precinct show – but they don't usually work because the precinct they choose does not have the same universal and heroic potential. Law courts, care system, probation service, river police – we are much less likely to step into this precinct in reality, and 'saving a life' is less likely to be portrayed as a single heroic act. They could work as settings for non-continuing shows – the law courts in particular have worked well. But they don't have the same capacity to run on and on and on and appeal to a broad audience.

RETURNING SERIES

Returners come back in seasons of episodes, usually annual. Episodes will generally tell a primary story, but there may be serial arcs across the season. For *Life on Mars* and *Ashes to Ashes* there was a crucial high-concept serial arc, though it still only comprised about 5–10 per cent of the story in most episodes. In some shows, such as *Hustle*, there may be only one major difference or development per season – a character leaves or a new one joins the team – and the rest is all episode story.

The key thing about the returner is precinct and world – cop show, crime show, school, sixth-form college, period rural village, housing estate, building site, hotel. But it's also about genre, sub-genre and variations on genre. Take cop shows. There's the intelligent, measured pace of *Morse*; the shadow of *Morse* in *Lewis*; the high-concept nostalgia of *Life on Mars*; the aging cold-case ex-coppers in *New Tricks*; the dark world of *Messiah*; the fight against male northern prejudice in *Prime Suspect. Trial and Retribution. Inspector Frost. Dalziel and Pascoe. Inspector Lynley. The Sweeney. The Professionals. Cops. City Central.* The list goes on and on – all cop shows in one way or another. Then there are the 'detective' shows: *Cracker, Kingdom, Rosemary and Thyme, Jonathan Creek*, right back to *Sherlock Homes, Poirot* and *Miss Marple.* And the forensic crime shows: *Silent Witness, Waking the Dead.* (And this is just British shows, never mind American ones.)

The variation within a genre is potentially endless. Shows can change over time – from the single heroine to the team in *Silent Witness.* But the central format – using forensic evidence to solve a crime – remains the same. The episode story-driven format of genre-driven returners must have the ability to live on – even when core characters leave or die. The format would tire were it to continue every week rather than return for a season every year.

Returners centred around a precinct/world rather than a genre – school (*Waterloo Road*), village (*Lark Rise to Candleford*), family home/

neighbourhood (*Shameless*) – invariably have a greater emphasis on serial arcs over the series. But successful shows will still tell a very strong episode story that could conceivably stand up without the absolute necessity of seeing the previous and next episodes.

A word about high-concept and Saturday-evening family shows – *Doctor Who, Merlin, Robin Hood, Primeval*. The same principles apply. These programmes, perhaps more than any other returner, show the power in, and clamour around, the 'season' – the limited run that we await with eager anticipation until it comes and then miss with a real sense of loss when it ends. They are designed to give you a more intense 'hit' and perhaps a bolder or higher-concept experience than the continuing and other returning shows. They are meant to be much larger than real life.

Finally, there are the 'anthology' series – a weird kind of development of older formats such as *The Twilight Zone*. In these a core precinct/world – an 'ordinary' street in *The Street*, the factory in *Clocking Off* – act as the place from which stand-alone stories with their own heroes and villains will be told. The show won't have core characters in each episode – rather, it will have an ensemble of characters. An anthology is an umbrella: a way of bringing various stories together under one canopy. Done well, they will feel like powerful singles embedded within a returning series format.

RELENTLESS MEETS FORMAT

The specific nature of format defines the level, scope and tone of relentlessness in TV storytelling. You need different kinds of formats and ingredients to keep different audiences hooked in different kinds of ways – to make them watch and then come again for more. What the format does is define the nature of the relationship between, and experience of, story and audence. This is at the heart of the medium of TV.

'It's a very addictive medium. I always thought I was going to be a movie writer but once you've had those immediate, big audiences, once you've heard people discussing your work on the bus the following morning . . . it's hard to go back into that movie ghetto of dreams and maybes.'

Ashley Pharaoh

2
The Beginning

WHAT ARE PRODUCERS LOOKING FOR?

This has to be the single most repeated question out of the mouths of aspiring writers (and/or desperate ones). And it is impossible to answer in a way that would satisfy them – because if it were that simple, half of us in the 'development' industry (and a fair few writers) would be out of work – commissioners would simply go to the people they like and order a script like a made-to-measure suit. This is just not how things work most of the time.

Commissioners like to be surprised. They like to be seen to take risks. They like to be responsible for breaking new talent as well as getting the very best out of established talent. They like being able to identify a new idea as one worth commissioning, developing, selling, green-lighting, investing production money in – and being able to nip uninspiring ones in the bud. They like stamping their personality over their slate. But they know ultimately that it is not their job to come up with ideas – it is their job to know when to pounce on them and the people who generate them.

One thing I can generally say of the big players across theatre, film, TV and radio is that they are looking not only for ideas they have never seen before, but also ideas with which as large an audience as possible can fall in love. This is not crude populism or 'commercialism'. It is the meaning of storytelling – to reach, touch, move, entertain, enthuse, inspire, anger, haunt and surprise as many people as possible. If you don't have this ambition and urge, then you shouldn't be writing drama for an audience. The logic is very simple and compelling. Audiences justify drama, not the other way around. Whether it's studio theatre or prime-time TV – everyone wants a full house.

THE MEAT MARKET

Feeding an audience should not mean serving up fodder. Ever. Audiences are always more discerning, intelligent, hungry, critical, demanding, knowing than you suspect they are – and than we ever give them credit for. And although what we hear and see can turn out to not be as good as everyone involved hoped and believed it would be, nobody really starts with the express intention of grinding out bog-standard work. A poor commissioner serves up the same old stuff all the time. A good commissioner will take wild risks some of the time and both succeed and fail; and a good commissioner will also take calculated risks the rest of the time and both succeed and fail. Nobody can ever get it right all the time – not least because one person's right is another person's very, very wrong indeed. Getting it right more often than not is pretty good going.

The best thing you as a writer can offer in a meat market is a prime fillet steak. Don't try to second-guess what you think the commissioner wants, nor what you think the commissioner thinks the audience wants, nor what you think the commissioner thinks the audiences thinks it wants. It won't help you – you will end up serving competent fodder at best.

THE MARKET

So do you ignore the 'market'? Well, no. Ditching the word 'market' might overcome a mental block for some. But you always need to know what has and hasn't worked for audiences – and why – in order to know what has already been done and won't be done again in the same way. I have too often read scripts that I know (and the writer apparently doesn't) have already been pretty much seen and done before. Don't do what has already been done. Learn from what you see and hear. Dissect it. Analyse it. Criticise it. Digest it. Accept it. Even if you don't like it. And move on to what's distinct about your idea. If you want to write a Radio 4 'Afternoon Play', you need to know what that slot in the schedule is and does. It's better if you already love a slot. It's good if you can learn to love the potential in it. But if you feel nothing for it whatsoever, then you're just being expedient and little good will come of it. So it's not just about knowing what the market looks like – it's about loving your stall and knowing who might want to shop at yours rather than somebody else's.

SO WHAT ARE PEOPLE LOOKING FOR?

As I've said, it's the most asked question. The truthful answer? UK commissioners and producers, whether they are after original ideas or writers for soaps, don't really have a long list of uncommissioned ideas and subjects against which they can tick off Writer X or Writer Y. What they are really looking for is a writer with a distinct voice who can create and deliver an original story that will stay with us – a story that an audience will love.

A brilliant original calling card script is your first step on the steep and rocky road towards your writing actually being produced. The calling card may never be made – but if it's good, then it will get you noticed. And only then do you really start to get into all-important conversations about what people are looking for – and whether they think you might just be able to deliver it.

WHERE TO BEGIN?

'The end is in the beginning. And yet you go on.'

Samuel Beckett, *Endgame*

THE BLANK PAGE

Dramas about writer's block aren't intrinsically dramatic and only rarely do they work. But anyone who has seen *Barton Fink* by the Coen brothers can see in all its glorious tedium the futility of sitting in front of a blank page, waiting in vain for the words to come. Choose this road and before long you too will most likely be worrying about the endlessly peeling wallpaper in the corner or what might be happening next door.

Nowadays most people will sit before a computer screen rather than a page in a notebook or typewriter. But computer screens are even more dangerous; email, the internet and Facebook are only a click away. The blank page screen might work for a valiant few – but it will almost certainly fail for the inglorious many. So don't face a blank page until you are armed and ready to actually fill it with something.

Whatever you do – DO NOT START WRITING YOUR SCRIPT STRAIGHT AWAY. Start writing, for sure. But the actual script is what you do when you know what you want to write – not what you do when you can't work out what to do next.

KNOWLEDGE IS POWER

Are there things you know or know about that other people do not know so well? Are there things you know by proxy that give you an insight into the workings of a particular world? Material doesn't come from nowhere. This doesn't mean that the thing you happen to be an expert in will necessarily be interesting to other people – only, perhaps, if you make a great story out of it or use it as texture within a great story. It may be that the jobs you wish to forget, the time in your life you wish to leave behind, the itches you perhaps could never scratch, give you the material you need – unfortunately, it may not be an expertise you are proud or desirous of, or even willing to acknowledge. But don't ignore the things you know in minute detail. And be prepared to research the things you know you need to know – but just happen not to know yet. You always need to be master of your universe.

NEWS OF THE WORLD

Ideas often come from snippets of real stories and news that seed themselves in your brain and then just take on a life of their own (with the aid of a gentle nudge – or perhaps a crowbar). If you're really stuck, mine true stories. They are normally both stranger and stronger than fiction. But still they must really take hold of you as much as you take hold of them.

THE DEVIL IN THE DETAIL

You may be inspired to explore 'the contemporary human condition', and that is a noble objective. But without detail, specifics, concrete material, this theme will remain for ever universal and never really a story about people in the world.

Try to let real, identifiable, tangible detail and material stick to your idea as soon as possible. It may be images or pictures. A character's way of walking, combing their hair, tying their shoes. A sound. A voice. A turn of phrase. A piece of music. Even a smell. Or a scene. A scenario. A situation. An opening sequence or closing image.

Start collecting all relevant material as soon as possible and keep collecting it. This will prove crucial not just in the exploratory stage, but later on too. It will be the detail, the minutiae, the quirks that make your characters, world and story stand out from the crowd and come into their own. A basic idea remains just that until you have flesh, skin and clothes to put on its bones.

A HEAD FOR IDEAS

To write scripts that actors can play and an audience will watch, you obviously need powerful material. Some writers constantly bubble and simmer with ideas. Others are infrequently inspired, but once it comes they drive forward thoroughly and doggedly. Ideally you will be endowed with both qualities. But few things in life are ideal and you're likely to do one these two things:

> ➢ Struggle to cohere, focus and select from numerous ideas.
> ➢ Struggle to generate enough ideas that will withstand development and scrutiny.

Either way, what you need to do is develop a harsh, critical faculty that can as objectively as possible look an idea in the eye and decide whether it's worth the time and energy of development. For experienced writers, this faculty might become second nature and instinctive. For the greater, less experienced number amongst you, it may need to be a self-conscious act that feels uncomfortable and unnatural. The myriad questions you should ask 'in the beginning' form the bulk of this section of the book.

YOU

You are without doubt the best source and database for material – but you come with glitches, and data means nothing without the judgement to interpret it meaningfully. The things you have seen, done, felt – been happy, sad, angry, annoyed, confused about – are crucial. It's not so much writing what you know, as using what you understand about what you know and feel in order to write well about your chosen subject. You may never have been an international jewel thief, but if you remember a moment when you sneaked a piece of chocolate as a child and got away with it, then you know what that vicarious thrill feels like at least to a small degree.

However, if you find yourself trying to write 'your story' or writing yourself wholesale into a story, you need to ask yourself a harsh and searching question – will an audience find it as interesting as you do? I was developing a script with a writer-director who drew very much on his own teenage experience. There was a real story in there – but sadly it was not the one where he as a teenager was the hero of the story. Needless to say, this was a difficult note for me to give – and for him to take. Charlie Kaufman was extraordinarily brave to write himself into *Adaptation* – but at least he invented an alter-twin brother character to turn that inside out and upside down.

YOUR FEELINGS

More important than what you have done in your life is what you have felt in your life. It never fails to hit me just how much a passionately told and heartfelt story will always engage and impress and affect so much more than one that is just expediently, efficiently told. No one can tell you what you should and should not care about, what should and should not keep you awake at night, get under your skin, get its teeth into you and not let go. But if you don't feel this powerful drive to want and need to tell a story, your script will only be competent at best. You can't apply tactics to what you feel. And even if a reader of your script down the line doesn't neces- sarily share your passion for a particular idea or story, if it's passionately delivered there's still a stronger chance your script will stick in their memory – and this is precisely what you want your script to do.

Your feelings may be politically driven, a response to society around you, inspired by an observed moment or idea that you can't shake, an expression of a deeply personal perspective or deeply held conviction. None of these things by themselves will make your script great. But they will give you the purpose, drive and emotional authenticity potentially to make it great. And without them, the most it can be is an exercise in craft, tech- nique, form, style.

> 'Your best script will touch on something you care deeply about.
> Something that you probably find hard to talk about easily. So
> writing it is the only way to get it out – you have to write or you'll go
> insane. But it's a bit like being a doctor. If you don't care enough
> you're a bad doctor. If you care too much you just go insane and
> you're no good to anybody. You need to filter your subjectivity

through a skin of objectivity, i.e write what matters to you – but keep it as uninflected and as universal as possible.'

Joe Penhall

YOUR VOICE

Voice is the non-quantifiable thing that commissioners, producers, developers always look for in writers. They can't usually explain it or break it down, but somehow they know when they do (or don't) see it, hear it, read it. Are great writers born with a 'voice'? Or can you make a great voice through effort and exercise of craft alone? I've already stated my case on this. I believe 'great' writers have something in them – insight, instinct, talent, whatever you want to call it – that effort and exercise will never fully generate or account for; but I believe that great writers only become or remain great by dint of effort and exercise as well, regardless of how talented they intrinsically might be.

THE X FACTOR

I generally think that mass-audience talent shows are a gloriously hollow distraction through which certain kinds of brilliant singers could never be found. But what's interesting is how we define the 'X Factor'. When a singer auditions, the judges and audience ask themselves questions. Can they sing? Can they hold a note and carry a tune? Do they have rhythm and phrasing? Is the sound they make pleasing? Is the sound they make interesting and unique? Is the sound they make irritating yet compelling? Is the sound they make nice but dull?

Can they *really* sing? Can you have the X Factor but not really be able to 'sing'? What about Leonard Cohen, The Pogues, Tom Waits, Bob Dylan? Why do we disagree about who does and does not have it? Is it purely subjective? Do you just somehow 'feel' that a singer is great, regardless of the various constituent factors that go into their voice? Or do we just like watching them sing, which is using another sense entirely?

Is there a 'something' in them or about them that can't be defined, explained, broken down, replicated, reconstituted, that is at the heart of why people love to hear them sing?

WHAT IS A VOICE?

A voice is a physical instrument. It is the sound made by the vibration of the vocal chords projecting into air, modified by the mouth, tongue and breath. All human voices are necessarily physically different because no two human bodies can be physiologically exactly the same. When we talk about a writer's voice, it's worth remembering that voice is physical, real and distinct – not obviously visible, but audible, perceptible.

A voice has 'condition'. It is a quality and, perhaps, a technique, that must be kept in condition, practised, trained, flexed like a muscle. A voice also has a natural condition defined by the greater physical personality of the being it expresses – softly spoken, kindly, melodious, aggressive, acerbic, grating. Can you change the natural condition of a voice? How much range can a voice have through conditioning and craft?

A voice has distinctive tone. It is physically unique, individual, unlike any other. Is vocal tone equivalent to a writer's distinctive, individual style, such as that of Pinter, Beckett, Brecht, Potter, Kaufman?

A voice is an expression of feeling and opinion. A voice can have passion, force, purpose, drive, desire, wish, need. A voice is the expression of theme – the central message of your desire to tell a story, your attitude, your passion, the thing you are trying to say and the things you have to say for yourself.

Voice is the human right to express an opinion and a feeling – a will. In politics, the vote is (ideally) the elector's voice. Is the right of an individual to articulate their voice equivalent to the right to be heard by many? Or is the right to a platform earned by the quality of voice more than simply the effort that goes into using it?

'Certainly as a writer, all you need is a pen and paper and a chair.
The one thing you don't need is permission.'

Toby Whithouse

CAN YOU HEAR YOUR OWN VOICE?

Voice is crucial to great writing. But can you ever objectively hear your own voice yourself? Do you know what it is you have to say or want to say? Are your opinions, attitudes, purposes and desires ever fully clear and coherent?

Can you apply your own voice consciously? Or is it something that you must allow to shine through of its own accord?

There are no right or wrong answers to any of these questions. And sitting around thinking too self-consciously about what your voice is could well be counter-productive. But in there somewhere along with the choices you make, the instincts you follow, the ideas you generate, the way you tell stories, the things you get right and the things you get wrong, the things that are universal and the things that are utterly you, is your voice. And it must be yours and yours alone – because that is what producer and audience alike are looking for. Remember, everyone else is an audience – we need to hear your voice.

'All I've ever wanted to be was a writer. It's more like an addiction now. I don't write to change things, I don't write because I'm angry. The opposite, perhaps: I write because I love this life and I love us all for trying to survive it, for trying to make meaning and love out of chaos. That's almost the definition of a writer, isn't it? Making story and meaning out of chaos.'

Ashley Pharaoh

KINDS OF STORIES

ARCHETYPES

There are probably a finite number of story archetypes. Opinion will always differ about exactly how many there are and what we should call them. In Western culture there are, for example, tragedy, comedy, satire, romance, rite-of-passage, epic, revenge. Such essentials form the basis of what stories tend ultimately to be.

Archetype is not genre; it is not a kind, classification or sort of story, but an original, originating model. You will never find *the* original, of course. Stories have been spinning off from archetypes since long before they were ever committed to paper. But there are some originals in terms of the first versions recorded for posterity: Homer's *Odyssey* and *Iliad*, Aeschylus' *Oresteia*, Sophocles's *Oedipus Rex*, Virgil's *Aeneid*, Ovid's *Metamorphoses*. And there are modern archetypes that come around through the ages –

Kyd's *The Spanish Tragedy*, Beckett's *Waiting for Godot*, Osborne's *Look Back in Anger*, Potter's *Pennies from Heaven*, Adams's *Hitchhiker's Guide to the Galaxy*.

From there, the big question is – what do you do with an archetype? What is your particular setting/context? What is your fresh take on it? What is your unique perspective? What is your original touch that will set this apart, even though the archetype still sits at the heart of it?

A favourite example of mine is the film *O Brother, Where Art Thou?* by the Coen brothers. On one level, it is a relatively straightforward version of Homer's *Odyssey*, an archetypal journey in Western epic storytelling – it has an Odysseus figure, it has his wife Penelope and her new suitor, it has the physical journey, the seductive sirens, the one-eyed monster Cyclops and so on. On another level, it places them within the specific context of the American deep south in the early twentieth century, with Blue Grass music and an expanse of land to traverse rather than an ocean of sea (though there is a deluge of water at the end). On another, crazier level, it turns Odysseus into the Three Stooges, and makes them comic petty criminals and prison escapees who become unlikely pop stars rather than victorious warrior heroes. And all because the Coen brothers thought the original story was 'funny'. Nobody but them could possibly have read, understood and reimagined the archetype in this way. It drips with their idiosyncratic and unique take on the world.

Shakespeare was especially brilliant at drawing on a range of archetypes and source materials to weave new stories that show their influences but create something new. *Titus Andronicus* is at a formative stage in his writing career and inspired by Kyd's massively popular Elizabethan revenge tragedy, influenced by Marlowe's *The Jew of Malta*, and a kind of prototype of his own later play *King Lear*. But it is fundamentally inspired by the transformative Roman poetic tale of Procne and Philomel from Ovid's *Metamorphoses*. The resulting play is pure Shakespeare – yet he wears his influences, inspirations and source materials proudly on his sleeve. To greater and lesser degrees all his plays come in this form – and this from the most famous, the most revered, the most brilliant playwright in history.

So. Have you seen your basic idea before? What's different and surprising about your version? What will you do to make the archetype your own? Surprising an audience (and reader) is crucial at this fundamental level.

LINEAR

Linear stories are in the majority by a long way because, I suppose, many a storyteller's instinct is to start at the beginning and end at the end. And this in turn, I suppose, is because forwards is the direction in which life runs; in linear stories consequence and causality has a forward momentum that corresponds to the recognisable reality in which, in all our lives, the clocks tick on and on. In these stories the reason for everything that happens is an accumulation of everything before it. What happens in the story, therefore, must follow on from what has already happened. If you throw in a narrative hand grenade – an alien visitation or some other trick that appears only once, comes out of nowhere and has no seeding or logic or relevant context (sometimes known as a *deus ex machina*) – then you corrupt the fundamental form of the story.

If you decide your story is not linear, you need to consider and justify why that need be the case – why the deep structure should not correspond to the dominant archetypal structure.

EPIC

Epic stories tend to be linear in form. But what distinguishes epics is the sheer scale and size of the reach and vision in their seeming presentation of a whole world/universe – one in which the events of the story seemingly have an effect on that whole world. What also distinguishes them is the scale of heroism/villainy in the characters' actions. In most linear stories, the events will not necessarily change lives beyond those of the core central characters; in epic, they will necessarily do so – thus the *Star Wars* saga, *Lord of the Rings* and tales from the Bible and other religious texts and traditions, such as the *Ramayana* or *Mahabharata*.

Theatre has been epic since the biblical medieval mystery plays and Shakespeare's histories. In *Hamlet* and *King Lear*, the end of the play marks a point at which nothing will be the same for world it presents. More recently, *Oh What a Lovely War!* and *The Seven Streams of the River Ota* reinvented epic in brilliant ways – the former as political polemic, the latter as a tapestry of intimate stories woven across continents and cultures.

Film has always been able to operate on an epic scale, from *The Birth of a Nation* by D.W. Griffith through *Battleship Potemkin*, *Lawrence of*

Arabia, Gone with the Wind, to Sergio Leone's 'spaghetti westerns', the *Godfather* saga, *Braveheart* and *Elizabeth*.

TV epic is perhaps different. Shows such as *The West Wing, Edge of Darkness, State of Play* and *Rome* are traditionally epic, but *Twin Peaks, Doctor Who* and *The Sopranos* also present a world (or multiple universes in the case of The Doctor) outside which nothing else is significant, at least for the time you are watching.

With radio it is very difficult to operate on an epic scale solely through the medium of sound. It is perhaps easier in radio comedy, where the imagination can take a freer, comic approach, as in *The Hitchhiker's Guide to the Galaxy*. But the potential for intimacy and the difficulty or presenting a large cast of voices makes sweeping epic a challenge for radio drama.

FULL CIRCLE

Circular stories end where they begin, in some cases literally, in others more metaphorically. Some literal circular stories can have a negative or disorienting effect, whereby whatever happens and whatever we do, we are bound to a certain destiny or pattern. In *American Beauty*, perhaps Lester can never really break out of the American way, even if he does quit his job, smoke pot, and chase a girl the same age as his teenage daughter; his demise is preordained by virtue of his attempting to drop out but never really leaving it all behind. In *The Lesson*, the message is absurdist – the teacher and pupil are locked in a surreal, repeating scenario from which neither can escape. In *Flashforward*, circularity is a fundamental element of the premise – where everyone in the world gets a brief flash-forward to their life six months hence; it isn't rigidly and exactly circular in shape, but the sense of having a destined point in the future that even with foresight the characters might not be able to change, is central to the premise.

Other more metaphorical circular stories have the opposite, comic effect – for example, traditional sitcoms (that do not have an ongoing narrative arc), such as *Fawlty Towers, Steptoe and Son, Porridge*, where at the end of each episode the central characters find themselves trapped in the same place or position as at the beginning. Curiously, though, the best sitcoms of this kind also tend to have a contradictory undercurrent of sadness and poignancy (Basil Fawlty trapped in an awful marriage, Harold Steptoe bound to his father, jailbird Fletch stuck in prison).

FRACTURED

In fractured and fragmented stories, life isn't a logical, linear reality – but though disorienting, that existence can be as wonderful and poignant as it is weird. *The Eternal Sunshine of the Spotless Mind* manages to surprise, delight and move all at the same time as it reinvents the 'love story'. In *21 Grams*, the utterly non-linear structure tells an extraordinarily moving, tragic story in which the overwhelming emotions of love, grief and guilt are simply more important than chronology. The fragmentation of *The Singing Detective* is a kind of desperate attempt to escape from the prison of a hospital bed and a debilitating condition.

REPETITIVE

A small number of stories set up patterns that repeat with tiny variations. As such they can be optimistic and comedic, like *Groundhog Day* – where we can change the repeating pattern if given a chance and/or if we set our mind to it. Or even as in *Run Lola Run*, where the heroine gets the chance to save the day. But it's most often a device in sci-fi and supernatural TV series, where it is either a surreal, inescapable loop or a surreal, escapable loop – from *The Twilight Zone* to *Star Trek*, *Doctor Who*, *Red Dwarf* (and even Monty Python's 'Déjà Vu' sketch). The point being that if there is no variation, then it's simply repetitive – a circular story played out again and again, with no further, developing meaning.

REVERSED

A tiny number of stories that simply run backwards from end to beginning in mostly linear fashion. Pinter's *Betrayal* does this; the play is not so much about the consequence of actions as about the gradual stripping away of those consequences to the origins of the three characters' relationships. The effect is to give the audience a sense of dramatic irony about what is about to happen at any given moment, because they see the consequences of actions before the actions themselves as we work backwards through narrative and time.

A large and fundamental part of the narrative of *Memento* runs in reverse. The effect is to put the audience in a sympathetic relationship with a central character who is unable to form new memories, since neither audience nor hero know what has just happened; both are therefore disoriented, and this is where the tension in the story lies. *Memento* is more complex than this, though; concurrent with the reverse narrative is an intercutting, forward-running strand (in black and white) showing the events that lead up to the chronological beginning of the main narrative (in colour) that run in reverse, which we will therefore see (non-chronologically) at the end of the film. It is brilliantly, bewilderingly simple yet complex, and a deadly effective narrative technique.

The key thing about both of these examples is: would the story work if it were played forward rather than in reverse? The answer is no – a straightforward linear treatment would not have the same tension and would not tell the story of either play or film.

THE IMPACT OF SHAPE

The first point is – what effect do you want to have? Do you want to satisfy an audience from beginning to end? Overwhelm them? Entrap and frustrate them? Disorient them? Surprise them? Subvert time for them?

The second point is – do certain kinds and forms of story structures lend themselves to certain genres of story? Or rather, can you help yourself by making your kind of story and genre of story correspond?

GENRE

Genre is often presumed by aspiring writers to be a limiting, simplistic, oppressive thing – an unforgiving box in which 'marketing' will confine your creativity. As such, it is easily misunderstood by the novice and can tend to show how distant from an audience that writer's mind is. You should use genre to help you do something that is recognisable yet original – to orient yourself and your audience without being derivative and slavish.

Genre is a means of classification. If I want to go out and see a film or play, then the need to set a date (when I think I will still have some energy left after a day at work), to make the booking and to arrange a babysitter means it must be worth the effort. To decide whether or not it might be worth it, I use genre. Do the write-ups, trailers and publicity tell me that it might be the kind of thing I would like to see? If a film is implied to be a taut thriller yet turns out to be a quirky romantic comedy, then I will have reasonable cause for feeling like I have been conned out of my hard-earned money. Genre tells us what *kind* of story a story might be, whether it might suit our general tastes or our preference on a particular occasion.

Robert McKee's overview of film genre in *Story* is excellent and there's no point trying to replicate or reinvent it here. The thing about genre is not to obfuscate or to deconstruct stories into endless sub-genres, but to clarify, to tell an audience something that is useful for their understanding and enjoyment of your story.

The essential genres McKee identifies are the kind of stories you can and will see in any medium: love story, epic, war, coming-of-age, comedy, crime, social drama, adventure, historical, biographical, musical, sci-fi, fantasy. Some you are less likely to see in other mediums: sports, western, horror, mockumentary, docu-drama, action and animation are certainly not staples of theatre and radio. Some are particular to film alone, such as the 'art' film. The same sort of logic goes for other mediums, but their relationships with genre aren't exactly the same as that of film.

THEATRE AND GENRE

Modern British theatre tends not to define genre rigidly, other than to broadly say whether something is West End (usually big, showy or to the popular taste, often musical, and often with star-name actors in the leads), off-West End (new writing at the Royal Court or Hampstead, mixed programming at the National or the Almeida), fringe/pub or regional repertory. In the ritual rites of ancient Greece, theatre took the form of either comedy, tragedy or satyr play. In *Hamlet*, Polonius bumbles his way through the various English Renaissance conjunctions of tragical, comical, historical and pastoral. Since then, genre has tended to be characterised by a particular style, era and place – Jacobean tragedy, Restoration comedy, post-war Theatre of the Absurd, British kitchen-sink drama of the fifties and sixties.

Classification by style and subject is now the norm – new plays are in-your-face/edgy (usually tragic), warm/popular (normally comic), intelligent/intellectual (sometimes political), documentary/verbatim (often political), or denoting a minority perspective in society (Afro-Caribbean, British-born Asian, gay/lesbian, disabled – also sometimes very political). The theatre industry doesn't tend to spend its time dividing and sub-dividing genres, it takes a much broader and more relaxed position because, ultimately, there are far fewer new plays to choose between at your nearest theatres (even in London) than there are new films to see at your nearest cinemas.

RADIO AND GENRE

Radio nods towards the essential film story types rather than eras or movements. But it also uses elements that are more in use in radio than elsewhere and, as such, it tweaks the genres – such as epistolary, diary, monologue. So you may be listening to a biographical drama that combines letters and diaries with dramatisation to tell the story.

TELEVISION AND GENRE

Television is where genre sub-divisions tend to have their most extreme but also most meaningful expressions, and these tend be a combination of genre with format. So for example there is the 'returning crime show'. This can be an adapted famous-author detective (*Poirot*); an updated famous-author detective (*Sherlock*); an intellectual detective (*Inspector Morse*); a psychological detective (*Cracker*); a period detective (*Foyle's War*); a time-slip detective (*Life on Mars*); a magician detective (*Jonathan Creek*); old-school cold-case coppers (*New Tricks*); general police precinct (*Cops*); specific police squad (*The Sweeney*); forensic live case (*Silent Witness*); forensic cold case (*Waking the Dead*); police procedural (*Law and Order*); court procedural (*Judge John Deed*); police/court procedural (*Trial and Retribution*); rural police (*Hamish Macbeth*); rural period police (*Heartbeat*); slick criminal POV (*Hustle*); comedy criminal POV (*The Invisibles*).

The reason for such seemingly endless variations on how we describe the TV crime genre is because there are so many shows that are either going out or being repeated across the many, many channels available that it helps an audience distinguish between them and hit on the one they want. Other central TV genres include: precinct (from soaps to schools to offices), ensembles (*Auf Wiedersehn Pet*, *This Life*), comedy-drama (*Cold Feet*, *Shameless*), hi-concept (*Doctor Who*, *Torchwood*), adventure (*Merlin*, *Robin Hood*, *Primeval*), supernatural (*Being Human*, *Apparitions*), thriller (*Spooks*, *Edge of Darkness*, *State of Play*), state of the nation serial (*Our

Friends in the North, Boys from the Blackstuff, Sex Traffic, Criminal Justice).

Some are an intriguing blend of various genres. *Being Human* is a supernatural comedy-horror combining flat-share ensemble with an epic battle between humanity and non-human beings on earth; the writer created a show that would cut from flatshare comedy to vampire horror in a heartbeat, and that's what makes the genre of the show unique – and the tone of the show unique. But as the writer Toby Whithouse says, this wasn't for the sake of being different:

> *My ambition for* Being Human *has always been to write as realistic a show as possible. The conceit has always been: if these creatures really existed, what would their lives be like? Consequently I had to incorporate all the different tones and shades of real life, from the comedic to the tragic. To do anything else would have been deliberate decision to move even further away from reality.'*

TONE

Wedded to genre is tone – the timbre, sensibility, feeling and style that suffuses your whole story. A mishmash of tone is almost certainly just as bad as a haphazard throwing together of genre. It usually indicates a lack of clarity in the writer's thinking rather than a revolutionary intelligence. As with Toby Whithouse's *Being Human*, only rarely will a writer pull off a clash of tone (and genre) – Dennis Potter's *The Singing Detective* (musical with detective fantasy, medical realism and childhood flashback), Shakespeare's *The Winter's Tale* (pastoral comedy with a tragedy of envy and a romantic reconciliation). And even in these instances, the overall success and coherence is a matter of subjectivity and taste – it will work for some but not for others.

But tone isn't simply about the kind or sort of story it is, but the way in which the writer will characterise it in the moment (no matter what the genre). Realistic. Naturalistic. Heightened. Comic/farcical. Dark/black. Surreal/absurd. A particular, distinct stylistic and tonal treatment can set a story apart, especially if that treatment is somehow in contrast with what you expect of a premise, idea and genre. What is brilliant about the zombie story in *Shaun of the Dead* is that it is funny; what is distinctive about the comedy is that it is set against the context of horror; what is surprising about both is that they run concurrent to a romantic tale of a boy losing, pursuing, saving and getting the girl. *The League of Gentlemen, Nighty Night* and *The Thick of It* are TV comedies that are so shot through respectively with the surreal, the dark/weird, and the most biting of satire that it sometimes feels like comedy is the last thing on the audience's (and writer's) mind. Yet they are funny – brilliantly, mind-bendingly, gut-wrenchingly funny. And they are all unique in tone.

THE RIGHT FORM

Many aspiring writers start out saying 'I want to write a political thriller' or 'road movie' or 'prison-cell two-hander for the stage' or 'tapestry of voices for radio'. Which is fine. But what can then happen is they start throwing obvious stock characters and clichéd scenarios at their chosen genre- or medium-driven idea. It's important to let your idea/characters gestate and see which genre/medium they suit best. Stories are too often shoehorned into the wrong form. Great ideas can ultimately live in many forms – but they always start in just one. Allow your idea to find the right form rather than have one foisted upon it. The point of all this is that your idea, world and story should hold and hang together as one, rather than be incoherent and jarring. And again, for the maverick-minded out there, I'm not simply advocating the obvious and what has always been done before. Surprising and distinct is great. Strange and weird is fine. But confused and incoherent is simply not good storytelling.

WHAT'S THE BIG IDEA?

'DROIT MORAL'

'Droit moral' is the author's right to claim and retain authorship of a work. It won't give you power or control but it does recognise you as creator. I won't dwell on the legal complexities of ownership, options, moral rights and theft. But there is one thing to say that's worth remembering: YOU CAN'T COPYRIGHT PROTECT A BASIC IDEA OR PREMISE. You can copyright specific detail – such as that which goes into a synopsis, outline, treatment or script. But you can't claim someone has stolen your idea about setting a drama series in a postal sorting office, or a comedy series in the world of film extras or an office smoking room. I saw versions of all these basic ideas before *Sorted*, *Extras* and *The Smoking Room* appeared on the BBC. The only real similarities between the unproduced and the produced versions were in the basic set-up and idea, which anyone could have come up with.

The point is that writers will independently come up with extremely similar ideas all the time. Ideas are cheap. It is the delivery of a singular vision, the wholly distinct take or version of an idea, that is coveted by producers. The big idea is what you make of it, and you alone could ever make of it. Don't ape something else or try to second-guess what you think people want. It never really works. What works is when you hit on an idea or theme that has taken hold of you, and therefore takes hold of character, story, script and audience.

THEME

A 'theme park' is pretty much the lowest common denominator of what 'theme' signifies: taking a successful idea and franchising it in fairground rides, cuddly toys and out-of-work actors dressed 'in character'. However:

> ➢ Theme is not subject. Subject is the thing you choose to write about and explore. Theme is the thing you have to say about that subject – the thing that no one else has to say in quite the same way that you do.

> ➢ Theme is your central message – even if it is complex and contradictory.

> ➢ Theme is your attitude – even if it is divided, or hypocritical.

> ➢ Theme is your passion – even if you don't exactly know why you feel the way you do.

> ➢ Theme is the thing you are trying to say – even if what you are trying to say cannot be reduced to anything smaller than the entirety of your script.

> ➢ Theme is the big idea. *Your* big idea.

> ➢ Theme is voice. *Your* voice.

UNIVERSAL

The problem with a 'theme' is that it can easily seem very vague, universal – conceptual. It's all well and good to want to write a state-of-the-nation, contemporary tale about politics and the media. But this in itself doesn't say much about the story or the writer. However, a post-watershed TV serial about an ambitious and idealistic investigative newspaper journalist whose dogged enquiry into the death of the young political aide to an equally ambitious and idealistic 'new generation' MP (of whom the journalist is an old friend) is a brilliant foray into an emotionally and politically gripping world of people trying to square their ideals both with their work and with their failings and weaknesses.

The former idea is by nobody; the latter is by Paul Abbott. The basic idea could be done a hundred ways; *State of Play* could only have been written by Abbott.

The other big problem with theme is that writers don't necessarily know what it is they are trying to say when they begin and may never be able to lock it down neatly. You don't need to be able to boil down your theme into a handy platitude – you just need to feel and know that it is in there somewhere.

If a story, idea, characters are bugging you and keeping you up at night, demanding to be written, then theme will be in there somewhere. So learn to recognise when a story has taken hold of your instincts to communicate something to an audience – even if you're never sure exactly what it is you mean to say.

CONCEPT AND WORLD

Most stories don't really have a 'concept' – most stories approximate to perceived and received human reality and history; therefore there's no need to conceptualise them. They are tales of people being people in the world.

Concepts are dangerous things in that it is easy to get stuck and lost in them – stuck because every element of story and plot has to fit, lost because in order to make them fit you can dig yourself in deeper and deeper with rules, sub-rules and micro-rules that justify the concept to the *n*th degree.

'High' concepts work best when they are kept fairly simple, such as the time-travel in *Life on Mars*, the supernatural flatshare in *Being Human*, the cloning in *A Number*, the end of fertility in *Children of Men*. Or when they are turned inside out, such as the completely and strange realities of *Being John Malkovich* and *Lost Highways*. Generally speaking, the more time you spend conceptualising the rules and regulations of your fictional world, the less useful time you spend on character, story, drama, emotional depth.

Remember, if you are inventing a universe not quite like or very unlike this one, then the rules can be what you want them to be – but they must cohere and make sense with one another. Weird places are fine – jumbled ones are not. Set your perameters clearly and simply, then concentrate on making what your characters do ring true within them.

The world you create must be coherent with itself and on its own terms. It must hang together, even if what it constitutes looks very weird. The world of *Being John Malkovich* is pretty bonkers, but it doesn't feel incoherent – just very strange indeed.

PREMISE

The premise is essentially the dramatic starting point of the story in your idea. It isn't: 'Imagine a vampire, werewolf and ghost share a house.' It is: 'What if a vampire and werewolf were helping one another to not kill people while sharing a house with a ghost who doesn't yet understand why she isn't dead.' The former is an idea. The latter is a dramatic premise – with desires and needs, journeys to go on, obstacles to surmount, drama, conflict.

A good premise asks a dramatic question about the characters. Why are the werewolf and vampire helping one another to not kill people? What brought them to this, despite their killing instinct? Is it only their instinct they must fight against? Are they the only vampire and werewolf who live this way in this curious but familiar universe? Why is the ghost here? What is it she doesn't understand about her death (or life) that has made her a ghost, bound to the house in which she died? How will finding out the truth change her? How will this strangest of house-shares impact on the three characters? How will they keep their extraordinary secret in a normal street, in a normal city, on any given, normal day?

PREMISE AND CHARACTER

A good premise isn't just about asking dramatic questions of characters. It is about creating the kinds of personalities for whom dramatic questions arise – whether once in their life or every day of it. For Willy Russell's Shirley Valentine or Rita, it's a fundamental question that arises once: is this it for me and my life? Can I aspire to something more? Dare I aspire? Dare I live with the consequences, bad and good?

For others the question returns and/or develops. For James Bond, film by film, it is: how do I avert the disaster posed by the villain and come through it unscathed and fundamentally unchanged at the end? For The Doctor, incarnation by incarnation, it is: why do my travels across the universe always bring me back to earth and humanity? What is it that makes humanity worth saving? For Jane Tennison, crime by crime, it is: can I keep on catching the criminal on behalf of society without it ruining me as a person and a woman in the end?

PREMISE AND EMOTION

A character premise is only as strong as the emotional engagement an audience has with their story. If we don't care whether or not Shirley, Rita, James, the Doctor or Jane will succeed, then the premise has no meaning and no legs. The writer can't anticipate who will or won't engage with any given character. But you can invest your characters and the traits that propel them into a dramatic journey with the potential to connect with us – to make us fearful, hopeful, relieved.

You need to home in on what is universal about that emotion. We need not know intimately the details of unemployed ex-steel workers in Sheffield in order to understand and share the pain of disenfranchised, emasculated men deprived of a wage, a vocation and self-worth. Most cultures will understand the story of hope winning out over hopelessness in *The Full Monty*.

Without emotion, a premise is just a story option.

With emotion, a premise can become compulsive viewing.

Without emotion, you have: how does a Mafia gangster keep his friends, enemies, partners, competition, family and lovers on his side?

With emotion, you have: how does a contemporary Mafia gangster keep everyone on his side when his kids are going off the rails, his wife is distant, his mother despises him, his uncle craves his power, his friends and 'employees' are a mixed bag of thuggish fools and foolish thugs, his own violent temper is his greatest enemy, and therapy with a smart female psychiatrist creates as many problems as the low self-esteem that sent him there seeking help in the first place?

On the face of it, it should not be easy to engage with a dangerous Mafia boss. But in practice Tony Soprano pulls you in because he is human, flawed, recognisable, and never stops raising emotional questions wherever he goes and whatever he does. He may be the unlikely lord of a criminal empire, but he's also a man who starts out feeling like a failure to his kids, wife, mother – and himself. Each of these relationships has potentially endless dramatic possibilities – they hooked a big audience for a long, long time and *The Sopranos* is regularly voted the best-ever TV drama.

THE BIG IDEA

The big idea, ultimately, is what you say about the world through what your characters do in every moment we see them. It is the expression of the universal and the essential in the minutiae of human want, need, desire, love, hate, anger, hurt, hope, despair – and, most importantly, action.

IDEA AND MEDIUM

What is it that makes an idea better for one medium than another?

It depends what you want to do with your idea. The complexity of *State of Play* and *The Singing Detective* lent themselves perfectly to TV serial drama over a number of hours and weeks. Both have since been adapted by Hollywood as feature films and they necessarily had to change. What Abbott and Potter wanted to do on the small screen was ultimately different to what Hollywood wanted to do with the same ideas on the big screen. You must match the scale, experience and volume of material you have to what works in a given medium. (For what it's worth, both were much, much better in their original TV form.)

Some stories will work (for better or worse) in every medium – including novels, many of which adapt into theatre, TV and radio alike. Other stories don't necessarily work in every medium, and are perfect in only one. The beauty of great adaptation from one medium to another is not that you wrench an idea into a new form, but that you breathe a new life, expression and form into it.

THEATRE

Theatre is the place where the physical, spatial dialectics of two (or more) characters in a scenario and the conflict or tension between them can be enough to make a play – which has been increasingly the case in new writing in and since the twentieth century (from Mamet's *Oleanna* to Enda Walsh's *Disco Pigs* to Mike Bartlett's *Contractions*). *Revolutionary Road* is a lovely film (adapted from a book) but it could work well on stage because it is so focused on a limited number of characters in mostly stageable 'scenes', where dialogue and emotional dialectic are the primary driving forces. *Dead Man's Shoes*, however, would not work in the theatre – the flashbacks, the visual backdrop, the loan avenger, are all pure cinema.

RADIO

Radio is where you can create a singular relationship with a listener that has the potential fluidity that only sound, audio and voice can bring. If you want to express your characters in ways that seem strange anywhere else, then radio is the place where all voices – even those that are not human, animal or alien – can be justified and made real. A good radio idea is one that will come to true life in the listener's head.

FILM

Film is the medium where visual scope is key and where you can use the canvas of a huge screen to zoom in close and zoom out wide to tell the story through images. It is hard to imagine how one might evoke the true scale of *Lawrence of Arabia* emerging alone from the desert, a shimmering speck on the horizon slowly coming into focus in the foreground, in any medium other than film. You could tell a different version of his story elsewhere, but the desert and 'Arabia' will never receive so bold an expression of their overwhelming scale.

TELEVISION

TV is where stories can develop an ongoing relationship with an audience that exists in the privacy and heart of their living room – of their family and home life. You can do continuing series on radio (*The Archers* is the world's longest-running soap of all time, having started in 1951), but TV is where they find their most intensive, audience-pulling expression and life. A great TV idea is usually one that will reach out to and grab hold of an audience in their home on a regular basis, whether for a few days, a few weeks, or for life.

WHAT'S THE STORY?

As I have said, the need to engage an audience through character is fundamental. Story is what you do with that character, that engagement, and that need to say something.

Story isn't: what scrapes can I make up for a character who travels through time and space in a telephone box? Or: what 1970s crimes can I throw at a twenty-first century policeman who has gone back in time?

Story is: why does a Time Lord care so much about the human race and what lengths will he go to in order to help it save itself? Or: how can a strait-laced twenty-first century DCI solve crimes in the corrupt 1970s without twenty-first century technology and techniques, knowing that he must solve them in order to get back home?

The former is a basic idea. The latter is story – an engaging character focus with conflicts, problems, tensions and obstacles to achieving the things that confirm who they are and why we stick with them.

The plot is the order in which you structure the events of a story to reach a particular end and have a particular effect on character and audience. The story is why we should care, why we stick with it – the effect and meaning you seek to have.

The plot is the route that we take.

The story is the journey that we make.

BEGINNINGS AND ENDINGS

Getting lost and distracted by plot is very easy. Don't be disheartened. It's easy to mistake the detail of plot for the fundaments of the story. Plot is where so and so happens, and then they do this, and then that happens, and then they say this or feel the other. Story is where things happen as a consequence of what a character says, thinks, believes, feels, and – most crucially – does.

I have read many scripts – probably thousands – where the story does not work because the beginning and ending are not absolutely, necessarily, essentially and inextricably connected. In strong stories, the end is a necessary outcome of the beginning, and the beginning is the necessary starting point for the end you wish to reach for the characters you have created.

Many inexperienced writers say they don't like to know what the ending will be because it spoils the writing process and they get bored. Well, people don't commission writers to have fun, but to tell stories that have an impact. And if you get bored that easily, then perhaps your characters just aren't worth spending that amount of time with. So, think again.

KNOWING WHERE YOU ARE GOING

I don't know any professional writers who write scripts without knowing (or without having a very strong feeling for) where they are going. They may not know at the exploratory outset while the idea gestates and develops, and while they gather together their material – but by the time they start writing an actual script they should, because otherwise they will waste a lot of time and energy working out where they are going as they go. They change their minds. They get it wrong. And they still get lost down highways and byways. But they fundamentally know where they are going in dramatic and emotional terms because the idea they have gestated and the characters they have created have a meaningful existence, purpose and direction.

DIRECTION AND PURPOSE

The clearer you are about who the characters are, why they do what they do, why we are watching them, why it is important to see them go on this particular journey over this particular length of time in this particular way, the better grasp of story you will have. Details may change. You may change your mind. You may still get lost. But you should know why you are travelling in a particular direction and taking us on a particular journey. You should have a purpose. The better you know and see this direction and purpose, the clearer the story, the more necessary the beginning and ending you choose – because for the story to work, the beginning and end must have a necessary, causal, consequential relationship. Beginnings and endings are not plot – they necessitate plot, they motivate and define the getting from A to Z.

I have read many scripts that feel as if they begin or end in the wrong place – or both. It is usually a lack of thorough understanding about who the characters are at their heart that makes writers not know where the narrative best begins and ends, and ultimately what their story is.

Don't try to fit story (or plot) around character. Your character must necessarily generate story and plot as a consequence of who they are, how they think, what they feel and what they do.

➢ Know your characters to know your story.
➢ Know your story to know where you are going.
➢ Know where you are going to know where to begin.

This way you won't get as lost, distracted or confused as you otherwise might.

FOCUS

Knowing your story is about focus. So what about *M*A*S*H*, *Crash*, *The Wire*, *EastEnders*? I'm not saying you must have only one main character focus. But that however many characters you believe your story is about, the audience also has the necessary character focus at any given time.

Which is to say – whose story is it at any given time? In this episode of *EastEnders*, whose story is it? *M*A*S*H* was about an ensemble, but it was more about a core few than it was equally about everybody. Which is to say, it was more often from their POV than from other POVs.

POINT OF VIEW

POV is a technical film-making term that denotes the viewpoint of the camera and/or a particular character's physical standpoint. But it's crucial for all stories in all forms. Not simply so you can feel sure about whose story it primarily is, but also so you can, scene by scene, work to put the audience in the shoes of particular characters – emotionally, psychologically, physically. For stories to really work, you need to know what the POVs are and put your audience in their shoes.

POV can be literal, as in a camera position. But more than that, it should be dramatic and emotional in that we might go into a scene knowing what has preceded, motivated and necessitated it, and with the knowledge of what might be achieved or what might be at stake. With this in mind, we can see dramatic consequences unfold and their emotional effect on character. (Non-linear stories are necessarily different in that we do not see the chronological order of consequence – but this doesn't mean you are dispensing with dramatic causality, only that you are rearranging and manipulating our viewing of it.)

So the key thing is to let an audience in on what matters to your characters and to follow that through. You need to make the audience see the world through your character's eyes. Everyone sees the world differently – some slightly, some extremely. You need to develop your characters with a clear sense of what they see when they look out at the world, and look out at any given moment and situation. The same scene told from a different character's POV is fundamentally a different scene because people see things in different ways. If you don't think about character POV early on, then the audience might remain outside the story, observing it rather than inside it and experiencing it.

Strong POV can utterly and brilliantly define what your story is by defining whose story it is and what we therefore feel about that definition and focus. Andrea Arnold's films *Fish Tank* and *Red Road* have an unswervingly tight focus on the POV of one character; we see the world from the POV of the female lead in both films to the extent of following them so closely (via hand-held camera) that the proximity is almost oppressive. The story is their story – it never really belongs to anyone else.

MOVIE ENSEMBLES

Lots of screenwriters wish to emulate films like *M*A*S*H**, *Short Cuts*, *Gosford Park*, *Magnolia*, *Crash*. The simple fact is that the multi-strand single drama is an extraordinarily difficult genre to do well – a challenge to the greatest minds and practitioners, never mind aspiring ones. Think hard about whether you yet have the material, the ability and the dexterity to pull this off.

I've seen a lot of such scripts try and fail because there's no defining focus in their story. In *M*A*S*H*, the wartime emergency scenario pulls the characters together. In *Crash* and *Short Cuts* it is the way unconnected characters overlap with dramatic effects. In *Magnolia* it is the tenuous connections that make isolated stories build together to a shared climax of a biblical shower of frogs (and in *Short Cuts* there's an earthquake). In *Gosford Park* it is the murder mystery and class divides within one country house that connect the disparate characters. In each there is a meaningful reason why so many POVs can coexist. In each you are seeing storytelling at its most difficult and remarkable and auteurist. The multi-stranded separateness still must be focused and tied together.

The other option, of course, is to make a TV show out of your multi-stranded idea instead. Which is exactly what they went on to do with *M*A*S*H* (and usually it's the TV show people tend to recall).

HOOK

The stronger the sense of character focus and POV, the clearer the dramatic and emotional hook will be. The 'hook' is the thing that justifies us watching – the thing that says it's worth watching this story because it will take Character X on a journey from beginning to end. It's the premise – the conflict, the dramatic question, the character's need and desire, the purpose – that will keep us hooked. It's the question that requires an answer that will only be delivered by watching through to the end.

POV TURNED UPSIDE-DOWN

So that's how it's supposed to be. Then there are the wild, maverick exceptions – the ones where storytellers do something weird, radical, upside down. Here are some favourite films that do it well:

In *Psycho*, we begin following Marion Crane as she robs her boss, leaves town, checks into a motel – and then is suddenly, shockingly killed off. Then Norman Bates takes over the POV. Hitchcock's mastery of suspense and tension was the ultimate play on expectation and POV.

In *Fargo*, we spend the first third of the film wondering whose story it is, who we're supposed to connect with, who occupies the moral centre of the world. And we struggle badly, faced with an awful father, his awful wife, their awful child, his awful grandfather and the awful kidnappers who turn up on the doorstep. That is, until Marge the plain, pregnant, small-town cop arrives. The Coen brothers push to the nth degree our sense of finding an emotional heart and POV. (They also tell us their film is a true story and a thriller, neither of which is true.)

In *Memento*, we follow a man who can't form new memories in his quest to find out the murderer of his wife, only to be ultimately told that there is no killer, that his quest is an invention to give meaning to a life that can have no meaning because nothing more in it can be remembered. Except that this bombshell might not true. We don't know. The hero doesn't know. The whole story might be a falsehood, a fabrication. But in that moment we are closer than ever to the POV of the hero and the hopelessness of a future in which nothing new will be remembered.

In *The Usual Suspects*, we spend an entire film intrigued about and terrified by the neo-mythical Kaiser Soze, and then in the mother of all twists we realise we've been watching him all along, pretending to be someone else, hearing the tale from his POV, but one that apparently is someone else's. Or have we? It is one of those rare films where the twist and ambiguity either works for you or doesn't. The writer and director simply did not know until they saw it in a cinema with an audience whether the twist would work.

In all these films, our connection and engagement with a focus and POV is given a unique and genre-bending treatment. They are all also 'thrillers' (except of course *Fargo*, which says it is – but isn't really). There's something about the intrigue, surprise, twists, turns and manipulation of expectation of this genre that can allow for – perhaps even demand – a different understanding of what character focus means. The point of this diversion is to show that even in genre-driven but also maverick and utterly distinct films like these, character focus remains crucial to what the story is and means at its heart of hearts.

In these films the drive towards the ending is utterly crucial and central too because it fully expresses the story: of a young man whose sinister, complex relationship with his dead mother has turned him into a monster; of a man who can't form new memories realising for only a moment (that he will soon forget) that his life possibly has absolutely no meaning; of a policewoman who simply cannot understand why people do such bad and stupid things for the sake of money; of the ultimate truth over whether a petty criminal is in fact a mythical criminal or the mythical criminal is invoked to help the petty criminal escape the law.

GETTING INTO CHARACTER

TEST OF CHARACTER

Strong characters that we want to engage with, spend time with, root for, cry over, laugh at, fear for, from whose POV we see the world, are the indispensable heart of all great scripts. They are also often the central problem with scripts that don't work. The big test of all scripts is ultimately whether the characters are strong and compelling enough to carry the story, idea and audience along with them.

We've all heard the popular cliché of an actor 'getting into character' – whether that's psyching up before a performance or a method actor 'living' the role. It's something we like to sneer at: doesn't so-and-so take themselves seriously? But it *is* deadly serious. If you haven't created a character worth 'getting into' then you are already in deep trouble. There are plenty of things you can get wrong, or at least that can be fixed – plot, structure, narrative, dialogue. But if your characters don't live, your whole story is dead. Neatly crafted, coherently plotted, perfectly formatted, market-ready scripts are meaningless if they don't have great characters at their heart.

I have read many carefully wrought thrillers that push every necessary button but are forgettable because the character doesn't stay with you; the difference between *Die Hard* and many a dispensable action flick is the central character at the heart of it, an ordinary Joe doing extraordinary things in very individual, personality-driven ways. I have read a much smaller number of messy, flawed, unproducable scripts that have stayed with me because the characters stand out and stick in the memory.

Characters are the beginning, middle and end of what makes or breaks a great script and a great writer. With strong, engaging characters, no matter what other problems you might have, you will always have somewhere to go.

'Once I've had the headline idea, then the very next thing I'll explore is the characters . . . This is the bit I love most. This is the truly creative part of the process, where anything can happen . . . It's very easy for me to get bogged down in the characters . . . But I think the bedrock of any decent drama has to be character, and devoting time and energy to getting those right usually pays dividends.'

Toby Whithouse

DRAMATIC VS COMIC

There is a fundamental difference between straight-dramatic and straight-comic characters. Great dramatic characters can reach *anagnorisis*, or awareness – the realisation and recognition of who they are, how they have changed and the meaning of what they have done. Comic characters tend to remain blinkered and unchanging, never fully able to comprehend what it is about their personality that gets them into comic trouble. However, between these two 'straight' extremes is every other shade of character, and the classic straight comedy characters usually exist only in traditional TV sitcoms and classic farces for the stage and the big screen. And I think that you need to invest the same amount of energy and create the same strength of story wherever your characters sit on the drama–comedy spectrum.

SPENDING TIME

We must want to spend time with them. We need to feel their desires, soak up their energy and joy, share their pain, fear for their safety, laugh at their shortcomings. We must want to see what they will do next – or we will stop watching and caring. It might be the vicarious thrill in the mania of Frank Gallagher or the calculation of Iago. It might be the heroic thrill of Billy Elliot winning a place at ballet school against the odds or Theo keeping the only pregnant woman in the world and her unborn baby safe. It might be the comic thrill of Basil Fawlty failing to keep the hotel inspector at bay or David Brent never quite realising how embarrassingly bad a boss he really is. It might be the domestic thrill of Angie lying about her terminal illness or what Dirty Den will do when he realises she is lying.

EMPATHY

Whoever they are, whatever they do, we need to empathise with them – to stand in their shoes and understand what they think, feel, do – regardless of whether or not we agree with them or would do what they do ourselves.

Empathy isn't diversion, a take-it-or-leave-it distraction from other more important things. It is a fundamental compulsion, a need to engage with another human being (and in stories, with a character), no matter how unlike us or far from us they appear to be. If it isn't there, your script is simply plot without story.

We don't need to like your characters. Or admire them. Or agree with them. Or wish we were more like them. Or want to take them home to meet our parents. Or wish we lived next door to someone like them. But they must have a human, emotional life. No matter how bad, selfish, arrogant, blinkered, stupid they appear to be, we need to connect with at least one part of their personality that is engaging or vulnerable – the chink in their armour that takes them beyond two-dimensional stereotypes.

Even if your character is not human. I don't know of any great characters driving a story or at the heart of a story that are not suffused with human traits – even robots like the Terminator, Wall-E, Hal or the Replicants. The only characters that can get away with a lack of humanity are the pure and unadulterated villains and nemeses – because it is precisely their selfishness and lack of humanity that defines their role in a story.

Shakespeare's Coriolanus is a much-maligned but interesting 'hero'. Seemingly brutal, granitic, driven by pride, military virtue and a disregard for the common people, he is not an easy hero to connect with. But in saying goodbye to his mother, wife and child when going into exile, and when they are later used to deter his returning vengeance, we see the chinks in his armour that make him as human as any other character. He is not simply a killing machine – he is a man who is out of place and anachronistic in a world that is changing around him. That is his tragedy – his heroism is in fighting for what he believes in, even if and when it kills him.

DEFINITION

Character is so important that it's worth asking what the word means, where it comes from. A character is a person portrayed in a literary or artistic work. The markings I am using here – and we all use every time we write any language of words or symbols or numbers – are characters of an alphabet. This is the root of it – a set of symbols arranged to express information. The word derives from the ancient Greek term, χαρακτήρ, a tool used for inscription or engraving. For your script to work, that 'inscription' of character must be indelible, clear, strong, expressive, literally impressing them into our hearts, minds and memories.

In contemporary terms, 'character' is defined as a number of things:

➢ The qualities/features that distinguish one person from another.
➢ A peculiar, eccentric or unusual person.
➢ Status, role and capacity.
➢ Public estimation and reputation.
➢ Moral/ethical strength and fortitude.

It's also interesting that we provide 'character references' in work and 'character witnesses' in court – as though the person we describe or recommend is a kind of fiction or construct of the elements that we believe constitute them.

ARCHETYPES

Before working out what 'individual' means, it's worth thinking about what archetypes are. In the work of Christopher Vogler, as inspired by Joseph Campbell's seminal anthropological research, he identifies common character and story archetypes that recur in stories ranging across the world, time and cultures (the hero, the mentor, the threshold guardian et al). Archetypal characters perform archetypal functions in stories – but when they become simply a regurgitation of what has been seen before, they stop being archetypal and become derivative and clichéd.

So in *Star Wars*, a modern reworking of the Arthurian 'hero's journey', you have the young, naive, foolhardy but brave hero plucked from apparent obscurity (but with a 'purpose' he doesn't yet understand) who embarks on a quest after receiving a call to adventure, mentored by a hermit-wizard-guide, to save a princess from the clutches of a dark knight serving an evil emperor, and aided by a freewheeling bandit-pirate, passing through wild places as he goes. He is lured inside the emperor's terrifying castle and must use his faith, courage and swordfighting skill against a faceless horde and even a dungeon monster in an epic battle of good against evil.

But this isn't an Arthurian tale set in medieval England. It is a sci-fi adventure set in deepest space where the call to adventure is a hologram, horses are spacecraft, castles are space stations, swords are light sabres and faith is 'the force'. Luke Skywalker's petulant desire to escape his rural prison is set against the context of repairing droids, twin moons, hovercars and the scale of the journey into the unknown taking him through space at light speed with an intergalactic smuggler and his big, hairy sidekick. The quality of his emotions and experiences are Arthurian – the detail of the world of the story is literally intergalactic.

So, is Luke simply an archetypal 'Sir Percival' naïf on a quest for the Holy Grail? Yes and no. His character is archetypal and much more than archetypal. His function is archetypal, but his personality is Luke Skywalker and only Luke Skywalker.

Not all your characters will or should necessarily have such a clear and identifiable archetype from stories past. But there will be something archetypal in their experiences, traits, attitudes, journeys, desires, flaws and relationships. Don't be afraid of this or fight it unnecessarily. Use it. Archetypal functions are there because they have been tried and tested – and have worked and satisfied. What will make your story is not trashing archetypes but developing them, growing them, reinventing them, giving them your own unique stamp in your own unique story.

FEATURES

Physiognomy is important. Characters need a physical presence and you should give them one in your script – even if the actor who goes on to play them could end up looking very different. A simple indication of sex, age, size, manner, dress, ability/disability, tic/quirk or characteristic action (e.g., never looking anyone in the eye) usually suffices. But it rarely helps to be too detailed, unless the detail is crucial in the story.

You also need not be literal and obvious – metaphor and simile can be powerful indicators. The point about a feature – whether it's a big nose, a pronounced limp or an excruciating shyness – is that it's noticeable, perceptible and something that makes this character stand out from the other characters around them. And it's fine to give us a simple, clear, tangible first impression. If they have much greater complexity and depth, then we will look beyond the initial wrapping in due course. It never helps to give long-winded explanations of personality and backstory in the introduction, so don't do it.

One of my favourite introductions is in Matthew Graham's opening episode of *Life on Mars*, where Sam Tyler is described thus on page one: 'SAM himself is smart, lithe, mid-thirties. If he were a flavour he'd be spearmint.' This neat description does an awful lot of work. A fairly specific age. Smart means not just smart-looking, but intelligent and sharp. Lithe means flexible or supple – which in turn mean resilient to physical pressure, graceful and mentally flexible. But my favourite part is the flavour. Of course, Sam does not literally taste of spearmint – but there's something about this which tells us about his too-sharp, too-cleancut, too-anal personality in an age where forensic technology can give police work some definite, clear, evidential meaning. The point being that the 1970s, where he will soon find himself, are not spearmint-flavoured – they are cigarette, sweat, booze, chip and grime flavoured.

ECCENTRICITY

It is natural to hit upon eccentricities, peculiarities, unusual tics and quirks that will speak your character loudly, clearly and distinctly. And in comedy, soap opera and genre-driven stories they are crucial – from the 'types' of sitcom and theatrical farce to the catchphrases of *EastEnders* to the goodies and baddies of the movies. But be careful that your character isn't simply a construct of tics, quirks, catchphrases and stereotypes. Eccentricity will only get you so far, especially with the main, lead characters driving your story. The peculiarities need to be at the heart of a character, not simply sitting on the visible surface. They need to be a quality, not just a feature; that is the difference between any number of forgettable quirky geeks and the unforgettable Napoleon Dynamite. Napoleon isn't just weird on top – he is weird in the middle too.

QUALITIES

What qualities can be attributed to your characters in the things they do and have done? What physical abilities and achievements? Or, alternatively, what disabilities and limitations? What do your characters – and audience – see when they look at another character? What perceivable, recognisable qualities – positive or negative – do they possess? What talents?

Confident, aware, intelligent, charming, persevering, tenacious, ambitious, enthusiastic, faithful, believing, honourable, generous, patient, understanding, empathetic, reasonable, rational, sensible, selfless, steadfast, honest, pure.

Self-defeating, blinkered, stupid, ignorant, sarcastic, lazy, doubting, cynical, mean, envious, jealous, covetous, irascible, uncaring, unsympathetic, irrational, arrogant, vicious, selfish, fickle, dishonest, licentious.

These lists are largely positive against negative. However, it isn't simple extremes that are most interesting, but complex combinations. The charm displayed by a trickster seeking to swindle someone out of their cash is not a positive quality; and there can be a fine line between confident and arrogant, or ambitious and covetous, or tenacious and unsympathetic. Various qualities can lie in seeming contradiction. Nobody is singularly anything.

The point about qualities is not in the first instance what characters try to be or show to other people, but what they revert to when the mask slips, when the heat is turned up, when they are threatened, when they are tempted, when they step outside their comfort zone and into the unknown. Who are your characters really when they can no longer pretend, blag or hide?

CAPABILITIES AND FLAWS

Capability is what a character can do; a flaw is a weakness that limits that capability.

Capabilities need not necessarily be morally qualitative – for example, the Christian virtues set against the seven deadly sins. They can simply be the outcome of what a character does and does not do. Abilities and weaknesses are multi-layered – they can figure on a moral, emotional, psychological, physical or social level. Complexity comes, for example, when physical ability (dancing) is countered by social, emotional and psychological handicaps (poverty, bereavement and lack of confidence), as in Billy Elliot. Billy can never change where he comes from socially or culturally, nor can he undo his mother's death, but the sheer force of physical ability alongside the qualities that makes us engage with him (charm, cheek, persistence, passion), mean he can still get to ballet school, excel, and make his once-doubting father and brother proud.

Tony Soprano is capable of cold-blooded murder – a truly deadly sin – in the name of 'honour' as set against a mafiosa code of morality, yet he is beset by psychological doubt, depression and the feeling that he will always somehow be a failure to someone. This doubt is almost in diametric opposition to the confidence required to know that a hoodlum who does the 'wrong' thing deserves punishment.

No person is perfect. No person is all bad. Everyone is complex.

ESTIMATION

The natural extension of what can be observed in characters is the estimation people have of them and the status they are given in the world of the story: what is presumed of them and how this affects how much power and influence they have, whether real or imagined. One character's estimation of another can form the basis of the conflicts and tensions in their relationship. Mistaken assumptions by one character about another can form the basis of their actions and the consequent repercussions.

Othello is a good example in that 'estimation' and 'reputation' are central ideas in Shakespeare's play. At the start, the world around Othello makes massive assumptions about him – he has the renowned status of a powerful military leader of men, yet his 'blackness' marks him out as an unsuitable husband for the daughter of a white man. This unsuitability and the fact that he does secretly marry the daughter of a prominent white man sets in motion a series of events that lead to tragedy. Iago plays on Cassio's sense of 'reputation', Iago soliloquises on what people see of him as compared with what we know of him below the surface, and Iago manipulates Othello's sense of Desdemona's 'reputation' as a faithful wife. Public estimation (in contrast to the truth that people might not immediately and clearly see) is at the heart of the conflict, story and tragedy.

So, what are your characters like when people look at them, observe them, judge them, compartmentalise them – and interact with them. What are the distinguishing features that set them apart? And then, what do your characters see when they look at themselves – and when we see beyond what is visible on the surface to the other character?

ATTITUDE

Capabilities and flaws are relative to the POV of a character (and audience member). One person's ability is another's flaw – to some empathy is strength, to others it is weakness. What makes characters increasingly distinct and interesting and complex is their attitude towards themselves, other people and the world around them. No two people will fully agree in every detail or about everything in the real world. It is attitude, perspective, point of view which makes them not just an assemblage of characteristics, but an expression of who they uniquely are in the world you create.

POV

As I have already said, POV is a film-making term – what the camera sees from a particular place, and what a character sees from their standpoint. But POV isn't just physical – it is emotional, political, social, psychological, gendered, sexual, intellectual, religious. It is subjective, personal, individual. No two POVs are the same – no two beings could make their responses to one thing exactly correspond, never mind their responses to everything.

The key thing for the writer is to make that character POV individual by making it complex – by making it as wide and full as possible. The audience needs to understand what the world looks, smells, tastes, sounds, feels like when that character interacts with it. To stand in their skin, step inside their shoes, use their eyes, ears and touch.

This is empathy – seeing the world from another person's POV. Empathy is the emotional tie that binds audience to character and story. We don't need to like them – just to see the world from their POV.

This does not mean POV should be logical, neat, tidy. On the contrary, POVs are illogical, messy, unordered, perhaps involuntary, inexplicable, conflicted, compromised, contradictory. A character – a person – can for example wish and yearn for the stability of a family to love, yet fear and avoid the responsibilities of supporting one.

Characters don't need to fully, clearly recognise all the various elements that make up their full, complex POV. They don't need to understand why they feel the way they do when they look out at the world at the start of the story. On the contrary, if they have full clarity at the start, there will probably be nowhere for them to go, no understanding to achieve, no *anagnorisis* – no journey to complete.

Most likely, the less neat, tidy and logical they are, the more human and interesting they will appear to be. They may believe their POV makes sense at the start – but does it? And what will change about how they see the world by the end of the story?

HISTORY AND BACKSTORY

Certain kinds of stories and characters tend not to demand a detailed, informed sense of where they have come from, what their history is, what their backstory is, and what has formed them as a person; surrealism and absurdism in particular, but sitcoms too and most kinds of broad comedy and farce. Their psychology appears more existential, focused entirely on what they do and what we can see with little psychological regard for what has gone before. There may be implied pasts – we perhaps presume Didi and Gogo have waited for Godot before, but that doesn't tell us many details about where they came from, while we might presume or even know of a fundamentally formative experience that has helped shape sitcom characters (such as Mum dying in *Only Fools and Horses*).

For other characters in other kinds of stories, audiences (and actors) tend to want to feel that there is a history that has formed and informed their psychology. The audience rarely needs to know that backstory in detail, unless it becomes a pivotal point of story and plot. For example, in concluding-twist psychological thrillers the revelation of backstory is frequently a fundamental part of the genre and character storytelling (as, for example, in *The Machinist*). But generally speaking, you can have as much backstory and character profiling in your notes and preparation as you want and deem fit.

The trick is to utilise and show to the audience only things that are crucial in the present-tense story. Writers far too often waste valuable, irretrievable time bringing the backstory into the present tense when frequently it just isn't necessary. But for the audience to feel the character has a fullness of history and personality, you as a writer need to know that history first in order that you can keep it in reserve. I often read characters that just don't seem to have anything to them beyond what is on the surface of the script – and often this is because writers haven't done the legwork.

You won't get any brownie points for all this unseen work on backstory and history, because most of it is meant to remain hidden. But if you do it well and do it thoroughly, it will serve your characters and story in unimaginable ways. As in any other element of the process, though, you need to resist cliché and the obvious as if under scrutiny from an audience. I've read a million scripts about troublesome and troubled characters that were beaten / abused / ignored / abandoned (delete as appropriate) as a child; this is an obvious, linear observation to make and by itself doesn't offer anything new about character that we haven't already seen.

MORAL COMPASS

Backstory and POV help define the direction to which the needle of the character's moral compass points. Characters with no moral instincts are impossible to engage with on a human level. Without some level of self-consciousness about the meaning of their actions in the world, they become like animals, literally inhuman. (Even anthropomorphised 'animal' characters display human moral characteristics.)

What codes do your characters live by, whether conscious or unconscious, acquired or intrinsic? How do differing codes contradict one another? Again, how do Tony Soprano's Mafia 'ethics' square with his potential to be brutal? How do Frank Gallagher's opinionated, neo-politicised rants square with the apparent amorality of many of his alcohol-fuelled acts? Does the avenger in *Dead Man's Shoes* (or indeed in any revenge tale) lose the moral high ground the moment he crosses the line and punishes those who have wronged his brother?

Within the moral POV will most likely be found not only your character's defining strengths, but also their flaws and the roots of conflict in their story.

MORALITY AND CONFLICT

When a character has a strong POV, you necessarily create a tension whereby anything that contradicts that standpoint is a cause of possible conflict. If you put a moralistic, Christian, virginal policeman on an island that celebrates fertility in pagan ritual, then you set him on a course for a fundamental clash of moralities – thus *The Wicker Man*. If you put an anachronistic, autocratic warrior hero in a city that has developed democratic principles then you set him on a collision course of world views – thus *Coriolanus*.

If your characters don't have a strong moralistic POV – whether moral or immoral – then nothing will challenge them and there will be no conflict, no tension, no story. Amoral characters tend to be a void, a vacuum, with whom we do not engage, for whom we do not feel.

THE 'AGON'

You will probably have heard the terms 'protagonist' and 'antagonist' – often misappropriated as 'hero' and 'villain'. The 'agon' in both terms is the conflict, but although the term derives from a contest in ancient Greece (such as in athletics or music, where prizes were awarded to the winner), a conflict is not just a physical conflict. It describes the verbal dispute between two characters – the dialectic. But it also means a test of will, a test of personality, the attempt to surmount whatever obstacles stand in the way of a character's wants and needs, whether physical, emotional, psychological, social, political. Hero and villain are qualitative terms – nowadays they tend to mean good and bad, light and dark, beautiful and ugly, right and wrong. But a protagonist doesn't have to be a good, handsome hero, they just have to be the character that sets out to achieve or realise a goal; an antagonist doesn't have to be a bad, ugly villain, they just have to be what stands in the way of the protagonist.

HERO AND VILLAIN

What does fundamentally characterise the hero and villain in western storytelling is what the character does as a consequence of who that character is. A hero is selfless, willing to suffer sacrifice on behalf of others or for what they believe to be right and true. A villain is selfish, willing to inflict suffering on others in order to get what they believe they want.

Anti-heroes are trickier beings because they subvert the usual course of heroic behaviour and can do bad, wrong or weird things – yet their POV gives them the dramatic, heroic focus.

Alex in *A Clockwork Orange* began life in a novel, but is one of the most infamous anti-heroes of the big screen, a charming, intelligent young man who appreciates beautiful music and the feeling it inspires in him, yet who is a violent gang leader capable of deliberate, extreme, sickening physical and sexual violence. He is manipulative, self-centred, even self-pitying. But in the book, film and stage versions alike, it is the strength of POV that makes this difficult personality compelling.

The same goes for Carlin in *Scum*, Stanley in *The Birthday Party*, David Wicks in *EastEnders*, Willy Loman in *Death of a Salesman*, Dexter, Napoleon Dynamite, Frank Gallagher. In all of them, it comes down to POV – what the characters want and believe, and the things they do as a consequence.

DESIRE AND NEED

The stronger your character's POV – even though complex and contra-dictory – the clearer will be their desire and need to the audience. What your character wants and needs may not be clear to them at the beginning, and may only become clear at the very end, but wherever that recognition comes, it is a crucial and indispensable part of great dramatic character writing.

Characters who want nothing and need nothing will come to nothing in dramatic terms. Pursuing want and need is what constitutes their journey forward. Without this journey, you don't have a story. Ask this of your characters: what do they want/need not simply now (in the scene), but by the end of that day, the following morning, a month later, in a year's time, and ultimately at the end of their lives?

Desire is what a character believes they want. They may be wrong, they may change their mind or heart, but they must desire something.

Need is what a character requires, whether they want it or not, whether they are aware of it or not.

Desire and need are utterly relative – a question of scale not impor-tance. Theo's desire to protect the only pregnant woman in a world without babies in *Children of Men* is, from the character's POV, equivalent in mea-ning to Shaun's desire in *This is England* to create a new family around him after the loss of his father in the Falklands War. The success of the former affects the world on a macro, epic scale; the success of the latter primarily affects just Shaun. The scale of desire in the worlds of the two films are different, but the dramatic importance of their desire to the character is fundamentally the same.

DESIRE VERSUS NEED

Character can become complex when desire and need have a necessary, causal connection. In *Star Wars*, Luke wants adventure but needs purpose; the former he already feels, the latter he isn't aware of until Obi-Wan Kenobi reveals he is a Jedi. He cannot truly realise his desire for adventure until the need to become a Jedi is realised too.

Characters become more complex when desire and need are in conflict and tension. In *Shameless*, Frank Gallagher wants oblivion but needs clarity; avoiding the fallout of the former and resisting the sobriety of the latter is the engine that drives his character and the story he generates. At the outset of *Prime Suspect*, Jane Tennison wants acceptance as the southern woman heading up an extremely masculine police department in the north, yet she needs a sense of conflict and abrasion in order to bring out her best policing and managerial instincts. And vice versa – she also in a sense wants conflict because that is how her personality best expresses itself, yet she needs acceptance because conflict will eventually drive her to the edge.

Characters become multilayered beings ripe for ongoing reinterpretation when such complexities pile on one another. Hamlet wants justice over his father's death yet he needs endless justification to realise that; he wants answers to justify revenge yet what he really needs is faith in what to do next: he thinks he wants evidence but what he really needs is resolve; he wants to escape Elsinore and other people yet he needs to stay and put the world back in joint; he wants the confusion of others not knowing what he feels by believing he is 'mad' yet what he really needs is clarity of knowledge and purpose; he wants the book and the library yet what he needs is the arena and the sword; and in the final irony, he both wants and needs peace, but can only reach it through death, destruction, tragedy.

If the wants and needs of your characters are too simple – the want is revenge, the need is a gun – then they will remain one-dimensional, cardboard cutouts, and the story will remain flat. In *Dead Man's Shoes*, Richard wants revenge but he needs peace, and the two simply can't coexist; this is what makes it a tragedy.

ACTION

From POV, desire and need come action. Passivity is the death of character – or rather, a severe limit to the dramatic life of character. Only masters of craft can push the limits of characters delaying action or appearing to avoid it, as in *About Schmidt*, *The Man Who Wasn't There* – and, indeed, *Hamlet*. In all three, action and the mistaken appearance of being passive is at the heart of what the story is about.

Drama without action is not drama. Drama stems from the character's need to show and be itself at the start of the story. If you tread water at the start, you are wasting time. Cut to the action.

By 'action' I do not mean big explosions, wild car-chases or crunching fight sequences (although it can be these things in certain genres, or at certain times in any genre – and if you are writing an action thriller then you'll probably need all three).

Fundamentally, action is the true expression of character through what they do or don't do – however big or small that action might be or seem. Again, the scale of action is relative to what is important to the character in the world they occupy.

To Shaun in *This is England*, wearing flared cords in 1983 when no other kid does is enough to spur him to get into fights, join a 'gang' and adopt a radical new look – because he hates standing out in the wrong way. The subtext to this is that he is searching for something that will assuage the loss of his father. In fact, though, it's not the flares that make him different and stand out – it's his personality, his POV, his actions. Which is why Woody and Combo are both so impressed by him despite his youth. It is this that makes him a compelling hero. At the start, you know he is a character who feels, thinks, believes, and who acts upon all three.

VULNERABILITY

Character-driven action makes characters vulnerable as well as making them engaging and compelling, because, as I have said, want/need brings about not only action but conflict too. In *This is England*, Shaun puts himself in ultimate danger when he joins Woody's gang of mates, even though the danger (racism and violence) at that point from his POV couldn't really be anticipated. The moment Billy Elliot hangs back to watch the ballet class, he sets on course a series of events that could lead to total breakdown in his relationship with his father and brother.

Characters without real vulnerabilities that are driven by their personality are, in a sense, not really in any more danger than you or I – we could all be hit by a bus tomorrow because accidents do happen. But great characters make their own jeopardy, not necessarily out of foolhardiness or bravery, but because they do things they feel they ought to do, whatever the reason, because of who they are. This is what binds us to them.

Even characters who appear to have an impenetrable armour around them need some kind of chink that exposes the flesh beneath. Hence the notion of an 'Achilles heel', for without a physical weakness Achilles would ultimately be more killing machine than human warrior hero. Frank Gallagher has an extremely thick armoury of drink, drugs, bad behaviour, opinion, cowardice and aggression. But he also has crucial moments where the guard drops and the sorry, bewildered, incapable father that any man is potentially capable of being is laid bare. In fact, the first time we see him in episode one of series one, he is utterly comatose and incapacitated – one huge chink in the armour we will come to see in all its grubby glory.

Feeling for and fearing for a character's vulnerabilities is not 'feeling sorry for them'. This kind of 'pity' is the lowest denomination in the possible scope of our relationship with a character. Vulnerability is not about bad things happening to characters and us feeling sorry for them; it is about characters creating jeopardy through the force of their personality and us being taken along on the ride with them. The former is drippy sentimentalism; the latter is dynamic drama.

CHARACTER AND MEDIUM

Great characters are great characters and perhaps there's no fundamental difference in how you should approach them in different mediums. But there are differences in how they play and how we relate to them.

THEATRICAL CHARACTER

Theatrical character relies on what an actor can perform, and is limited in the amount of technical resources that might be available in radio and on screen. In theatre, characters are physical beings in a physical space in relatively close proximity to an audience. This pure physicality can (and arguably should) be at the heart of your characters.

RADIO CHARACTER

Radio character is curious. It is fundamentally no different to any other, except in the crucial fact that we cannot physically see the person. Therefore all the simple clues and signs that one can pick up on stage and screen cannot be relied on. You only have their voice, their actions, and the reactions and indications of the other characters around them. There is, therefore, a huge pressure and reliance on the word – on what is said and what you write in order to delineate what happens in the acoustic environment. In radio, the voice must go a very long way in characterising who the characters are, how they project, what they feel, what they think. You should try hard not to state (or at least overstate) them through exposition. In radio, character is voice.

FILM CHARACTER

A great film character need never actually speak words, as in the greatest silent movies. So too in theatre or TV – but in film, the cinematic canvas speaks character action from the minutiae of extreme close-up to the panorama of the long, wide shot. *Walkabout* has very little script and dialogue – it is primarily visual storytelling, and powerfully so. Film need only have one character – as in *Moon* (though that one-ness is strange and complex). So too theatre, radio and TV – but film has the ability to follow a character, observe them, detail them without them explaining anything to us. In radio, theatre and TV, a single character almost certainly means a monologue – in film, it means visual storytelling. Not many films do this in such an extreme way, but it's worth remembering that it's something that films can do uniquely.

TV CHARACTER

On the smaller screen, in the corner of the room, characters need to be big. We don't have physical presence, visual scope and breadth, or (usually) a short cut into their mind/voice. Instead, they need to stand out, be writ large, bully their way into our living rooms and our attention. Soaps can be quite Dickensian, upfront, immediately appreciable. Extreme subtlety does not necessarily play as well or as successfully on TV, though this of course depends on the genre, format and what an audience demands from a particular slot and channel at a particular time. But being 'big' is always essential.

HITTING THE GROUND RUNNING

PAGE ONE

So you have developed your characters, explored the form, world, idea, story, theme, genre, focus, POV, and you know where you are trying to go by the end of the story. If you have set about this work well, and by virtue of knowing the ending, you should have a sense deep in your gut or brain about where to begin. But the writing process is never so logical and simple – beginnings are notoriously difficult to get right and a great many scripts don't manage to hit the ground running on page one, scene one, line one.

When I say 'hit the ground running', I do not mean an action chase or a literal interpretation of speed – unless of course your story is in the action or thriller genre. I mean that the story should be under way straightaway. Page one, scene one, line one, is where the audience touches down. The last thing you want them to do is then collapse in a heap of confusion, tedium or emotional disconnection. It is extremely easy to lose an audience. In TV and radio, this can literally mean them turning off, turning over or surfing back and forth in prevarication. In film and theatre, it's unlikely they will actually leave unless they believe it is truly awful – but you can still lose your hold on their attention, engagement and enjoyment. And once you have lost the audience, you face a hard climb up a sheer rock face to get them back.

KNOW YOUR STORY

As I have already said, it's hard to tell a story well and to know where a story is going if you don't know what you think it is about. It is even harder to know how, where and when to set a story rolling if you don't really know what it is and you don't really know it thoroughly. You can't ultimately fake this thoroughness and you can waste a lot of time doing, undoing and redoing your script because you have leapt into it before you know what kind of story it is, what kind of effect you hope to have, what is original about it, who the characters are and why we would go on their journey with them. I'm not talking about knowledge of plot details and narrative minutiae; I'm talking about what the story fundamentally is at its heart. With this knowledge should come the instinct and the clarity to clear the decks of clutter and find the right beginning for the story, characters and audience.

HOOK THE ATTENTION

Reel the audience in straight away – don't wait. The kind and genre of story you are telling will greatly influence the style and manner in which you do this – Bond movies always start with a bang, whereas *My Summer of Love* started with a teenage girl freewheeling an engineless moped through remote roads and fields – but you still need to identify what is the intrigue, or mystery, the conflict or tension, the sense of captivation and compulsion that will exist and develop throughout.

Jack Thorne's play *When You Cure Me* begins with a teenage boy and girl in a bedroom. The girl is bedridden, though it is unclear why. The boy appears to be her boyfriend but their close proximity is very awkward. He is trying very hard (too hard) to help and care for her; she is finding this uncomfortable but it quickly becomes clear that she doesn't want her mother to take over, she wants him to be there with and for her. In the opening moments, we see him awkwardly help her use a toilet in a bedpan and this simple action effectively allows the themes and emotional relationships to come immediately into play.

But it isn't just miserable or depressing – the scene has a tender, gently comic awkwardness as well. In the play, we will never leave this girl's bedroom and she will never leave her bed, even though it isn't evident on medical grounds why she is incapable of doing so. The boy will try to stay with her as much as possible and their relationship – which has only really just begun but has instantly been turned upside down by a stranger raping her – will be put through the kind of pressure that no teenage relationship should have to endure.

Shane Meadows' film *A Room for Romeo Brass* begins with an unassuming but lovely sequence in which Romeo is taking home bags of chips for his family's tea. His friend Knocks tags along. But Romeo can't resist starting to eat his chips on the way. He then decides to 'balance out' the three bags by eating from the other two bags, until all three bags are depleted. All the while, he refuses to let his pleading friend have a single chip. This is a film about a simple but strong relationship between neighbouring teenage boys that is turned inside out when an older man appears on the scene and events look like they will take a sinister turn for the worse.

The opening doesn't give away this change and turn, but it does hook us straight away into the relationship between the two boys and does hint that the bond is vulnerable in Romeo's insistence on not giving his friend a single chip while he gobbles them up himself. And it does show that Romeo has the capacity to make very wrong decisions about the consequences of his actions (when he gets home, Romeo gets a deserving bollocking from his mum and sister). The moment is both endearing and revealing. This sequence sets the central characters, relationship, world and theme of the film from the start.

In Matthew Graham's opening episode in series one of *Life on Mars*, we begin with the turning wheels of a police car on the way to apprehend a murder suspect. It is immediately clear that this is a cop show. Sam Tyler, a young, clean-cut, besuited copper knocks on the door of Colin Raimes and gives chase when Raimes takes to his heels. Sam catches up with him and, in a back alley of a Manchester red-brick estate, it seems for a split second that Sam is perhaps out of his depth and not cut out for a hand-to-hand fight. That is until he floors Raimes using a textbook manoeuvre with his retractable baton, and without breaking a sweat or scuffing his suit.

Then we cut to the interview room where it looks as if Sam has the evidence neatly stacked up against Raimes. That is until a very big hole that Sam had missed in the evidence is pointed out and Raimes is set free. So our expectations are neatly upturned twice in quick succession – as we would hope in a crime show. The twenty-first century police practices that will soon disappear as we travel back to 1973, along with Sam's personality and his reliance upon those practices, are set out at once in brilliantly economic television scriptwriting.

In Dennis Kelly's radio drama *The Colony*, we are drawn into the apparently curious place of Paul Henry's inner world and a moment in time after which nothing will ever be the same again. He tells us in monologue the tale of how as a boy in 1975 he came to call John Noakes from *Blue*

Peter a 'prick' live on television. The tale is in a sense a complete diversion from the magnitude of what we will come to see in this story. But it's one that tells us a huge amount about the character, and not simply because the character is 'telling' us – but because he is telling us in the middle of a moment, in his flat, with the noise of a loud party in a flat opposite (he occasionally breaks off from his monologue to scream at them to turn the music down), moments before a tragic accident changes the lives of every-one who witnesses it or is close by. Clearly a tragic death is in a sense not comparable to a youthful moment of indiscretion on live TV; but to Paul Henry, it is on the same life-changing scale from his POV.

THE MIDST OF A MOMENT

Cut straight into the action. Open in the middle of an event, conflict or moment. In the above four examples, we begin mid-moment – using a bed-pan, failing to deliver supper, apprehending a suspect and screaming at the neighbours to turn the noise down.

The best way to do this is to show characters in action. Again, not an action sequence – rather characters actively being themselves, making decisions, doing things. These things can be monumental. In the first scene of *King Lear*, the hero divides up his kingdom between his least favourite daughters, falls out spectacularly with his once-favoured daughter, displays his vanity and sets in motion events that will lead to terrible tragedy for himself, his family and his kingdom. But doing very small things is 'action' so long as they are things that express the character and feed into the story that follows. Making a cock-up of buying chips is a very, very small action, but one that tells us a huge amount about the wilfulness and naivety of Romeo Brass that will get him into such trouble later.

A FOCUSED WAY IN

Multi-stranded stories do pose a particular problem for the writer, and the larger the cast of characters the harder it will be to hook the audience. The temptation can be to give the audience a snapshot of all major aspects of the world at the start. *Five Days* is a good example, where a TV serial opens very quietly but surely and deliberately draws you in through seemingly insignificant but in fact very precisely chosen and important moments that glimpse at most of the main players in the drama to come. But in episode one of *Shameless*, a gang show about a wild family squashed into a small house (or 'the Waltons on acid', as the creator Paul Abbott pitched it), we are given a neatly focused way into the world and series.

After the opening credits, episode one could have spent the first ten minutes giving us various glimpses of the whole family in action, or even a chaotic breakfast table tableau that would throw us into the melee of their world. However, the episode is focused through Fiona's POV (the lynchpin, elder-sister, substitute-mother in that first series) and is filtered through her meeting Steve for the first time at a nightclub in Manchester, away from the Chatsworth estate – where Steve spots his ideal girl across the dance floor, gives chase to the thief who steals her handbag, and punches the bouncer who refuses to let them back into the club afterwards. Then they go back to the Gallagher house, where they find Frank comatose on the floor – an auspicious first meeting if ever there was one. Then they spend the night together. And then, next morning, we meet the rest of the family . . .

'GETTING TO KNOW' THE CHARACTERS

Try not to consciously preface, set up or introduce the characters and world. If you are showing your characters in engaging action then we are getting to know them and the world they inhabit in the best way possible. But if you are trying to 'ease' us into the characters and world before or outside the action of the main story, you just won't hook our attention anything like so well. We get to know the characters by seeing them doing meaningful things, not by seeing them go through meaningless routines. If they are going to do an everyday thing (the son buying chips for the family), show them doing something meaningful or unusual with it (eating half of everyone's chips before even making it back through the front door in the knowledge, surely, that it will get him into trouble).

EXPOSITION

Beware the obvious exposition of backstory at the start. This is, of course, easier said than done. The opening scene of *King Lear* might set rolling all the main events of the play, but Shakespeare isn't averse to crowbarring us in with an expository exchange between Kent and Gloucester (although in truth he wrote worse dialogue than this in his time). Audiences are much more capable of piecing together information and going with the flow than we usually think – what they struggle to do is stick with a story if they are immediately laden with static information and explanation in undramatic scenes.

If you have chosen to start the story in a particular place for a meaningful dramatic reason, then do you need to throw in lots of detail about how the characters got there? If information is important in the story, then it should come out in the story. Don't shoehorn information in at the start – find an action, conflict or incident that shows it. Ask yourself how much an audience really needs to know to orient themselves and be interested enough to want to find out more. The more your genre relies on intrigue and withholding information – as in detective, mystery, psychological thriller – the more manipulative and playful you will need to be with information. But blunt opening exposition which is there purely for the benefit of 'setting up' the story for the audience, as opposed to being there for a dramatic story-driven reason, is never good writing.

THE CAPTIVE AUDIENCE

Some say that in theatre in particular, but also in film, once the audience has bought their ticket and taken their seat, you have them captive and you can do what you want. I agree that in these mediums you are afforded some space with the audience. It would have to be pretty bad for you to get up and leave before the end, surely? That's true. But audiences can also form quick and lasting impressions at the beginning and, as I've said, once you have lost them and they have lost faith in your story, you face an uphill struggle to get them back on side.

The other thing is – the reader of your script can put it down, can choose not to bother reading to the end, can make an instant judgement and decide that's enough for them to make a decision. The reader is not a captive audience. If they are busy, even less so. And if they have a steady stream of other scripts to plough through, less so again.

So if you think you can get away with not hooking the attention in your stage play or art-house film, think again.

STRUCTURE AND THE BEGINNING

Structure is not an add-on to story. It is not something you 'apply' to story. It is intrinsic, essential, fundamental – indivisible from story, inseparable from storytelling. Much of what I have discussed regarding medium, form, format, archetypes, genre, idea, premise, beginnings and endings, direction, focus, POV and character is another way of exploring structure – the kind of story you choose to tell, the way in which you choose to tell it. Without an engagement with these other elements, all you will have is plot – a route that you take. But with them, what you will have is meaningful story structure – a journey that we make.

'ACT ONE'

This term was filched from theatre quite some time ago and has become the standard language of Hollywood movie-speak. I'm using the term loosely to mean the overall beginning – the movement from the opening to the middle. Even if you are writing a 'one-act' short play for the stage, it should still have an 'act one' – a beginning – within it.

STRUCTURAL DIAGRAMS

Many screenwriting books propose diagrams and formulae – some elaborate, some bewildering – setting out how good and/or popular film stories have been and should be structured. They are invariably American, and invariably refer to American movies (though they do by extension apply to British films and a great many films across the world).

Some are an interesting read and can be useful. But I am not going to stipulate a complex, precise and prescriptive template, not simply because I am working across various mediums, but because I think that if you start applying complex structural blueprints to ideas you are still struggling to formulate (especially at an early stage of your mastery of the craft), then it's easy to get distracted by plotting the detail of events rather than concentrating on structuring the fundamentals of the story. The best of these books and writers argue that their templates are not necessarily prescriptive, and they are absolutely right – but unfortunately aspiring writers will use them in prescriptive ways, as a kind of crutch or exam crib rather than as a way of feeding and flexing their writer's mind and muscle about how best to tell the stories they have to tell.

I read far too many scripts that have clearly followed a template and are utterly forgettable because the slavish application of that template won't make up for a lack of great character writing and a structure that develops from it. Inserting a piece of formula won't make your script work better. I also think that it's easy, with a template, to start editing and developing out the things that are unusual, distinctive and original about what you are doing with your story, the things that instinct tells you to do. Treading the line between acknowledging structures that work and making a structure your own is always difficult to do, full stop, at any point in your career – never mind do with elegant and sophisticated success.

THE UNIVERSAL FORMULA

I will, however, give you one universal formula (and yes this *is* an entirely prescriptive template) that is absolutely, one-hundred-per-cent indispensable:

BEGINNING + MIDDLE + END
(not necessarily in that order)
= STORY

Yes, I am stating the obvious – and doing so a little facetiously. But I do really mean it. Many writers forget this fundamental principle of engaging character and story, and instead lose themselves and their stories in the intricacies and trickeries of plot design and narrative complication.

The middle is a consequence of the beginning and the ending is a consequence of the beginning and the middle combined. Not necessarily in that linear order as it is shown in the story (as in reversed and fragmented forms) but in that dramatic order in terms of causal relationship between the actions and events of the story. Only in the most surreal, absurd, experimental and downright strange stories does this not necessarily happen – and only in the writers that show mastery of craft and form (as opposed to wilfully maverick behaviour) does challenging the idea of dramatic causality actually work, as in Samuel Beckett, David Lynch, Charlie Kaufman.

If you re-plotted the fragmented events of *21 Grams* into a linear telling, you would see a story of actions, reactions and consequences. It wouldn't be the same film and it wouldn't be half so powerful, but the dramatic core of beginning, middle and ending would be there. A drunken man from the wrong side of the tracks runs down and kills a respectable father and his children on the street. The father's donated heart saves another man who has barely bothered to keep going while he awaits a suitable heart for transplant. The saved man seeks out the bereaved wife/ mother and their growing relationship in turn leads them to seek out and confront the killer, who is now a reformed and zealously godfearing man following his time in prison. And this journey leads to an ending where reform, remorse, forgiveness, anger and revenge meet in a true climax of fundamental human dilemma and conflict for all three characters. The film succeeds in its fragmented non-linear form because the linear dramatic story that underlies the form works.

THREE IS THE MAGIC NUMBER

BEGINNING → MIDDLE → END

DESIRE → OBSTACLE → FULFILMENT

NEED → RESISTANCE → RESOLUTION

PROBLEM → CONFLICT → SOLUTION

ACTION → REACTION → OUTCOME

QUESTION → ARGUMENT → ANSWER

I think story magic has always come in threes. So in terms of genres and kinds of stories, you get this:

HEROIC JOURNEY: Call to adventure → journey → elixir (*Star Wars*)

LOVE STORY: Desire → test of love → marriage (*Four Weddings*)

THWARTED LOVE: Desire → test of love → parting (*Breaking the Waves*)

TRAGEDY: Misunderstanding → failure to understand → death (*Othello*)

CRIME: Misdemeanour → detection → capture (*Inspector Morse*)

MYSTERY: Intrigue → investigation → clarity (*Jonathan Creek*)

REVENGE: A 'wrong' → pursuit → payback (*Dead Man's Shoes*)

EPIC: Old world → struggle → new world (*Elizabeth*)

COMING-OF-AGE: Youth → maturation → awareness (*Kes*)

ACTION HERO: Challenge → battle → victory (*James Bond*)

TRAGIC ACTION HERO: Challenge → battle → defeat (*Coriolanus*)

AGAINST-THE-ODDS: Goal → plan → achievement (*Billy Elliot*)

CIRCULAR: Beginning → middle → ending/beginning (*Fawlty Towers*)

REPETITIVE: Beginning → replayed beginning → ending (*Groundhog Day*)

REVERSED: End → middle → beginning (*Betrayal*)

If you have fewer than three parts then you have one of three things:

➤ Only a beginning and ending where a need/desire is fulfilled or frustrated with no meaningful conflict or journey in between (lots of scripts get lost or grind to a halt in the middle).

➤ Only a beginning and middle, or a story with no ending (lots of scripts fail to deliver the right ending or any ending at all).

➤ Only a middle and ending, with a sweep of events but without the motivation, instigation or logic for them (lots of scripts don't give us a meaningful reason to engage in the first place).

If you get this fundamental triangulation of structural meaning wrong in the first place, I think you just don't have a story that can satisfy – and therefore no real story at all.

BUT THREE IS NOT A SIMPLE NUMBER

The problem with three being the magic number is that beginnings, middles and endings are not necessarily of equivalent lengths. The journey of the middle normally comprises the larger part of the story as a whole. The ending can be a brief affair, though of course it depends where you 'draw the line' between act two and act three. Sometimes trying to draw definitive lines between acts is a fruitless and pointless exercise because different strands will effect their separate changes at different points in the overall story. Or because people disagree about what the story (and therefore structure) really is. Or because there is enough complexity in the story to mean that the structural blueprint that marked out the foundations have been absorbed into the form you have gone on to build above and beyond them. And the audience doesn't necessarily want to have the architecture still on show in the finished story; most audiences want a story in which they can lose themselves.

The point is that while theories are interesting, they won't necessarily help you write well. Theory naturally requires all elements to fit, otherwise it has no value – and this is where people tie themselves in knots trying to make their story correspond to a blueprint exactly and at all costs. You need to take a flexible approach to where the act divisions fall and where the lines are drawn according to what story you are trying to tell, and not stretch and bend your story to fit a template that seems to have worked for some other box-office-busting film that made billions of dollars across the ocean. If you are writing television episodes for a commercial broadcaster with exactly demarcated ad breaks then you do ultimately have to conform – but that's what a script editor is there to help you do. You don't write ad breaks into your calling card script. You tell the story.

THE BEGINNING

So taking in the first part of the three-part sequences above, you need to work out what at the beginning of your story is the fundamental desire, need, problem, tension, question, mystery, call, goal, challenge or action that takes your characters from the ordinary world that precedes it to the new one that will unfold within it. There are some fundamental elements that story tends to use and expect, but they won't necessarily come in a set order. And for some forms and genres, longer will be spent on certain parts than with other forms and genres. But without them, the audience and story will struggle to orient themselves.

DISORIENTATION VERSUS CONFUSION

Disorientation may be your intention, and if you want to be radical and maverick then be so – but don't mistake chopping out story functions for setting up an engaging intrigue, mystery or disorientation. You successfully create a disorienting effect through decisions about order and juxtaposition rather than through reinventing or ignoring structure and replacing it with confusion, chaos, ambiguity and gaping holes in the story.

Many crime and murder mysteries open with the crime/murder and then go on to establish the context in which the crime has occurred because the intrigue and disorientation created by this juxtaposition in the opening is part and parcel of the genre and tone. This did not happen in *Criminal Justice I* (or *II*) because it is not in the crime or murder mystery genre – it is a state-of-the-nation TV serial about the criminal justice system as investigated through a crime and a miscarriage of justice. The tension is in our relationship with the accused young man who does not remember the murder but does not believe he can be guilty (rather than in 'working out' the crime like a thrilling crossword); he does not remember the crime even though he knows he was present; therefore we do not see who commits it until the evidence finally comes to light and the truth is made known to the world (and not because we want to see how clever the detective, criminal or writer are). What distinguishes the two kinds of 'crime' story in these terms is the juxtaposition of events, not the disregard of structure.

ESTABLISH THE WORLD

This does not mean set up the story, preface the story or deliver story exposition and backstory. It means establish the principles of the world you are presenting. For the majority of naturalistic, realistic worlds, this may take very little time because the rules do not fundamentally differ from the real world we inhabit, and therefore the conceptual leap is small. For high-concept, supernatural, sci-fi, futuristic, surreal worlds it will almost inevitably take longer because they do differ from the world we inhabit. But the key thing still is to not do it through static, undramatic exposition, but through action, in the moment, in the story – and to do it as simply and clearly as possible.

In *Hamlet*, scene one immediately presents a world where the perturbed ghost of the dead king walks the ramparts of Elsinore and terrifies the guards. Then we see the seat of power where his brother Claudius has taken the place of the dead king by marrying his widow – and where the bereaved son is still in deep mourning and anguish. We see this world in action – the ghost appears before our eyes, the new king directs the 'court' as to the new-found (and short-lived) security he has apparently brought to the state of Denmark. It is clearly, quickly established that a world of both state power and private grief are so out of joint that a ghost is haunting the living.

DELAYED ESTABLISHMENT

Sometimes the central characters do not realise the world is something very different from what they have experienced every day so far, in which case the full establishment of this hidden world may not come until rather later. But in these cases of delayed clarity, the establishment performs other and rather different story functions: the call to adventure (*Shaun of the Dead*) or the climax and turning point of the beginning (*Being John Malkovich*) or both (episode one of *Life on Mars*). In *Shaun*, there is a comic-dramatic irony in us realising that zombies have taken over when Shaun in his daily morning stupor does not. In *Malkovich*, the world is already pretty strange and heightened, so the discovery of a portal into a famous actor's brain comes as a weird surprise rather than an entirely random shock. And the change of world in *Life on Mars* is a smart shift from clinical twenty-first century policing to the unreconstructed world of 1970s coppers, this tension being the central hook of the show.

DESIRE, NEED, PROBLEM

Structurally, we need to see in action what the characters desire, what they need, and what is the fundamental problem in both. Hamlet wants for his father to not be dead; he needs to get over his father's death; he also needs to right a wrong; but his father *is* dead, he can't get over it because he can't ignore the wrong that he must set right. He wants for his mother not to have married her brother-in-law so quickly (or at all); he needs his mother to continue grieving with him and acknowledge that nobody could ever replace his father; he also needs to accept that she must move on for the sake of Denmark; but his mother *has* remarried, his father *has* been replaced, and he cannot accept that her grief appears less than his own or that she could conceivably move on. He wants to escape Elsinore and return to his studies in Wittenberg; he needs to find peace rather than to run away; he is pressurised into staying to fulfil his duty and function as Prince of Denmark. He wants to die; he needs to stay alive; suicide is a mortal sin. In the first scene and soliloquy we spend with Hamlet, all these wants, needs and problems are established.

You won't necessarily need to stack all the needs into one scene like this. But they need to be there in the beginning as a whole. In *Life on Mars*, Sam's initial desire is to catch the criminal. When the suspect walks free, he thinks he needs to draw a line between work and his personal relationship with Maya in order to focus and resolve the error made in gathering evidence. But the real problem is that he needs to stop relying on his clinical take on evidence alone and listen to her appeal to go with his gut instinct.

When Maya goes missing as a consequence of standing her down from the case, he wants her safely back. He needs to use his instinct and his forensic brain to find her. But his emotions take over and he hits a metaphorical wall. And, after about ten minutes of story, a real car hits him and somehow sends him back to the 1970s. At which point, a whole new set of wants and needs and problems join his initial ones.

CALL TO CHANGE/ACTION

There are various ways of characterising this fundamental storytelling function and you may get a number of them in your script:

> ➤ The instigating incident – the event that shows/tells the characters that change is afoot (even if they don't realise as much).

> ➤ The inciting action – the cause through which change is brought about and begins to emerge.

> ➤ The call to arms or adventure – the literal rallying cry or another kind of appeal to the characters to take up arms and/or take to their heels in pursuit of change

What can throw writers is when they confuse instigating or inciting action that brings about the events of the story before we begin watching – the backstory – with what we experience within the story. All good stories will have backstory that is dramatic. But you need to make sure that there is this crucial action within the story, visible to the audience.

You might say that the incitement for Hamlet is the murder of the king before the play starts. But then what incited that action? And the one before? The instigating incident of the events of the play that we see is that first appearance of the ghost at night in scene one. When Hamlet is told of this haunting, it is a call to him. But it is the second appearance of the ghost that Hamlet witnesses, during which he is told of his father's murder, that becomes the true call to arms – the call to revenge – that sets in motion the subsequent events of the play. Of course, Hamlet famously does not set straight on this course of revenge like many avengers before and after him. His journey is much less direct, and this is what makes it distinct.

In *Billy Elliot* the instigating incident is Billy watching the ballet dancers after the boxing class his father forces him to take and which he so despises. The inciting action is his decision to take part in a subsequent ballet class. The true call to adventure is when, despite his clumsy attempts to join in, he is told that he should keep going, that he does have the potential, that he could be a dancer.

The incidents, actions and calls are not necessarily external and visible. They may be from within, a kind of growing consciousness of what a character wants and/or needs. They may even remain immediately unaware and unwitting of the extent and meaning of that call.

THE COMPLEX CALL

The call should be the root of complexity rather than just some scenes to tick off on a checklist of what you are supposed to do in order to have something that resembles a story structure. This is the point. Don't just throw in an incident, an action, a 'call'. They need to derive from your characters.

Just as Othello returns to Cyprus a military hero, Desdemona's father accuses him of stealing (eloping with) his daughter. The instigating incident is the accusation, Othello's assured and honourable response to it, and society's apparent but perhaps tenuous acceptance of this. This feeds into the complexity that follows. For it is not simply his ability to retain his status and respect while also being a black man in a white world (which he does for a while), but his ability to retain his honour in the face of insinuations that Desdemona has cheated on him. These insinuations of infidelity are not public like the first accusation but private, planted in his head by the scheming, plotting Iago.

This is the real story of the play and the opening scene is the start of that story, but what follows is more complex than was suggested at the start. It is not just about the difficulty of him being black or of being a soldier in polite society, it is also about his inner strength of character, his strength of mind, his faith in Desdemona, his trust in his own instincts and emotions, and the decisions he takes that eventually unravel both. His 'call' is to be the man Desdemona believed him to be (and he believed himself to be) when she married him. In the beginning, nobody (except perhaps Iago) realises that this is the journey he is being called upon to make.

THE UNCERTAINTY

When a three-dimensional character is called upon to undertake a journey, take up a cause and step outside their ordinary world of safety and security, if they have any depth in their character then there will inevitably be some form of uncertainty about what they do: a reluctance to take up the call, a fear of that change, uncertainty over their ability to handle change, a desire to return to the security of ignorance or insignificance – otherwise known as 'the refusal'. Again, this isn't a 'refusal'-shaped scene or block that you insert here. It is character-shaped, personality-shaped, story-shaped.

Hamlet spends much of his tragedy veering back to the uncertainty and refusal of the point before which he made a pact with his father from beyond the grave to avenge murder. Perhaps this is because there was simply no time to think in between the call to revenge and the promise to pursue it? Hamlet only has the opportunity to question his decision once he has already made his promise – hence his dilemma.

In *Life on Mars* Sam spends a full two series' worth of episodes solving crimes and trying to get back 'home' before finally and truly taking up the call in the penultimate scene of the final episode to leap off a building and back to the 1970s and the 'real' him – a call that is entirely different to what he thought it was in the beginning.

In *Criminal Justice II*, Juliette takes up the call of defending in court her action to kill her abusive husband. But it is a complex response because it is only in the final stages of the fifth episode of the serial (and a number of months later) that she is finally pushed to acknowledge why she did it – and in a sense this is the call she refused to take up from the beginning because she is ashamed of the admission that her husband buggered her, because she doesn't want the world to know it, and most of all because she doesn't want her daughter to know.

For some characters, often the more subsidiary ones, this uncertainty or this status of reluctant hero is core and is present throughout. Han Solo in *Star Wars* is a classic reluctant hero, never willing until the final heroic moment to take up the cause of the rebels against the Empire. In Han's journey as a character, the reluctance and refusal *is* the story.

Hearing the call, taking up the call and then succeeding or failing in the journey are not things you 'come up with'. They are essential to the story, fundamental to the characters, integral to the reason for watching the play or series or film, and as such they should not be simplistic and a box to tick, but complex – and a question to keep asking your characters throughout.

THE POINT OF NO RETURN

The end of the beginning (and also the beginning of the end, ultimately) is when events reach such a point of no return that change in the world of the play and character's life is inevitable. This is the point at which there is some form of cementing of the situation or turn of events that confirms the direction in which the story is heading. As such, it is normally climactic (a crisis) or at least pivotal (a definite shift of direction), and can mean identifying the opposition to (or the consequences of) not taking up the call.

At the point of no return too much has already happened in the story, too much has already changed in the world and for the character. At the point of no return the events have already gained a momentum that cannot simply be stopped or ignored, though they can still be influenced – otherwise taking up the call would be the equivalent of a certain suicide mission.

In many action thrillers, a seeming suicide mission is exactly what things might appear to be at this point. Does it really seem likely that John can foil the terrorists and save his wife in *Die Hard*? Well, not until we see him being heroic and invincible in action and slowly come to believe it might just be possible – that's the hook, that's our connection with him, that's the tension. The terrorists won't go away just because he's been down on his luck and doesn't feel prepared for this battle. Yet there's a chance, however slim, that he can find a way at least to do *something*.

Billy Elliot could stop taking the ballet lessons and give up his 'secret'. But the point of no return is less that events are unstoppable than that his desire and passion beyond a certain point is unquenchable – *therefore* events are unstoppable. His desire to dance is clear from scene one, where he fails to babysit his senile grandmother, but it isn't until he chooses to keep the ballet shoes, promises to return to the class and begins hiding his secret from his father that the unquenchable desire becomes fully clear to him.

In every good story there is a moment, whether climactic and world-changing or quiet and unnoticed by everyone but the central character, in which the threshold between hearing the call at the beginning and taking up the call in the middle is crossed. Wherever it falls in the design and shape of your story, this more than anything is likely to be the end of the beginning.

TENSION

For the beginning to have a causal relationship with the end, a tension between the two must exist. The tension from the beginning onwards is in the possible outcomes of the events and actions of the opening on the spectrum between comedy and tragedy – between either managing to resolve or failing to avert the danger or problem that exists for the characters. What could be the ultimate effect of change?

Tension also exists in the shortfall between what a character wants and what they get. What they need and what they get. What they realise and do not realise, understand and do not understand, believe and do not believe.

The distinct possibility of the ending is in the beginning, otherwise there would be no tension to carry us from the one to the other across the story. What is the causal, necessary and inevitable ending of your story?

Hamlet is called upon to avenge his father's murder. He calls upon himself to do so, at the start and throughout. Yet he struggles throughout to attain the confidence, surety and conviction that it is the right thing to do. This is the tension – can he bring himself to do it? And if he does, what will be the consequences?

EPISODE AND SERIES BEGINNINGS

Beginnings (and middles and ends) are all well and good when you are writing a single, one-off, finite story. But when you are writing a continuing series, returning series or serial drama, the episode must have not only a beginning, middle and ending of its own, but also be the beginning of the longer or ongoing format.

If your calling card is for a series then you will need both to tell a full episode story and begin the series as a whole in your episode; if the series is in seasons (i.e., returning) then you will also need a beginning, middle and end to the season.

If it is for a finite serial then you will almost certainly not have a defined 'story of the week' episode narrative that comes to a strong sense of closure; however, you will still need a shape to the opening instalment, a sense of building towards an episode climax, even though we know there is more to come.

Striking the right balance between internal episode structure and the way the episode sits within the larger series and serial arc is always difficult. You need to be sure and clear about what kind of show you are writing. But whatever kind of show it is, you need to tell an episode story that does have a beginning, middle and ending shape to it.

Episode one of *Life on Mars* is a very smart example of when a returning series strikes that balance perfectly – although it did take nearly forty drafts of the script over a number of years from an experienced writer (Matthew Graham) collaborating with other very experienced writers (Ashley Pharoah and Tony Jordan) on the series as a whole. In the opening fifteen minutes, Sam Tyler goes from his 2007 pursuit of suspect Colin Raimes, to failing to keep that suspect, to Maya being kidnapped, to being sent back in time to the 1970s and finding himself amidst an unreconstructed police squad immediately supervised by Gene Hunt, the über-seventies copper.

By the end of the episode he has solved the crime, probably prevented Colin Raimes from turning into a future criminal, racked his brain trying to work out why he has gone back in time, and nearly leapt off the top of a building in desperation because he doesn't know what to do next. The tension that is created in the opening fifteen minutes feeds both the episode story of solving a crime and the series arc of Sam working out why he is there, how to get home, and whether home is what he believes it to be. It is a fantastic beginning to a fantastic show.

THE PLAN OF ACTION

WHEN TO START WRITING?

At the very beginning, I said not to start writing your actual script straight away. If you have been developing and working through all the questions raised thus far, then everything you have done is 'writing'. There is no magic scheduled moment when you start filling a blank page with words in a scriptwriting program. But many people do start committing words to page in a scriptwriting program before they have really taken stock, worked out where they are going and given their idea the time and space to breath, gestate and take a form of its own in their head out of the preparatory material they have collected.

TREATMENTS

Detailed prose treatments are tricky things, often on the one hand grudgingly accepted or on the other despised and rejected. I've never met a scriptwriter who genuinely enjoys writing treatments. They might value them, need them, believe in them, but they never seem to love them. Because they are not drama – they are a way of organising the story in non-dramatic form and therefore in a way counter-intuitive to the dramatic writer.

A detailed treatment is often now a requirement in the script commissioning process in TV and film. So if you are serious, you may well have to get to grips with them, like it or not. But when you are writing your calling card script, I would advise against using a detailed prose treatment unless you feel or already know that it's the kind of preparation that will work for you. Even so, I would question how useful it would be. They can be deadening to the not-yet-hardened professional.

In practice, treatments give all interested parties – writer, script editor, producer, commissioner – an opportunity to clarify the story before they are carried along on the wave of a script. If the commission is for a proven scriptwriter, the danger of getting swept away is even greater and it can be easier for all involved to remain on more equal terms in dull prose at the earliest stage. But with a calling card script, you are the writer, script editor and commissioner of sorts all in one. I would stick instead with a road map that feels malleable to you, and worry about treatments later.

CLARITY

At this point a useful thing to do is to test clarity to see if you can boil it down into three things:

➢   A one-sentence logline.
➢   A one-paragraph pitch.
➢   A one-page outline.

They might not read beautifully and elegantly but they don't have to (and nobody else need ever see them) so long as they tell a coherent, abbreviated version of your story as you see it at this stage. This is a test. It can show you whether all the great stuff running through your head actually coheres into meaningful, story-shaped wholes that are small, very small and miniscule. (It may also be that you aren't very good at them – yet – but you don't know until you try.)

Don't write out the plot or list events in narrative order. Don't try to get out every detail. Don't try to explain every element and idea. And don't act like you are hawking your idea to a Hollywood mogul. Just get down the story – the idea, the kind, the form, the characters, the beating heart of it, the reason to tell the story, the things you think you are trying to say, what it is that's distinct about it, what it is that makes it yours. In the logline you won't have the space to express much more than the heart of the idea. Gather together everything you have gestated thus far and set it down in a heartfelt expression to yourself.

Now put them away in a drawer for a week. Do the other stuff you have neglected in your writerly preoccupation. Ignore it as best you can.

COHERENCE

Now go back to them as objectively as you can and see whether they are a statement of clarity and coherence:

➢   Does the story work?

➢   Is it the one you wanted to tell?

➢   Would someone else who doesn't have access to your brain get it?

➢   Does it hang together as a coherent whole?

➢   Does it have the right form and shape?

➢   Is the tone unified?

➢   Are you trying to do too much in your story?

➢   Is it focused enough?

➢   Does it feel original?

➢   What is it that is distinctive about it?

➢   Does it have strong characters and strength of character?

➢   Is it what you wanted it to be?

Don't sidestep these questions. Try to resolve the apparent problems now before you weave yourself a tapestry that will prove impossible to unpick and stitch back together again in a different pattern. There will always be things that can, do and will change, things you get wrong, things you don't notice, things you change your mind about – that is true for all writers. But if at this stage you do know there's something major and crucial that doesn't click, then don't plough on hoping it will sort itself out. It won't. Only you can sort it out. And that will be harder when you are already well and truly into an actual draft of the script.

BUILDING A BLUEPRINT

A section of spare wall. Scene cards. Colour-coded Post-it notes. Diagrams. Maps. PowerPoint presentation. Spreadsheet graph. Use whatever works best for you. Set your blueprint down in a malleable, movable, editable form.

This is not final, definitive or right. It is adaptable, fluid, plastic. It's a road map that should set you in the right direction and will hopefully help you when you get stuck. Don't be tempted to keep holding it all in your head in a supreme effort of memorisation and information juggling. When information and material is broken down into separate parts, it means you can move it around and see whether another shape works better.

The point of these blueprints, maps, charts, whatever you want to call them, is that they allow you to see the foundations clearly before the form that builds on them clouds your view of what the story fundamentally is and whether it works. Detail is a devil. Begin to set down the big picture clearly before the devil starts trying to distract you from your purpose.

3
The Middle

The Middle

THE MUDDLE IN THE MIDDLE

Philip Larkin once said that the joy of stories is in losing yourself in the 'muddle in the middle'. He was describing great novels but his notion is a truism for all stories. This doesn't mean all your work and effort should be concentrated in the middle. In this book, I advocate spending a dispropor-tionate amount of time to the beginning of story and process because it's where everything that will subsequently unravel is set on course towards that muddling. But the middle is no less crucial, and it is certainly no easier to get right. In fact, I'd say the middle is where a great many stories and scripts unravel – in the wrong way.

MANAGING THE MUDDLE

The muddle is a double-edged sword. Your characters and audience must in an engaging, dramatic way get lost in the middle. But in order to do that effectively, you, the writer, must be in control of the muddle, knotting every strand, engineering hazards and hurdles in the way, leading characters towards the quicksand that threatens to suck them in.

If the writer gets lost, audience and character will be lost for all the wrong reasons – because of incoherence and chaos, lack of clarity, lack of direction and purpose. Be careful you don't mistake muddling the charac-ters' journeys with losing your own way with the story.

A frequent complaint about the second act of a story – the middle – is that it sags, loses a sense of direction, gets complicated rather than com-plex, fails to follow through strands and creates new ones out of a loss as to what to do next – that it fails to take us meaningfully from beginning to end.

The point about losing the way is that 'the way' is ultimately found again – whether that means a tragic outcome, a comic one, or something in between the two. 'The way' is not necessarily happiness and resolution – rather, it is the ending that the characters inevitably had to reach as a consequence of their desires, needs, actions, decisions through the story.

MUDDLED METAPHORS

It's good to have a metaphor or image or idea of what your middle is, means, looks like, feels like:

➢ The beginning and the end are the foothills – the middle is the mountain to climb.

➢ The beginning and the end are the winding path into and out of the trees – the middle is the increasingly dense, dark, foreboding and tangled forest through which it struggles to wend its way.

➢ The middle is a hole – the characters must dig deeper and deeper.

➢ The middle is a state of becoming – between two different states of being at the beginning and at the end.

One reason why many middles sag and many writers lose their way is because the mountain/forest/hole is not of the character's own volition and doing but a contrived hurdle they are traversing without a strong enough sense of consequence or causality from their actions at the beginning.

In the middle, the plot thickens – the story of the beginning becomes more complex, more intriguing, more mysterious, more exciting, more terrifying, more entertaining, more necessary.

FAIL BETTER

'Ever tried. Ever failed. No matter. Try again. Fail again. Fail better.'

This is a quote from one of Samuel Beckett's last works, *Worstward Ho*, one of the most enigmatic expressions of the avante-garde existentialism for which he is so famous.

Try again. Fail again. Fail better.

If ever there were a mantra for your characters to pursue in the middle, then perhaps this is it. But there is also perhaps an alternative, even more tragic version of this:

Try again. Fail again. Fail worse.

'Try again' is the basic way forward in the muddle that is the middle. The characters must try. They are bound at some points to fail. And whether they ultimately fail better or fail worse is a consequence of what they do as they keep trying again, and again, and again. You need this propulsion and momentum and dynamic. The momentum may take your characters into deep, dark pits from which it appears they may never escape but in the middle it is the trying that matters. The ending will show whether the result of that trial is a concluding failure or success – or something in between.

DIG DEEPER

In the middle, you must dig deeper into the conflict, the characters, and the complexity of both. You don't want more of the same – you want what we have already seen to grow, change and deepen. Many writers panic and create new strands, new plotlines, bring in new characters. They complicate the story. Complication means overcrowding the picture with unnecessary material, ideas, plots, subplots, details. Complexity means giving the existing picture more depth, texture, layering – more meaning. It means developing the consequences of what we have already seen, not generating swathes of new ideas and directions that are not consequential from what we have seen.

STRETCH THE LINE

You also need to develop the tension – stretch the line tauter and tighter. Whatever it is your characters want and need, the likelihood of them achieving this must seem less and less, and must be harder and harder to achieve. The trying must become more and more intense.

The greater the danger, the greater the tension, the greater the muddle. 'Danger' doesn't necessarily mean that in a thriller or tragedy or war film. If your story is a romantic comedy, the danger must still be there – will he/ she get their girl/boy? When you're in love, this is no throwaway question – it is the epicentre of everything you feel. The danger is that characters will not get what they want or need. The tension is in not knowing what the outcome of their trying will be. The longer and tighter you stretch that line of not knowing, the more captivating the middle will be.

DOMINOES

The thing about the muddle in the middle is that it isn't just a big swamp into which you just dump your characters after the beginning. It will come about in increments, the line will stretch one notch at a time, the hole will get deeper one spadeful at a time. Each increment will have a causal, cumulative effect going forward. Each domino will knock forward and the line will fall one by one inevitably towards the end. And if you miss out any crucial dominoes, then the run will stop, the momentum will stall – and the final pattern of collapsed dominoes will not unfold before our eyes.

The muddle is something that you must orchestrate with meticulous care, and yet will seem as chaotic as possible for the characters caught up in the middle of it. There will be false starts, short-lived successes, and unexpected failures along the way – but there will be a sense of inevitability in where they and we end up.

The muddle is fraught with contradiction. The muddle will be difficult. The only option is to face up to this difficulty, not to avoid it, complicate it or seek to circumvent it. Without the difficulty, there is no journey. Without the difficulty, there is no story.

DEEPER INTO CHARACTER

THE 'ARC'

Great characters are not simply in what you create at the outset, but in where they go, where you take them, the way they develop and grow, the journey they go on. Characters that go nowhere aren't worth spending time with.

Through over-use, perhaps, 'arc' feels more like simplistic jargon than a useful term. If it feels too 'Hollywood' for you, then replace it with 'journey'. But both 'arc' and 'journey' can throw writers because they presume it means an exerting physical journey or a story spanning a significant length of time – both of which are mainstays of dramatic storytelling. Yet journeys can be as much emotional, psychological, religious, social, political, and so on.

Story is not just who characters are but who they become and remain once they have undergone a journey that tests who they are, what they want, what they need, what they feel, what they understand, what they believe.

An arc can span a lifetime at one extreme or run in pure real time at the other. In actuality, most character arcs are somewhere between the two. It's difficult to select those necessary parts that represent an entire lifetime, and trying to do too much rarely works – *Citizen Kane* is an extremely unusual achievement. It's also difficult to take a character on a meaningful journey in real time because you necessarily push the bounds of how much they can realistically, convincingly, meaningfully change in a very short space of time – *Abigail's Party* is likewise a rarity.

The clearer you are about the timescale and span of your character journeys, the better. Whatever you choose, make a virtue of it. Each instalment of the *Harry Potter* saga represents a year in the school life of Harry. The whole series takes him through school from childhood to young adulthood. The arc in each 'episode' and the arc across all episodes are both crystal clear.

CHANGE

Great stories dramatise times of change for a character. That's why we see some things and not others. Some aspiring writers nobly set out to 'tell it like it is' and mistake realism (the interesting and extraordinary reality of a life) with tedium (the uninteresting and ordinary realities of an existence). Audiences don't want to see basic, boring existence – they want to see *life*. Some simply focus on the wrong parts of the life – the bits in which meaningful change doesn't really happen. Great characters never stay utterly and exactly the same. Even if at the end they are a more or less extreme version of themselves, that still means change – that still means a journey.

I once confidently said as much in a room full of aspiring writers and the reply that came back was 'What about Schmidt?' It was a good reply, because *About Schmidt* is a story in which the anti(ish)-hero doesn't seem to go on any great arc or journey of change. I use the word 'seem' carefully – because there *is* change. Schmidt certainly doesn't undergo a fundamental transformation of personality. But strong characters rarely do. Change is relative. For Schmidt, deciding to pee standing up – despite being trained by his recently deceased wife to do otherwise – is change. The anger he feels at uncovering his wife's affair with his old friend is change. The decision to set off in the Winnebago by himself, even though it was really his wife's dream, is change. Deciding not to say what he really thinks to a room full of people, microphone in hand, at his disappointment-of-a-daughter's wedding is change. The changes are not earth shattering. But they are Schmidt's. Because the story is about Schmidt.

STATE OF BECOMING

Everyone is born and everyone dies. Whatever we may believe about what that signifies or what (if anything) might happen next, it's a fundamental truth. It is the states and stages of becoming between the two that constitutes the story of everyone's life.

Great stories aren't just about the outcome. We usually know somewhere deep down how the story will turn out, especially if we know what the genre is (a romcom in which they don't get it together is not really a romcom; a tragedy without the death of the hero is not really a tragedy). Great endings are crucial, necessary, inevitable. But what we love about the muddle in the middle is how the characters get there – what road they take, whether real or metaphorical, and how lost they become in order to get where they need to end up. Whether it's a single heroic tale or twenty-five years' worth of strands and episodes for Ian Beale in *EastEnders*, both are states of becoming.

MUDDIED WANTS AND NEEDS

In the beginning there should be an identifiable set of wants and needs in your characters. If they remain simply the same, unchanging, then they run the risk of stalling, of not developing and growing and becoming more interesting and engaging the more we see of them.

At the beginning of *Star Wars*, Luke Skywalker is perhaps not the most complex of characters. He wants excitement, escape, purpose, and he also needs all three – though he is perhaps as wary as he is desirous of them. But as the story develops in the middle, his wants and needs change. He needs to save Leia but he doesn't know how. He wants to be the Jedi he is destined to be as fast as possible but he needs to be as patient as he is ambitious. He wants to be the hero, but he needs to think as well as act. He wants to grow up instantly but needs to learn through a wealth and depth of experience, which he cannot do overnight. He wants strength but he needs faith and control in order to gain it.

When Obi-Wan Kenobi dies, Luke instinctively wants instant revenge, but he needs to accept his mentor's act of sacrifice (which is also a major step in his maturity, patience, control) and channel his emotions for the ultimate revenge against the Death Star. And at the climax he wants and needs to use the 'force' rather than rely on a computer guidance system to fire the killer missile, but he also needs the help of the swaggering pirate Han Solo who has so often frustrated Luke's pure, simple, heroic aims, beliefs and perspective with realism, pragmatism, sarcasm, cynicism and at times pure selfishness.

The point is that Luke pursues each of these wants and so brings about each of the consequent and attendant needs. He tries and he changes. He is never really in control of the wants and needs. He is not necessarily always clear or sure about what they are, what he should do, whether it will work, whether it is worth it. But he always tries and so no matter how muddied his developing wants and needs are, they are constantly propelling him forward towards the ending that was in the beginning – to save Leia and destroy the Death Star.

MUDDLED CONSEQUENCES

If in the beginning a character says they want something and they then simply go ahead and get it, there is no drama. If a character struggles to get what they want then there is drama and story – but there isn't necessarily complexity and depth.

In the course of achieving their wants and needs, the most engaging characters modify, reappraise, examine what they want, why they want it, what it will mean to get it. The consequences of their actions are not simple and clear but muddled and complex.

In *This Is England* Shaun wants to not stand out. He gets a gang of friends with whom he fits in, but who collectively stand out from the crowd even more than Shaun did by himself. He embraces this – he wants the haircut, the clothes, the boots. Now he doesn't mind standing out if it means fitting in with a group of people that embrace him for who he is. But he doesn't anticipate the shift that occurs when Combo returns and displaces the warm-hearted Woody. Shaun's fearlessness marks him out to Combo as a kid to be trusted, a kid who really means it. And this brings Shaun closer to the previously unseen danger: racism and violence. Shaun is faced with a major dilemma that tests his understanding of what he wants and needs.

When Combo attacks Milky, Shaun is the only one left kicking and screaming in an attempt to stop him. What he wants and needs is to put the brakes on the gang hurtling down this very wrong, very dark road.

His wants and needs have changed and developed; the more muddled their outcomes are as the story develops, the more he must assert himself, be himself, become the 'himself' that he didn't realise he could be.

Hamlet is full of muddled consequences: the killing of Polonius and the sending away of Hamlet; the alienation of Ophelia and her eventual suicide; the engineered death of Rosencrantz and Guildenstern for betraying Hamlet; the demise of Gertrude as she drinks the poison to save her son, futile though that action is. None of these consequences were desired, planned for, expected or anticipated. All are ultimately a muddled consequence of Hamlet's actions as he tries and for a long time fails to take revenge for his father's death. But he gets there in the end. The end is inevitable.

BEYOND THE COMFORT ZONE

When a character answers 'the call' and goes past the point of no return, they are stepping outside their comfort zone – beyond what they know and understand, even if that comfort zone is not necessarily a pleasant or comfortable or happy place to be. Sometimes the danger of the new and unknown is more unsettling than the difficulty of what a character has experienced and dealt with in the past.

Beyond the comfort zone, characters cannot simply rely on who they were or how they dealt with things in the past. They must learn new strategies, new skills, new behaviours, new capabilities, new points of view. And they will therefore find new flaws and limitations, new inabilities, new seeming limits to who they are. For great characters, this is the muddle – where they have for better or for worse chosen to step beyond and take on the consequences of their actions and decisions. Not knowing necessarily what those consequences will be is the thrill of our engagement and the heart of the muddle. The muddle is not just a muddle – it is a consequential muddle, one driven by want, need, choice, decision, action and trying again and again until the inevitable ending comes about.

If you keep your characters inside their comfort zone in the middle, your story will simply run out of steam.

In *Withnail and I* the comfort zone is a drug-infested Camden – beyond it is a car journey to Penrith and into the unknown. In *Merlin* the comfort zone is the security of being Arthur's apparently hapless servant – beyond it is the secret use of magic that is forbidden by Arthur's father. In *Being*

Human the comfort zone is usually the flatshare – beyond it is the three characters allowing their secret life to come out into the open where other people might notice. In *Closer* the comfort zone is desire and eroticism – beyond it is love, intimacy, trust, commitment, need.

DEVELOPING THE 'AGON'

The 'agon' defines the role of character. Are they protagonist or antagonist? Pursuing something or standing in the way of that pursuit? But remember – to the antagonist, their own role as obstacle to the protagonist is in fact their own protagonism. They are not simply there to oppose another. If they are interesting, they will oppose another because they have wants, needs, a POV, an attitude of their own, whether it is towards positive or negative ends. And therefore the seeming protagonist is from that POV the antagonist.

The *agon* should not remain simple, obvious, clear. The *agon* – the conflict – should not remain static. It can shape-shift and develop as the story progresses. For Shaun, the initial antagonist is anyone who points him (and his terrible trousers) out. By the end, the antagonist has become Combo – or rather the pressures and anger and insecurity that have driven Combo towards an act of racist violence. The conflicts change and develop. They intensify. They mutate. In a sense, at the climax Shaun becomes the antagonist to the warped sense of alienation and desire to belong that has driven Combo to extreme nationalism. At the outset, it was Shaun's own alienation and desire to belong that had ultimately and ironically driven him as protagonist to this point of fighting against a consequence of precisely that want and need. This is what makes his journey so brilliant, so engaging, so unique, so complex.

DEVELOPING THE COMPLEXITY

By taking a complex character on a journey forward through conflict, you make them more complex, interesting and unique. The story gets better and better. Your story must get better and better.

'What about action films?' I hear you say. 'Are they ever complex?' The good ones are. In *Die Hard* the ordinary-Joe hero does not stay the same. The journey from entering the besieged building to penetrating the hostage-takers' lair is one that tests his character, personality, resolve, ability, stamina, desire, intelligence, confidence in increasingly intense increments. The tests are not just physical but emotional and psychological. It's not just about guns and explosions and fist-fights. Poor action films ditch any semblance or shred of complexity for complication and base sensation. They are *only* about guns and explosions and fist fights.

NEW WORLD, NEW CHARACTERISTICS

By taking a leap into the unknown or the little known, what new sides, facets, hidden depths and characteristics will your characters discover and uncover about themselves and other people? Are they new? Surprises? Unwelcome developments? Do the characters even see and recognise the changes at all? Are they new characteristics that only we and/or other characters notice?

From the isolated, lonely, uncool, irascible, grudging, miserable kid in the beginning, we come to see in Shaun a physical transformation, a confidence, a humour, a sense of place and worth, his first kiss, and a growing consciousness that the extreme nationalism he is seeing for the first time is wrong. Shaun blossoms and flourishes and matures but he also isn't able, strong or mature enough to prevent some things happening as the story climaxes. His personality doesn't fundamentally alter – but it grows and is given the opportunity to truly be itself rather than masked by a sense of unhappiness and anger as it is at the beginning.

QUALITIES

As your characters follow the call and their chosen pursuit, which specific qualities are altered, or newly appear, or even disappear altogether? What qualities do the characters consciously aspire towards? Which do they begin to acquire, whether desired or not, conscious or not? What are the accidental effects on personality?

Hamlet aims to become an avenging force, though not before he is confident that vengeance is a true and justified path. He attempts to put an 'antic disposition on', to pretend to be mad, so that he can draw out the truth without anyone realising that is what he is doing. But the more his behaviour becomes unhinged, the more eyes are on him, and ultimately the harder his task. His unhinged behaviour isn't just this 'act' – he become as genuinely unhinged, irascible and rash as he does vicious, dismissive, suspicious, calculating, deceptive; the way he rejects Ophelia; the way he 'tests' Rosencrantz and Guildenstern; the way he puts on a play to reflect an accusing mirror back at Claudius; the way he fails to take revenge as Claudius guiltily prays; the way he unleashes disappointed venom at his mother; the way he stabs Polonius without apparently knowing who the victim is (yet surely aware that his actions are extreme whoever that victim might be); the way he escapes the captors who are taking him to his death. Although there is complexity in the qualities we see in him at the beginning, there is much greater complexity and extremity and variation in the qualities we see him display in his actions throughout the middle.

CAPABILITIES AND FLAWS

Are any of the things that your character can and can't do severely tested in the middle? And how aware of this are they? For Billy Elliot, physical capability looms very large in the middle – can he learn to dance well enough to get a place at ballet school? But his journey is much more complex than this. Does he have the capability to do this in secret? Or does he have the strength finally to admit the truth and show his father what he can do, whatever the consequences? Can he steer his way past the temptations of a girl who fancies him? And can he rise above the inverted cultural snobbery that says to be a ballet-dancing boy must mean he is 'gay'? And when his best friends 'outs' himself as gay, how will Billy cope with that revelation? Does he have the ability to get beyond the loss of his mother? And when he does finally get the big audition and has danced his heart out for the panel, does he have the ability to express in words what dancing means to him and dispel any lingering doubts that his assessors might have?

Does Billy have the capability to handle all the complex things that will help him learn to dance and get to ballet school? What weaknesses and flaws will compromise and jeopardise those capabilities?

POV, MORALITY, ATTITUDE

Whatever happens in the middle, whatever trajectory your characters' journeys take, their POV, attitude and moral take on the world will be tested, challenged, be put under pressure and even altered. If they have stepped outside their comfort zone, then they will necessarily be seeing, experiencing, feeling, understanding, tackling things that are beyond their usual experience.

In this state of becoming one of four things is likely to happen. Their POV, attitude and moral sense will:

➢   Diminish and dilute.
➢   Harden and sharpen.
➢   Mutate and shift.
➢   Or appear to remain the same (until the end, at which point all the pressure that has been storing up will effect a more sudden and extreme transformation).

If your characters' perspective on the world does not change, not even the tiniest little bit, then what you are fundamentally saying is that even in extraordinary circumstances they do not have the ability to grow. (And if this is what you really *are* trying to say, then be prepared for whoever reads it to come back and say it is a negative, depressing, cynical view of the world that they don't want to take any further, thank you very much.)

The main exceptions are those rare heroes whose main function is to survive, Teflon-coated and immutable, for ever unchanging, like James Bond – though the character has changed with every new actor that plays him and every new era in which he exists, and his survival is ultimately intended to show the 'good guys' beating the 'bad' ones and so is not negative and cynical as such. The other exceptions are the true villains who refuse to acknowledge that what they have done is bad or wrong or anti-social or antagonistic – such as Iago in *Othello* or John Doe in *Se7en*. Many of the worst-seeming baddies do in fact have a death-bed conversion or at least accept that they have been evil, like Edmund at the end of *King Lear*. Utter villains are relative rarities but can often exist in the more comic-book-like stories such as action and superhero movies. Even Iago isn't just bad – what his soliloquies reveal is something inexplicable and complex, but not something that is simply pure evil.

For every other character, their view and understanding of and beliefs about the world need to be provoked, challenged, tested, pressurised.

Moon is an extraordinarily unusual, clever and poignant take on a character journey through the middle of the story. It's rare enough for a film to rely so heavily on apparently just one character. But when in the middle of the story it becomes clear to us and Sam 1 that he is a clone, the life, history, memory and everything else that makes up his personality unfolds as a fabrication, a pretence, a meaningless existence. For a man who has been counting the days and hours and minutes until he can return to a wife and child he believes he hasn't seen for three years and who are not in fact waiting for him at all, his understanding of the world and himself is thrown completely into existential, psychological and emotional disarray.

The fact that each clone is a somewhat different version of the original Sam, and the fact that two versions are accidentally thrown together on this claustrophobic moon base, is a brilliant way of externalising this journey as physical dramatic action and conflict. For Sam 1 the journey in the middle is the most poignantly earth-shattering muddle, where nothing is as it has always appeared to be. For Sam 2, the middle is in fact a beginning and his ending is something we don't actually see – which cleverly adds a layer of narrative complexity. So while the story is ultimately a heroic tragedy for Sam 1, Sam 2 is able to carry Sam 1's (and therefore his own) story forward in a unique way at the end, so that their secret cloned existence will be revealed on earth and not forever be a tragedy.

VULNERABILITIES

Moon is a great example of where vulnerabilities that were not immediately visible at the beginning are brought into sharp, painful relief in the middle. In the beginning Sam 1 seems to be going a bit stir-crazy; he is clearly missing human contact (ironic – since he's never actually had any), thinks he has seen a mysterious girl in and around the base, and feels exhausted. By the middle, it's clear that his physical longevity as a clone is running out, he is mentally breaking down, and he must deal with the collapse of his existential, psychological and emotional world. The clock is ticking on his fabricated life and he doesn't even have the pull of a home and loved ones to keep him going, because there is no home and there are no loved ones to go back to. The only thing he does have to protect the vulnerabilities that go to the core of his being and circumstances is the eventual, ironic support of Sam 2 as they try to fight their situation rather than simply accept it.

For Sam 1 and ultimately for Sam 2, absolutely everything is at stake. Even though Sam 1 realises he is doomed and dying, he heroically battles on so that no other clones after him will have to endure a meaningless existence – even though they may never have realised it was meaningless, like the other clones before him. It is the depth and extremity of the character's vulnerabilities in the middle that make this story so powerful and so engaging in character terms.

On a less earth-shattering level, the chinks in Frank Gallagher's thick armour are on show in any given *Shameless* episode in which he looms large as a character. Whether it's the chink that is failing to resist temptation from his son's girlfriend, or failing to keep his opinionated mouth shut when his daughter kidnaps a child off the street and Frank becomes the mouthpiece of the outraged mob, or failing to say anything paternal and useful when Debbie is under pressure to lose her virginity and all eyes are on him to say something useful. Despite being an extreme and perhaps grotesque character, the chinks in Frank's armour are the kinds of things that might make any of us vulnerable. When he fails to say anything useful to Debbie, he is in much the same position as any man for whom having a conversation with their teenage daughter about losing her virginity is just about the last conversation in the world they would ever wish to have. The thicker the armour, the more ironically susceptible is the heel that remains exposed where the plates of armour do not overlap. It is in the middle of the story that the plates are pulled apart and the heel begins to be truly exposed.

DEVELOPING RELATIONSHIPS

The journey of character is not simply about the depth of the vulnerabilities and wounds in their personality that threaten to gape open further. *Moon* is a rarity in its singular character focus. Depth of character is not simply an inward-looking phenomenon, but also outward-looking – to do with the relationships and the social journey of characters.

In some stories it is most obviously about just this. Love stories, wherever they sit between the rom-com and tragic extremes of the spectrum from *Four Weddings* to *Closer* to *Romeo and Juliet*, are primarily about a relationship between two (or more) lovers.

But relationships can have infinite variety: families (*Fish Tank*), friends (*Shifty, Pulling*), peer groups (*Skins, Misfits*), colleagues (*Casualty, Auf Wiedersehen Pet*), neighbours (*Coronation Street, EastEnders*), enemies (*Coriolanus*), flatmates (*Being Human, Withnail and I*), siblings (*Shameless*), husband and wife (*Nil by Mouth*), locals and outsiders (*The Wicker Man*), warden and ward (*Children of Men*).

A mistake some writers make is they have a conveyor belt of people passing through a character's story without any one relationship developing interestingly or meaningfully. Another mistake is that some writers wish to tell a story about loneliness and isolation and do so by simply cutting characters off from other people – when in fact they might dramatise it better through contact and relationships. A man alone in a cabin in the woods is remote; a man alone in a city constantly surrounded by people is perhaps more poignantly lonely and isolated by virtue of that proximity (Ed Hime's radio play *The Incomplete Recorded Works of a Dead Body* brilliantly explores this as Babak journeys further into himself the more he ventures out into the alien city of London).

So what is the journey of the character's relationship? What is the muddle that they face once a road has been embarked upon at the start? A character journey isn't in isolation – it is usually relative, contextual, social, associated with the journeyings of other characters.

JOURNEY TOWARDS AWARENESS

Whatever kind of journey it is – whatever unique combination of physical, emotional, psychological, social, political, religious, intellectual elements – dramatic characters travel in some way towards a sense of awareness about who they are, what they are doing, why they are doing it and what it all might mean. In ancient Greek tragedy, this position of insight and awareness is called the *anagnorisis*. It is the moment or point at which the character is able self-consciously to reflect at the very least momentarily on what has changed about who they are, given the journey they been on. In *Oedipus Rex* it is the moment where the hero realises he has unknowingly killed his own father and married his mother, and embarks on the irreversible punishment of stabbing out his own eyes.

If the characters reach *anagnorisis* – their sense of understanding and clarity – too soon, then the ending is reached too soon. There may be moments of false awareness, presumptuous understanding, mistaken clarity, deceptive insight, and these are part of the character's journey through the middle. It may be that there is no clarity whatsoever in the middle about what the true anagnorisis might be. But if your character never reaches any form or sense of *anagnorisis* then the dramatic journey has failed because it has no meaning, the change has no purpose, the story has no point. In the middle the characters must be journeying towards awareness, whether fighting to get there or kicking and screaming to avoid it.

CONTRADICTION

This journey towards awareness does not mean that points of clarity along the way need be clear and simple. Far from it. The complexity that comes from contradiction is crucial as the characters make this journey. As they try and fail, as their personalities are tested, as their vulnerabilities are exposed and as their relationships develop, the picture that will emerge *should* be contradictory because they have not reached an ending yet, and therefore have not reached the point of true clarity about what their actions have led them to – resolution, disaster or somewhere between the two.

For the deepening character, contradiction is an ever-present danger precisely because they have stepped beyond their comfort zone and are trying to achieve something that was previously beyond their capability or experience. If the path forward is too simple, straight, linear and non-contradictory, then what you will offer the audience is the sin of all story-telling sins: predictability and tedium.

Hamlet is full of contradiction between the grief of the beginning and the vengeance of the ending. Every step offers the possibility that Hamlet will contradict himself because he always has opposing wants and needs and thoughts and feelings. This is probably the reason why it is a role craved by so many actors and a play so popular with audiences ever since it first appeared at the beginning of the seventeenth century. It offers seemingly endless variations and possibilities of interpretation because there is so much contradiction and complexity and depth of character along the way.

SURPRISING THEMSELVES

Although some form of true awareness should come at the end, the capacity to realise – to display – new facets, whether good or bad, can come all the way through the middle. A useful way of using this to make the story surprising and compelling is to make the characters surprise themselves along the way – whether for better or for worse. Billy Elliot may surprise himself with his dancing capacity, but he also surprises himself with his failures, faults and follies. Sam Tyler, in particular in the earlier episodes of series one of *Life on Mars*, is in a constant state of surprising himself – not only by the things he is no longer able to do and achieve due to the lack of accustomed technology, but also by the things he *is* able to achieve in this 1970s world when he sets his twenty-first-century mind to it. Sam can tend to find himself in sticky situations due to the mind-set and policing principles that he has brought with him, yet he is able to surprise himself by finding ways to resolve or circumvent those situations without just ditching his convictions and morality.

Characters surprising themselves can mean a series of small moments of awareness and recognition along the way, but with the real truth and bigger picture not coming clear until the end.

CHARACTER AND ACTION

Some characters fade in the middle of the story, as though the plot has taken them over and their purpose is simply to people it rather than drive it forward. But the plot takes over like this when the character has lost purpose and lost their way. When they are not trying to get through the muddle – but have simply stopped moving meaningfully altogether. Again, it is all about failing better – it is trying and trying, again and again, with success never coming easily that keeps the muddle active.

In *Memento*, the hero may not remember where he has just been or what he has just done – or anything since the traumatic event that he seeks to avenge – but he always knows what he's searching for and that drive forward intensifies the more he searches and the closer he believes he is getting. The less he continues to remember, the more he must tattoo across his body as a record of his investigations and the more complex and muddied and muddled the journey and story and plot become – but his drive to find the man he believes took away his life cuts through it.

CHARACTER AND STRUCTURE

So remember that character action must keep on coming before plot. It is the continuing, developing and changing sense of character that continues to drive story, plot and therefore structure. More on structure shortly – but if you are losing your way with plot in the middle, you need to go back to character and make them lead us through the gloom towards the ending.

When the middle sags and wanders it is not because the plot has gone wrong, but because the character has failed to sustain the story.

THE 'MIDDLE' IN SERIES AND SERIALS

This stuff is all well and good when your characters exist in a single, finite, one-off story that ends at the end. But what about series and serials for TV (and radio)? Some series never end – so how do you conceive usefully of the middle?

Since I don't think writing a calling-card script for a new soap is remotely a good idea, I'm not going to dwell on the difficulties of managing short-, medium- and long-term arcs for soaps and continuing drama characters. Other than to say that you need three things: arcs across the short term (the length of an episode), one for the medium term (the length of a story strand) and one for the long term (the character's life in a show). In a sense, until they either leave or are killed off, soap characters are in a near-perpetual state of muddle in the middle, a pattern only broken by the conclusion of an episode, or strand, or ultimately their life on a show. And even then, some characters end up effectively coming back from the dead (like Dirty Den), so even the end isn't necessarily the end.

RETURNING SERIES

In a returning series the relentless demands are somewhat less daunting in terms of volume but no less difficult in terms of quality. But you need to make a similar distinction between the kinds of middles that you are layering and balancing.

There will be the middle-of-the-episode story, which is crucial but not necessarily as life-changing as that in a single drama – otherwise the characters' lives could well seem like an unconvincing stream of extraordinary moments. The muddle must be relative to the episode story. For crime shows, it will be crime-driven but also have some greater impact on the characters' lives than just being an ordinary day in their working life. For Frank Gallagher, it will most likely mean dealing with the messy fallout of his messy actions on the Chatsworth estate. For Merlin, it *will* involve averting some level of extraordinary disaster or misfortune about to befall Camelot by secretly using magic – because the Saturday early-evening audience expects that level of jeopardy every week.

Then there will be where exactly the episode sits in the wider series or season. For your calling card script it's most likely you will write (and people will want to see) the pilot episode, so you probably won't yet be embroiled in the mid-season muddle. But be aware that if you aspire to write series TV then it's a conundrum you are likely to encounter at some point (if you are very lucky).

Then there will be where the characters are at the end of the show. Unless you are the creator of a show being made, then you are unlikely to end up having to write this. But if you are creating a new idea and world in the act of writing your pilot episode, then that sense that the characters will spend much of their life in the middle for the duration of the show yet reach an ultimate ending eventually needs to be there somewhere. We need to know what the middle will feel like for them, and your pilot should show that. In episode one of *Life on Mars*, we had a clear, palpable sense of what every episode and week will feel like for Sam Tyler. Same with *Merlin*. Same, in its own way, with *Being Human*. And *Shameless*. And *Skins*. And the list goes on.

SERIALS

And then there are the serials – in which you will have a less defined sense of episode story structure reaching a conclusion, but a wholly finite and defined sense of a not-too-distant ending. So the characters are not in a near-perpetual state of middle-ness, rather they are in incremental story stages that are reaching a climax only a few episodes away. What this does tend to mean is that those moments of false clarity, momentary awareness, craven resolution, mistaken endings will probably sit at the end of your serial episodes as a way of concluding the instalments, while also propelling them on to the next stage along the way towards the overall ending.

This is the big challenge that faces series/serial writers and distinguishes what they do from what anyone writing singles does. It's not just about writing a great pilot. It's about writing a great pilot that shows the potential ongoing state of character being and character becoming that each new episode will bring. If this quality and depth and potential of character is not there, your script and idea will run out of steam even before the end of your pilot episode.

ABSTRACT ALTERNATIVES

I have already mentioned *Moon* and *Memento* – the oeuvre of story where the notion of the journey in the middle is given unique, unusual, strange, maverick, abstract, heightened, or surreal expression. This is perhaps easier to conceive in a high-concept single drama, whatever the medium. It's more common in theatre, where the artifice of space and experience can lend itself well to abstractness of experience – as in plays by Beckett, Ionesco, Pirandello, Pinter, Kane, Crimp and others.

But are abstract alternatives therefore random, non-consequential, without dramatic logic? Not as much as you might presume. In *Moon* the hero meets a new version of himself – yet the story has a wholly consequential, logical dramatic movement through the muddle. As also in *Memento* – even though the construction feels bewildering.

In Pinter's *The Birthday Party*, the narrow and claustrophobic world of Meg and Petey's guest house is heightened, odd and increasingly menacing. It is in many ways abstract, and plays out in abstract ways. Yet at the heart of its defiant uniqueness and seeming inscrutability is the story of Stanley, a self-aggrandising loser who, like a petulant child, bemoans his situation yet also craves Meg's overbearing mothering. When Goldman and McCann arrive to find him out and take him away – for what reason we will never know – his small world is turned inside out and he tries to resist them, but he cannot. His failure turns Meg, Petey and even Lulu's worlds inside out for the time we watch them. And when it's over, we're not sure whether they in any conceivable way live on beyond the lights up and lights down at beginning and end. But that doesn't mean we haven't gone on a journey with them through the middle to the end.

Charlie Kaufman's films can be a weird and unique take on character journey and development. But in *Being John Malkovich*, once Craig Schwartz has stepped into the strange new world of LesterCorp on floor 7½ of an office building and discovered a portal into the mind of John Malkovich, he embraces this new world in the confused belief that it will impress Maxine and in the confused desire to live someone else's life for ever (like Dr Lester's clandestine band who have been priming this portal for their journey into eternity). Yes, it is very, very weird. But the character journey isn't without logic, desire, need and a complex state of becoming. I'm not sure what the ending says and what the *anagnorisis* is, but the character middle isn't remotely as random as it might seem.

Twin Peaks, David Lynch's seminal TV series, is also very weird. But for the characters, it is always ultimately about who killed Laura Palmer – or put another way, *what* killed her. The opening discovery of her dead body and the arrival of Special Agent Dale Cooper is the opening of a Pandora's box for everyone in the town, and the whole show goes on that journey until the revelation (of sorts) in the dark finale.

Your world and your version of the characters' journeys and states of becoming can be as weird, skewed and unconventional as you want them to be. But they should not be without logic, purpose, meaning, vulnerability, change, complexity, wants, needs, actions, relationships or consequences.

Put another way, they should not be without an arc.

SURPRISE

Surprise is one of the things that keeps an audience hooked and engaged. Not simply plot twists and turns – though for certain genres, such as detective and thriller, they are a must – but where the characters' actions, reactions and decisions surprise the audience, one another and themselves, revealing something new as the story progresses.

Surprise is a hard thing to do well. It's too easy to write material that doesn't surprise the audience. It's too easy to write a script that plays out predictably, goes exactly where we expect it to go in a way that we have seen before a dozen times, and therefore says nothing new.

Surprise is a particular problem in the middle and many scripts fail to keep the attention because nothing (or not enough) that is surprising happens along the way. Surprise is all about change – if things stay the same or do not develop interestingly, then predictability and tedium will never be far away.

REVELATION

Many writers assume surprise means throwing shocks at the characters that seem to come from nowhere – from somewhere that isn't really generated by the actions. Affecting surprise does not come out of the blue – it comes from character.

A big mistake writers can make is to panic about the middle being exciting and interesting, and therefore to launch sudden revelations about who the character is or what their backstory is. You must be careful about what you reveal and about whom. If you suddenly reveal something essential and life-changing (i.e., story-changing) that the character knew but was holding back from us then you run the risk of making the audience feel cheated and lied to by a character they have connected and engaged with thus far. Central characters withholding information from the audience is a dangerous game to play, and is most likely a problem of clarity about who the central character is and who is making the revelation.

In *The Crying Game* there comes an infamous revelation in the plot about the gender of a character we have always assumed to be female. Fergus is the central character of this story and if the revelation had been by him and about something so fundamental as his own gender then the audience would be alienated by the surprise. But the revelation is about a secondary character, and as such the revelation is a powerful surprise, and one that has a massive impact on the 'hero' Fergus. And from this revelation Fergus surprises himself – not by his initial, instinctive response, which is revulsion and violence, but by his subsequent response, which is reconciliation and a realisation that he is still attracted to Dil despite knowing the uncomfortable truth and despite his position in a paramilitary organisation. Getting character surprise the right way round like this is crucial – because getting it wrong means confusing, tricking, losing the audience.

There is a pivotal moment in *A Room for Romeo Brass* when Knocks, who has had nagging doubts about the peculiar Morell, is taken by surprise. Morell has spotted these nagging doubts and suddenly turns on Knocks, threatening him to keep quiet. It is a horrible moment for Knocks because it is a jolt, it is an augur of things to come, he feels in danger but has to keep his fear to himself not only for his own sake but also for his friend Romeo. It is the moment the wedge between the two young friends begins to push them apart. And it is a surprise to the audience. We think

Morell is strange but also funny, off his head but probably harmless – yet at this moment we realise he isn't harmless and he isn't as oblivious to what's going on around him as everyone might think. This isn't so much a revelation of hidden information or unknown backstory, but of character, of personality and of conflict.

Occasionally a concluding character revelation works in the most twisting, turning thriller – such as *No Way Out* – but this is extremely rare and the hero keeping a major secret from the audience is simply cheating on them. Surprise is where the audience realises new things and gains understanding alongside the characters as they develop and grow. This is empathy and synchronicity. It is connection. And it is satisfaction. Make the audience and character connect by revealing new things to both as the journey progresses. Don't hurl random plot-grenades at them in the hope that it will be surprising; they won't resonate meaningfully and the audience won't thank or respect you for it.

DEUS EX MACHINA

Another version of this random hurling of plot is the 'deus ex machina' from classical theatre, which very loosely translates as 'the gods intervening from outside the action of the play'. At the end of Euripides' *Medea*, a chariot descends from the heavens and removes Medea from the scene of her murderous, vengeful actions. She does not face the immediate consequences of her revenge against her unfaithful husband – that is, the murder of her own sons. The ending is of the gods. But in contemporary drama, this is akin to aliens landing and preventing Carter from being got at the end of *Get Carter*. Chances are, the audience will feel cheated – and with just cause.

SHOCK TACTICS

I have already mentioned *The Crying Game*, where the major surprise comes as a real jolt but becomes the real story. One of the most effective story shocks I have seen is in the film *Hidden*. The tension in the story about a middle-class couple seemingly being blackmailed slowly creeps up on the central character right from the opening shot. The pace is generally measured and unsensational. And then there comes a moment when the suspected blackmailer invites the central character Georges into his apartment and suddenly, shockingly, irrevocably changes the course of the story by slitting his own throat. This instantaneously stuns both central character and audience. It seems entirely out of the blue – but only because we haven't had a chance to get to know this subsidiary character and understand why he would do something so extreme. We subsequently come to understand the reasons why he does so, but in the moment we are thrown, winded – stunned.

I don't know exactly why the director chose to do this quite as he does – but it perfectly compliments the sense that this is a middle-class character, secure in his life and sense of self, but suddenly jolted out of that security. And that's what the story in *Hidden* is perhaps all about. It's not a thriller, or a twisting, turning detective story – even though detection is exactly what Georges does to seek out his blackmailer. Rather it is the upturning of a secure POV into one that begins to see the world as the more complex and far less comfortable place that exists for all those people who lack that security. It is about what happens to people when something previously hidden suddenly opens their eyes and doesn't allow them to settle back into the safety they have always known.

There are other kinds of shock. The audiences who first witnessed (and still do when they are revived) young men stoning a baby in its pram in Edward Bond's play *Saved*, or the entirety of Sarah Kane's *Blasted*, came away shocked. In the former it was a seemingly inexplicable moment; in the latter it was the whole damn thing. But shock was the instinctive response, not necessarily the lasting one. Both plays were written as they were for a reason – to say something, to express something, to show something. These shocks are not the same as the kind of gratuitous movie violence that means nothing and makes me despair for humanity. Gratuitous violence is only about the unreal technicoloured red of movie blood and guts. *Saved* and *Blasted* are plays exploring the real worst that the real world can bring out in real people. They are not a comfortable experience but the shock actually means something and says something.

SECRETS

Surprise is essential; secrets are a way of generating surprise as an integral, organic part of the story. Shakespeare used secrets all the time to drive the story and plot forward. Iago tells quiet, secret lies to Othello. Hamlet secretly promises the ghost he will take revenge; Titus Andronicus makes a similar promise to himself. Romeo and Juliet marry secretly. Hermione is secretly still alive when most believe she is dead in *The Winter's Tale* – as is Hero in *Much Ado About Nothing*. Shakespeare's comedies are full of them and each works to unravel the world until it teeters on the precipice of disaster, before being pulled back to comedic resolution and safety.

The point about secrets is not that they are there or even that they are revealed, but that they make characters choose to do certain things in order to either keep them or expose them, whatever the consequence might be. From secrets can come power and fear – power being a knowledge a character has about another character, and fear being the possibility that a secret about a character will be revealed.

Secrets are a fundamental driver for long-term story arcs in TV soaps. For example in *EastEnders* – Angie pretending she only has months to live, Arthur Fowler stealing the Christmas Club money, the identity of the father of Michelle Fowler's baby, or the multiple secrets that culminated in the climactic live episode on the twenty-fifth anniversary of the show.

The power of secrets obviously isn't just in the middle. But planting a secret at the beginning and revealing it (or not) at the end of a story or strand is probably the simplest part – it's the journey between the two that is harder to manage. If the secret is not just a bit of plot trickery but character driven and essential to who they are in the story, then it will help drive the story through the muddle in the middle that is a necessary outcome of keeping a secret or exposing it.

DRAMATIC IRONY

Dramatic irony is when the audience can see or knows what the character cannot see or know. It's a staple of pantomime – 'He's behind you!' And of the horror genre – we can see he/she/it is behind the character, but in the cinema we are powerless to tell them, however much we scream. Dramatic irony is when the audience feels the tension and suspense that the character perhaps does not, because we are thinking ahead to the possible outcomes of what we know (and the character does not). Hitchcock framed suspense as the audience seeing a bomb ticking away beneath a table as two characters sit at the table talking, oblivious to the danger.

Effective dramatic irony, though, is when the character is surprised and we see it and anticipate it – but do not necessarily predict it exactly. At its best it isn't simply a surprise for the character, it is a surprise for the audience because it defies or exceeds or upturns what we expect, even with the benefit of foresight.

In the brilliantly unique film *Let the Right One In*, we know long before Oskar does that Eli is not just a curious girl he meets outside his apartment block but something much more sinister and complex. The moment when he realises what she is slowly sidles up to him, but when it does come his reaction is not quite what we might expect – he isn't scared exactly (except perhaps for her), he isn't stunned exactly (he must have sensed something all along). It is like a dawning realisation about what she is that brings a moment of clarity and *anagnorisis* for himself: before he was a bullied loner, but now there is someone who understands him and whom he understands, because she is a loner too.

It is a deeply affecting journey through dramatic irony towards the start of something much bigger – a young love that will inextricably bind them together, no matter what the cost. Here the surprise that comes from dramatic irony is not about shock, it is about empathy and journey and love.

UNEXPECTED OUTCOMES

Great dramatic irony is all about unexpected outcomes. But unexpected outcomes can come at any time without either audience or character anticipating it so long as you have characters that are proactively seeking something. The surprise of unexpected outcomes is when a character acts but what they consequently get is different from what they expected. Again, it is back to trying and trying and failing better. If the outcomes are simply as expected then there will be no tension and suspense in the actions because the consequences are simply predictable.

In stories where characters have truly stepped beyond their comfort zones and are pursuing desires and needs through the middle, the consequences will not be controlled precisely because the experience is new to them. For Oskar, although his burgeoning relationship with Eli gives him strength and confidence to act in new and surprising ways with his bullies, the consequences of that empowerment goes way beyond what he expected and builds ultimately to a dangerous climax where Eli must save him from a danger he did not foresee (in the extraordinary swimming-pool sequence at the climax). Oskar is not in control of the consequences of his actions. What saves him is not the confidence Eli has inspired in him but the strength of feeling he has inspired in Eli that she should come back for him even though it looked like their relationship was over. This is what makes it such a poignant story.

PREDICTABILITY

The opposite of all this is predictability. Knowing what is coming, seeing what is coming – the audience being one step ahead of the writing rather than the writing being one step ahead of the audience. Entirely predictable storytelling is lazy. But predictability is not easy to avoid, far from it. Remember that it is not the same thing as inevitability. Your story should have a sense of inevitability about where it ends up – but the surprise in how we get there is what will make it work rather than fail. We know that in love stories the couple either stays together or separates – we can call *Eternal Sunshine of the Spotless Mind* a kind of romantic comedy even though just about everything about it is unlike any other romcom ever made, and it is never predictable. We know that in revenge tragedies the hero will take revenge but lose some humanity along the way – *Dead Man's Shoes* is revenge tragedy through and through but there are things about it that are not like any other, and step by step right up to the ending it is not predictable.

The journey towards those endings is why the middle is so important and so easy to get wrong; the middle can define whether we come away from a story feeling that it was either surprising or predictable. A great beginning and a sensational ending will not to make up for tedious, long, unfocused middles that lose their way.

TEDIUM

Tedium is one of the deadly sins of storytelling. To paraphrase the TV writer Tony Jordan, audiences would rather have an hour of surprising, interesting mess than ten seconds of boredom. Avoiding tedium is about doing all the things well that I have described thus far. It is *not* about throwing car chases, explosions, fist-fights, melodramatic revelations or gruesome shocks at the audience. That is mere sensation. Sensationalism too becomes tedious when it has no meaningful reason to be in the story. You can't avoid tedium by chucking CGI at it and hoping it will go away quietly. It won't. It will continue to scream its blandness loudly and monotonously. Don't make your story 'exciting' as a desperate plot measure. Make it exciting in every element and everything you do in putting together your world and characters and story. And keep a very sharp eye on it in the middle, because it is here where tedium tends to creep up and set in.

CLICHÉ

Cliché is a bit easier to get to grips with. If you have already seen an element – character, scene, idea, dialogue, whatever – before more than twice (and you are not making a parody) then you know it's an unwanted cliché and you know you need to do something about it. Unless, that is, you want to lull the audience into a false sense of security only to surprise them by the radical thing you then do with the cliché. This kind of *coup de grâce* is not easy, but if you think you can do it well, then do it. But not for the sake of it. It's a dangerous game to deliberately tread a path between cliché and surprise without it being intrinsic to your idea.

In Joe Orton's brilliant play *What the Butler Saw*, what you see is essentially a classic bedroom farce replete with every cliché, but with each one turned into something altogether stranger, more interestingly histrionic, more unsettling, more deviant in the transposition to a psychiatric hospital. Subverting the cliché is what the play is all about. But you must be on top of your game to take this kind of path. As the theatre, radio and TV writer Sarah Daniels suggests:

'The two things I always tell would-be scriptwriters to beware of are overwriting and clichés.'

STRUCTURE AND THE MIDDLE

So you've probably worked out by now that (in my view) structure isn't something you simply apply to character or fit story into. Meaningful and effective structure is not divisible or separable from character journey and

story; it is generated by character and by the kind of story you have chosen to tell.

Again, there is no universal formula that will always work to get you out of trouble, apart from the most basic one: a beginning, middle and end that are inextricably bound together. But for the structural middle, the sense of muddle, character development, failing better, digging deeper, stages of becoming and the importance of surprise should guide you in the right direction.

One thing you must do, though – you must make sure your middle has *some* kind of structure that suits the story, because aimlessness and shapelessness will make it grind slowly to a disappointing halt. And as in the beginning, there are structural functions that you expect to see in all good middles, whatever their precise order in the genre of your story.

THE DIVIDING LINES

Unless you are writing a TV episode with prescribed ad breaks that precisely demarcate chunks of story, then you shouldn't be rigid about where exactly the three 'act' divisions fall and where the lines are drawn. You can have such defined divisions and lines, but you don't need them. Remember those basic principles of drawing you did in art lessons at school? There is no single outline that defines a shape as set against a background or against other shapes – it is the dimensions, contours, contrasts and colours of the shape itself that define it. I think it is fundamentally the same with dramatic structure.

What *is* the case with the structural middle of good stories is that it's the difficult (and often *big*) part that takes character from beginning to end. Be it a two-act stage play, a 45-minute radio drama, a 90-minute film or a 60-minute TV episode, the middle is a potential quagmire of story development. Keeping it an interesting muddle rather than an ill-defined mess is the challenge you face. And allocating specific page numbers to act divisions in a scriptwriting program will not solve the problem for you, no matter what some Hollywood movie scriptwriting manuals tell you. But knowing what the story is unfolding towards will guide you in the right direction.

In the pilot of *Life on Mars*, the shift between the beginning and the middle is strictly demarcated – Sam is hit by a car, he has a brief out-of-body interlude, and then he wakes up in 1973. But this is not for the sake of drawing dividing lines but of marking the shift between the present and the past – which only happens again at the end of the whole show. No other episode of the coming two seasons is structured in the same way.

In *Hamlet*, we could argue for eternity about where the dividing line, if any, falls. You might say the moment when Hamlet makes his vow to the ghost. But depending on what your 'take' on *Hamlet* is (and there have been a multitude, whether in terms of theatre production, film adaptation or academic study), it could fall in any number of places – and it wouldn't necessarily change what happens and the story of what happens.

MOMENTUM

The ending is the possible light at the end of the tunnel that your story is driving towards. If you don't know where you are going, then the middle just can't work. The beginning and middle don't exist in the vague hope of finding an ending. They make the ending happen, and that's what gives them momentum. It's the writer's job to make the story go somewhere, not to wait for that somewhere hopefully to turn up along the way.

It is for a very good reason that structure in the middle goes wrong when it feels like it has no momentum and isn't going somewhere. You don't have to state that ending clearly until the end – but it needs to exist all the way through the middle, just as it did in the beginning.

Look at any really great dramatic work whatever the medium. If it's great, then the journey from beginning to end will exist in the middle, no matter how hidden or warped or deceptive or complex that might seem to be. Road movies can be a great example of this. The middle is often where by virtue of the genre – a physical journey into the unknown – the characters necessarily get lost in some way or other.

Heartland. Butterfly Kiss. Badlands. Wild at Heart. Priscilla Queen of the Desert. Easy Rider. Little Miss Sunshine. The ending of each is inevitable both despite and because of the chaos of the muddle – it is there all the way through the trials and tribulations and temptations and perils of the middle.

DOMINOES

The stronger your ending is (in terms of dramatic inevitability) the easier it will be to set up character actions which, like a line of carefully placed dominoes, knock consequentially into the next situation and action. As your characters push forward, so will their actions have consequences and the story have momentum. So look again at what your characters want and need at the start, then make their changing wants and needs impact each action as they pursue and follow them. This is the only way to make it all really work.

Stories and middles sag when there isn't really a dramatic reason why characters do the things they do. Stories and middles sag when characters drift forward without a sense of purpose or urge. Again, they don't need to know clearly and transparently where their urge is taking them, but the urge needs to be there. The dominoes must fall for the pattern to emerge – they must hit one another continuously rather than fall over randomly.

In drama, things don't just happen after one another, they happen as a *consequence* of one another. If the dominoes are set right, then once the first one goes there is no stopping them until they reach the end. This is what you want your story to feel like throughout the middle to the end.

PEAKS AND TROUGHS

Dramatic dominoes are not simply about flat lines of consequential momentum. The point about consequences is not that they just happen ad infinitum, but that they rise and fall in peaks and troughs towards climaxes and lulls – towards dramatic intensities and pauses in the action. If you keep the levels of tension and intensity in the action on one linear flat line, then what you get is sameness. What you get is the dramatic equivalent to the intense beeping of the hospital heart monitor that indicates the heart is in shock. Or the regular beep indicating everything is fine. Or the monotonous drone that indicates the patient is dead. Whether it is all peak (action sequences), all trough (abject misery) or somewhere in between (the dull plod of ordinariness), the effect is the same – a flat-line line with no variation.

This can be a real problem in the middle of scripts. The momentum shouldn't simply be linear like this:

ACTION → CONSEQUENCE → ACTION → CONSEQUENCE → ACTION → OUTCOME

Rather, it might feel something a little more akin to this:

Each trough is the starting point of events that work towards the climax of the peak. But the whole middle won't be just be one wave, it will be a series of connected waves. Each wave is a sequence – or a movement, as in musical concertos ('movement' is a telling term in that it denotes momentum, journey, propulsion). So you need to break down the long stretch of the middle into more manageable movements or sequences of story. Each wave is a stage of the character journey and story. And each wave should consequentially follows the previous one, even if the gap between them is a year, ten years, a century or whole eras of time.

There are always apparent exceptions to this apparent 'rule'. You might say that the *Bourne* films are a relentless series of escalating events that never let up. But look hard enough and you will find the moments of pause, lull – trough. Or you might say *The Station Agent* develops in an extraordinarily measured, quiet, slow manner. But look hard enough and you will see the peaks in the waves. At both extremes of genre – action thriller and character drama – the scale of the wave is defined by precisely that genre. In *Bourne*, the waves are massive and noisy and frantic. In *The Station Agent*, the distance between the peak and trough seems much smaller in the quietly drawn world of the story and its not-very-demonstrative hero. Yet on a deeper emotional level, the peaks and troughs are ultimately just as high and deep and intense; raher they just show themselves in less histrionic ways.

The great thing about the wave as a way of thinking and visualising the story and breaking things down is that it is adaptable and malleable and can, I think, be applied in some form to any interesting character journey. The peaks and troughs can reach rapid highs and lows at one extreme, or measured, gentle undulations at the other – the line of the wave can be squeezed in or stretched out like a concertina. So as the story develops and builds through the middle, you might get something along the lines of this:

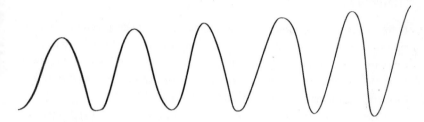

THE ROAD AHEAD

If everything in life went to plan, the road ahead would be a straight line and we would get what we want without any surprises, cock-ups, dangers or disasters along the way. But life isn't often like that. And drama can never be like that. So while there may appear to be straight roads, they usually don't last very long or stay straight for very long.

If the beginning is about a character stepping beyond their comfort zone and following a call, whether that is with excitable energy or fearful trepidation, then the initial urge in the middle will often reflect that feeling. The character(s) set out with some kind of plan or intent, however well- or ill-formed it might be, however confident or anxious they might be, and whether or not they are really seeing it and understanding it clearly.

In the middle, Billy Elliot sets out and applies himself to learning to dance and fulfilling the talent and desire he knows he has. In his mind, that appears to be a relatively straight road, even if it's one fraught with the danger of his secret being exposed.

Hamlet's plan is to flush out the guilt of Claudius, though at this stage he still doesn't know quite how to do so, which is why pretending to be mad and putting on a play seems like a straight road ahead to him.

Withnail and I flee to the country to escape the drug and booze-addled mess of their jobless Camden life – at that point, the M6 seems a very straight road indeed.

In episode one (and every subsequent episode) of *Bodies*, Rob Lake's plan is to diagnose the medical problems and do his job properly – the desire and principle is clear and, at this point, unsullied and uncompromised.

In episode one of *Life on Mars*, Sam's copper's instinct is to help solve the team's case, even though he still suspects it might all be a bad dream. The aim is simple – prevent the next crime, catch the criminals.

SHARP BENDS AND CHICANES

Before long, this straight road will hit some kind of sharp bend or chicane that throws the character and story. They may well find themselves back on the same road afterwards, but they will have swerved and veered away from the direction they are heading in to avoid an obstacle, and they will therefore be forced to work to get back on track.

The journey forward is not just about peaks and troughs, ups and downs: it is about twists and turns – not so much twists and turns in the plot for the tricksy sake of it, but twists and turns in the character's journey forward as they try to get what they want. Even in mystery and detective stories, it's not just about twists and turns, it's about the detective trying to find something out for a reason – to catch a criminal, to prevent the next crime, to rescue an imminent victim – not just for the sake of it.

Once he has recovered from his first meeting with Gene Hunt and the rest of the squad, Sam tries to call a mobile phone number – but the 1970s telephone operator is having none of it and the moment really throws him as it warps into what might be the sound of a hospital ventilator and heart monitor – is he in a coma? It is a sharp swerve in his journey forward, but it doesn't last long as the sounds are swallowed up by the bustle of the office and the news that just comes through about another body being found.

CUL-DE-SACS

In any story where a character is trying and at some point inevitably failing to get what they want, they will hit dead ends. Not necessarily insurmountable brick walls but cul-de-sacs in which they have to turn around and go back the way they came in order to continue on the road ahead. These are non-catastrophic set backs – moments of being sidetracked or false starts that bring the character's journey to a temporary halt.

You get these all the time in crime and detective narrative – the line of enquiry that leads nowhere. They can be clever red herrings that have been deliberately placed to distract and divert the detective. Or they can simply be moments of failure.

When Sam Tyler is left in charge of the squad for the first time in 1973, he attempts to get the team started in their investigations of Suzi Tripper's murder. But every idea, question and possibility that comes out of

Sam's mind and mouth is a cul-de-sac – it's a series of small dead-ends in one scene that show how far off he is psychologically and practically from the road ahead in cracking this case and therefore getting himself home.

A CLEAR VIEW OF THE DISTANCE

Then there are the moments where the character gets a brief but clear view of not just the road ahead but what lies at the end of it. Moments of insight, inspiration, clarity and understanding, where their sense of purpose returns and their faith is restored.

Sam Tyler cannot get his head round not only how to investigate Suzi's murder, but why he is doing it, what the point of it really is. Then in the mortuary he makes the connection between this case and the one he left unfinished back in the future. It appears to be the same killer – and therefore it is his ticket to getting back home. And his purpose is renewed. (And then he immediately hits a couple more very sharp bends – his behaviour means his colleagues think he's going nuts, he is taken to the ghastly bedsit in which he will be haunted by the TV test-card girl from the 1970s, and he begins again to questions his sanity and his purpose . . .)

QUICKSANDS AND HIGH TIDES

Then there are the moments in the muddle where it's not so simple a case of reversing out of the dead-end. Quicksands and high tides are the times when the character seems to be walking and walking but going nowhere, sinking slowly in the gloop or failing to fight back a rising tide of failure. These are more dangerous times, times when there is greater jeopardy than just a sense of surmountable bemusement and confusion.

Sam's investigation using the novel (at that time) approach of profiling and cross-referencing unsolved crimes is hideously slow when done in this manual, non-computerised way. As this process trudges on, he is still trying to reason out the reality he is in, caught up in complex and strange conversations with WPC Annie and enigmatic pub landlord Nelson. And meanwhile, Dora has gone missing, Gene and the rest of the doubting squad are questioning Sam's approach, and every attempt to make contact with the future fails. For Sam, it is like wading through treacle that is slowly but surely getting deeper and thicker and stickier.

THE CAVE

The cave is the 'big gloom', the moments where the characters ask themselves: can it get any worse? Where their confidence, faith, energy, ability, purpose, desire are at their lowest ebb and it almost seems easier to lie down and stop trying than to carry on. But it is also therefore in the cave where for better or for worse their journey forward is carved in stone – because otherwise, the story would just stop here with no ending.

For Sam, it is when Gene Hunt tells him (via a fist fight) that time has run out for Sam's line and method of enquiries, and he strides out determined not to bother any more, to stop trying to solve this case and just walk and walk until his mind can no longer invent any more 1970s wallpaper and props. He isn't physically inert and depressed, but he has had enough and doesn't see a way forward – and for a true-blooded policeman, being forced out of the police station is about as deep and dark a cave as you could expect to find. But as he questions the very fabric of life around him, his police brain does what it does best – it has an idea, it takes an observation from this fabric (the soundproofing in the record shop booth) that tells him something about the case.

CHASMS AND ROCK FACES

Just because there has been a flash of light about the way forward, this certainly does not mean the journey becomes easy again. Just the opposite. This is where the characters meet not just obstacles but deep, wide chasms to traverse and sheer rockfaces to climb. These barriers to the journey require not simply sheer effort, but a kind of leap of faith to just do it from the gut/heart. In these moments comes a renewed faith in the road ahead, one that isn't just desired but earned.

For Sam, having the flash of inspiration is not enough and it's not something he can even pursue straight away. First he must become a part of Gene's team – jump in the Ford Cortina and be and look and feel like part of the squad, out to catch a killer, despite everything about them that is alien to him. He must take a big leap of faith in them across a wide chasm of experience and attitude and opinion. And he must not only join the squad, but use their ways to get what he wants. When Sam questions Mrs Raimes, he fails; but Gene's charm and way with certain kinds of interviewees (as well as the violence and intimidation he uses with others) is something that does not come naturally to Sam and something that actually works. It is here they get the information they need for Sam's brainwave to become useful. At this point, the momentum towards catching the killer is absolutely back on track. But it's still a steep, winding, perilous track.

A SECOND POINT OF NO RETURN

If the middle is about taking the characters from beginning to end, then perhaps this moment or sequence of transition mirrors that from beginning to middle – it's another point of no return, where the pull of the inevitable ending is so strong that it drives or drags the character forward inexorably, whether they want it or not. Without this point, without the kind of momentum the characters generate and build, you can't really justify the climax of the ending – the conclusion that everything has led towards, whether or not it seemed like it.

THE (NOT SO) NATURAL ORDER

Episode one of *Life on Mars* is a fantastic piece where the order of the fundamental elements of structure in the middle tends to run in the order that I have discussed them here. They have a cumulative effect and build upon one another. And this will be the case in a lot of stories, especially the more genre-driven or format-driven they are, for whatever medium.

However, it doesn't have to be this way. And there are lots of maverick examples I could use. But instead I'll use the eternally popular one I have already referred to heavily.

In *Hamlet*, the structure of the middle is unusual. It reaches a point of intensity not in the final stretches but rather earlier on. When the play-within-the-play seems to Hamlet to show the guilt of Claudius, the momentum and intensity of events is high. Hamlet then steps up to take revenge – but steps back again, convincing himself that he cannot murder Claudius when he is at prayer because it will send him to heaven rather than to the hell he deserves. Instead, he unleashes an invective at his mother, during which he accidentally murders Polonius. From here he is sent away from Elsinore (and in Claudius's plan, to his death). While Hamlet is away, we see the descent into grief and madness that consumes Ophelia. (In the earlier, longer version we also see Hamlet soliloquise on the approach of Fortinbras's army, the distant threat that is seeded at the beginning of that version.) Then he returns in secret, famously contemplates Yorick's skull, and witnesses Ophelia's unconsecrated funeral, where the pace towards the end begins to pick up again because it signals Laertes's own desire for revenge against Hamlet for the death of both father and sister. You could say that the 'cave' is something Hamlet finds himself trapped inside much earlier in the story – in the grief of his famous early soliloquies. And when Laertes challenges him to a duel he accepts with a curious sense of calm, perhaps even of understanding, that this is where he has been heading all the time and this is where it will all come clear.

The structure in the middle in *Hamlet* is not generic – it is unusual and disorienting. As such, perhaps it better tells and expresses the journey of a character not quite like any other revenge hero we have seen before or since. Hamlet's journey forward is not just about putting together a plan of revenge – which he essentially fails to do. Rather, it is a journey of acceptance towards the inevitable conclusion – and it is only this acceptance, this sense of clarity beyond the antic disposition and the desperate grief and anger from earlier in the play, that ironically allows him at the end to be finally, irrevocably revenged upon Claudius – and to find a sense of peace where 'the rest is silence' and no longer 'words, words, words'.

CAUSING A SCENE

Here is a common scenario: a child is denied sweets and so has a tantrum in the supermarket aisle as the mother looks on. The child is, as the common phrase would have it, 'causing a scene'. Why is it called this? Because the child and mother are both refusing to back down from a moment of conflict, where two personalities with opposed wants and desires are at loggerheads. Writing a scene is all about causing a scene. It frequently will not involve something as spectacularly demonstrative as a tantrum, but it should involve some kind and level of conflict.

WHAT IS A SCENE?

If a dramatic story is a journey for the characters and audience, then a scene is a mini-story that moves your larger story forward, scene by scene, conflict by conflict. From conflict comes change – because in a story something must give, something must change, a deadlock can't exist unchanged for ever. If a scene is effecting a change, however subtle and miniscule it might appear to be, it is moving your story, characters and idea forward.

Scenes are the basic building blocks of a drama. They may be small and delicate or grand and cataclysmic, depending on their place in the design of your story, but at their heart is the importance of dramatic conflict, action and change that moves your story on. So if a scene isn't moving your story on in some way, you need to ask yourself this question: does it need to be there?

THE BASICS

A scene is essentially the time, the place and the setting you design to create a dramatic conflict. Scenes are unified by time and place. If the place changes, then it is for all intents and purposes a new scene. If the time changes, the same applies. Even if it isn't necessarily clear to an audience when and where a scene is taking place, the writer should know. It should generally be clear in your script where the scene is set. Stage and radio plays do not necessarily specify the time but in classic screenplay format, night or day is clearly stated at the top of each new scene, along with whether or not it is an interior (INT) or exterior (EXT) shot, and the specific location:

INT. SUPERMARKET – DAY

When writing the 'scene action' or 'stage directions', keep it as simple and focused as possible. If you can use ten words rather than twenty to describe an action, then use ten. And then see if you can get it down to five. Remember that you are writing drama, not prose – you are writing essential dramatic actions rather than exhaustively detailed minutiae or poetic description. Remember also that you are writing scenes that can be played by actors and shown to an audience – so don't tell us what the character is thinking and feeling if it can't be shown/played, or explain the character's backstory if it isn't integral to the scene.

There is one simple basic rule of thumb for drama across all mediums: show, don't tell. By 'show' I don't mean make it visual so much as make it dramatic. Don't explain what is happening – dramatise what is happening.

PICTURE AND MONTAGE

So what about pure visual or audio pictures and montages? How do you put drama and conflict into a simple image or tableau? Well, you don't. They are not scenes – they are not times and places designed to present dramatic conflict so much as links between scenes, texture, framing, pauses and breaths and transitions, ways of contextualising and juxtaposing and offering counterpoint to scenes.

The only reason you should worry too much is when there are too many of these and they take up too much time. I have seen films that are maybe only half story and half the in-between stuff. And although the director might say it's their 'style' or visual signature, it's usually because they don't have enough story and so are padding out the gaps with visual sensation. So if you find yourself resorting to indicating full-blown montage more than occasionally then let the alarm bells ring clear and loud – because reading such padding in a script is even worse than having to watch it on the screen.

DRAMATIC ACTION

Drama is all about conflict and change for the characters. You need specific actions that affect character. They need to be in some way unique, specific actions because repeating action without variation means your story is going nowhere; and going nowhere in drama means boredom.

It's easy to mistake dramatic action simply for action. Explosions or car chases are meaningful only if they tell us something about character. Action is dramatic when it reveals something new about the character to the audience, to other characters or perhaps to themselves.

A scene is a distinct piece of dramatic action and should be in some way distinguishable from every other scene in your story, because it should serve a unique, specific role in the story. The dramatic purpose of a scene is expressed in what the action uniquely shows us about the characters at a specific time and in a specific place in your story.

CONFLICT

'Conflict', like 'action', is an unsubtle term. Dramatic conflict does not necessarily (or even often) mean a stand-up row or fight. Conflict is not always or necessarily visible; it can be in the subtler frictions and tensions between characters or in situations. It isn't necessarily a physical or demonstrable action. It can be emotional or psychological in nature; it can be within a heart or mind or conscience or memory or instinct. It can be a contradiction within or choice/dilemma for a personality as much as a visible clash of swords.

GOALS

For the Hollywood-sounding term 'goal' you can substitute 'want', 'desire', 'need', 'urge', 'compulsion' or 'belief' – whatever works for you. What do the characters want? What stands in their way? What do they do to get what they want? You need to focus in on at least one crucial goal and/or conflict that must be dramatised in each scene in order to keep your story moving. Without it, your story will grind to a halt.

If you can in no way think of anything that a character in or connected to a scene wants or needs, then why is it there?

CONFLICTS THAT MATTER

You need to make the conflict in the scene resonate and cohere with what we see of the characters in your larger story. Don't make the conflicts random, episodic or for the sake of finding an action; make them meaningful to your characters, important in your story and engaging for an audience. Meaningful conflicts are the bricks that will make your building stand strong; if they are random sizes, shapes, designs, textures and colours then no matter how solid the separate bricks appear to be, they will not make for a strong or coherent or satisfying collective structure.

WHAT'S AT STAKE?

Meaningful conflicts engage us when there is something at stake for your characters – not just that a great battle must be won, but jeopardy on a human, emotional, individuated, personal level. If there's no hope of success or gratification on the one hand (goal), and no risk of failure or fear of loss on the other (obstacle), then there's no compelling reason for an audience to keep caring and keep watching to find out whether or not the character achieves that goal. If that compelling reason does not connect with us on a human, emotional level, the story will simply have no heart and no impact. So with every scene along the way, ask yourself: what is really at stake in this moment for the character?

Remember that raising the stakes for your characters applies as much to the silliest comic scene as it does to the deepest, darkest, tragic scene – as much to David Brent and Basil Fawlty as it does to Prince Hamlet and King Lear.

THREE DRAMATIC LEVELS

Conflict is a big term with big connotations, so it's useful to break things down in your thinking and clarify for yourself the dramatic levels on which you are operating within any given moment. There are three important levels:

➢   INTERNAL: where the conflict is within your protagonist, a battle with themselves. It might be emotional, where the character's feelings are confronted. Or psychological, where the character's understanding is challenged. Or about resolve, where their ability to make a choice and decision is tested. They may not even consciously realise the conflict is there at all.

➢   RELATIONSHIP: where the conflict is with other characters, a battle between personalities, and your characters' relationships are challenged and changed.

➢   GLOBAL: where the conflict is in the wider world and bigger than the individual character, though it is perceived by them and they do play some kind of part in it, however small.

All three levels will not be necessary for every scene, but the more crucial, critical or pivotal your scene is in the design of your story, the more likely will be the need for it to work on all three levels simultaneously.

SUBTEXT

Subtext is probably the single hardest thing to write well in drama because it requires your characters and story to have depth – hidden depths that you invite, even challenge, your audience to explore. In fact, subtext is quite literally impossible to write. It is not text. It is sub-text. It is what is not written as text. But although you can't write subtext, you can create it.

Subtext is what is going on behind, beyond and beneath what the dialogue and action on the surface of the scene tell us. Subtext is the secret life of the character's thoughts, feelings, instincts, intentions and fears that the best drama will seek to explore and express. Subtext is the unspoken conversation that is held between characters when words and acts are not sufficient. Subtext is the part of us that we are unable, unwilling or afraid to express openly – that we may not even be aware is there to express.

Subtext is the extra dimension that brings characters and scenes to fully-fledged life. You need to explore the extra dimension in your characters – the thing that makes them a personality like no other as opposed to a stock or archetypal character. You can't literally write subtext but if you make characters with depth and dimensions and contradictions then it will be there, somewhere.

SURPRISE

Surprise is probably the next hardest thing to write. Put another way, it's simply too easy to write a scene that doesn't surprise the audience. It's too easy to write a scene that plays out predictably, goes exactly where we expected it to go in a way that we have seen before a dozen times, and therefore reveals nothing new about the character.

Do you manage to turn the scene? Send the characters in a new direction, however slight that difference might be? Bring about a change in the characters and story, whether gigantic or minute? A scene isn't just about showing things – it's about showing things that change, that move, that develop, that do not remain exactly the same as they were.

Surprise is unexpected outcomes. What are the unexpected outcomes that confound the character's expectations of the consequences of their actions?

BEATS

A scene 'beat' is a measure of the conflict and movement within a scene. It is a way of breaking down the action structurally into smaller units. It is also an imprecise term and form. How long is a beat? How long is a piece of string?

Understanding beats is about appreciating the beginning, middle and end in your scene. Strong dramatic actions are rarely simplistic – they are complex and they move your story forward by dramatising a sense of movement. In its simplest form that dramatic movement is:

action   →   reaction   →   unexpected reaction

This form is expandable, depending on the scale of your scene:

action   →   reaction   →   action   →   reaction   →
unexpected reaction   →   outcome

If it is a major, climactic, pivotal scene, then it might break down into further manageable beats:

action   →   reaction   →   unexpected reaction
action   →   reaction   →   unexpected reaction
action   →   reaction   →   unexpected reaction   →   outcome

This is a way of charting how the tone of a scene might change, or the balance of power in a relationship might shift, or the decision-making of a character might be dramatised. From an unexpected reaction comes change. From change comes movement. And from movement comes the momentum to propel your story forward.

WHAT TO SHOW

Great scenes are composed, designed – crafted. Beginning, middle, end. Action, reaction, outcome. Goal, obstacle, solution. Problem, complication, resolution.

Need, opposition, plan of action. We don't need to see all three – we rarely see the immediate resolutions to conflicts – we just need to know all three exist within the context of the scene. The art and craft of writing a good scene is in the judicious selection of what to show and what not to show.

How much you choose to show and where in a sequence you choose to show it will go a long way towards setting the tone and feel, the pace and momentum, and the sense of tension and expectation.

JUXTAPOSITION

Scenes are defined by what surrounds and is left out of them as much as by what is in them. The judicious selection of material is crucial; the judicious placement of a scene is just as crucial. Scenes are normally part of smaller sequences, larger acts and superstructures that arc across the whole story. Knowing where and how they fit into your story as a whole is key to knowing what to show and how much to write.

When a scene doesn't appear to be working, look at the preceding scenes, because the problem might lie there – the conflict in that scene might have resolved itself too fully, or the conflict might simply not have been there at all.

LESS IS MORE

One dictum in screenplay writing is 'get in late, get out early'. Cut to the chase. Don't ease us into it. Don't 'set the scene'. Don't linger. Don't ease out of it. Don't write a beat, a line, a word more than you need – the crucial point being: than you *need*. If you know what the scene is about, the significance of the action and conflict, and its place in the larger design, then you should know what is necessary and what is superfluous. Whatever the medium, format and genre, it's useful to always aim to keep it lean, tight, focused, concise, succinct. Or in other words, keep it *essential*.

There are of course exceptions to every perceived rule. But as a writer, you should guard against indulgence and superfluity. Scenes are hard to unwrite once you have written dialogue and beats that you like. Deliver just enough to keep an audience satisfied. Deliver just enough to keep them intrigued about what comes next. Except for the final scene(s) – that's the one place where you need not continue to keep them at bay.

KINDS OF SCENES

Different kinds of scenes will tend to work in different ways at different points in your story – a series of short interplaying scenes work to build momentum and pace as you drive towards a climactic moment, whereas a single, long and unbroken scene will create the opposite effect and perform a different function in your plot. The terms I use below are a mix-and-match from theatre, screenwriting and archetypal storytelling traditions. They tend to come in pairings of related or opposing qualities and functions, though they probably won't necessarily (or even probably) sit together in a story:

➢   INTRODUCTIONS (prologues) and CONCLUSIONS (epilogues) can be formal, as in *Romeo and Juliet*, *Shameless*, *The Royal Tenenbaums* or *Incomplete Recorded Works*. All stories start and conclude – have an opening and closing scene. But deliberately and formally drawing an audience in and saying goodbye to them sets a particular self-conscious 'storytelling' tone. Is that the effect you wish to have?

➢   ARRIVALS (first meetings) and DEPARTURES (final goodbyes) can be simple. In *Romeo and Juliet* it is the ball where they meet and church where they die. In this example, they are also PIVOTAL in that they incite the love story and decide the concluding tragedy.

➢   INSTIGATING INCIDENTS are the primary actions that set the main story going. We often witness them and they usually come near the start of the story: Lear dividing up his kingdom and banishing Cordelia; Sam Tyler being hit by a car and seemingly going back in time in *Life on Mars*. But instigating incidents for different stretches of the story, or for sub-plots within it, can also come at other times.

➢   PIVOTAL scenes are where the story somehow turns on its axis and heads in a new direction. They can be pivotal in a large or small scene – and the extent to which the direction of the story changes will vary.

➢   THRESHOLDS are where a character makes a distinct step in a particular direction, either expected or new. The point is that we see the step or breakthrough being made – whether that is physical, emotional or psychological.

> OBSCURING scenes work to complicate the story and plot and narrative, and obfuscate what is going on to some degree. They will be those scenes in a detective or mystery piece that tangle up the story and leave us wondering quite what is going on. REVEALING scenes work to clarify obfuscation, to provide exposition about what has previously been unclear. They will be those scenes where Holmes, Poirot or Morse untangle what has happened, and reveal who the killer is and how they managed to work it out. Don't be deceived that they exist only in detective stories – all good stories need tangling and untangling. In Greek tragedy, the ultimate revealing scene was the *anagnorisis*, where the hero gained a true and tragic insight into their fallible humanity.

> TWIST scenes spring a fundamental surprise on an audience and character. Where a pivot turns the action in a new direction, a twist shocks the action to at least a momentary standstill before resuming quite possibly in a new direction, but almost certainly with a different understanding of the story and characters. Most twists come at the end as a final sucker-punch to the audience and characters, and they are most common in movies – *The Sixth Sense*, *Fight Club*. An infamous example would be the shower scene in *Psycho*, which shocks us by killing off early on the woman we thought was the heroine and takes the story in a wholly new direction. The crisis in *Chinatown*, where the truth about Evelyn's relationship with her daughter is revealed, is also a kind of twist and a pivot. But they aren't exclusive to movies. In soap and serial TV drama, the end of an episode might have a twist that will hook an audience to tune back in for the next instalment. And of course, twists are a staple of detective, thriller and mystery stories, whatever the medium.

> NAIL-BITER scenes build tension, either at a high octane or by manipulating a high fear factor. They are an obvious and common trope of horror, thriller and action movies. But on a more subtle level, great drama will often tease and stretch our nerves to breaking point as a story intensifies. The outcome will not necessarily be COMIC RELIEF, but if you are pushing a character, story and audience to its limit, then you'll need to find a way of releasing the pressure and tension, allowing all three to breathe again. The greatest tragic

stories frequently use humour and comic relief, from the fools in Shakespeare to the sexual exploits of Bess on a bus in *Breaking the Waves* to the heartbreaking comedy of Yosser Hughes in the confessional box in *Boys from the Blackstuff*.

➤ PINNACLE scenes are where the action soars to a dramatic, emotional height. This won't necessarily be a crisis scene – rather, it might be a moment of pure, unfettered flight and abandon – Shakespeare's Coriolanus single-handedly capturing a city, Tony beating a man to death in his rage in *The Sopranos*. The 'soaring' might well not be a happy or nice experience, but it will be a somehow simple, uncontrolled expression of the true character.

➤ CAVE scenes are where the character descends to the opposite extreme from the pinnacle. It is their lowest point and ebb – Coriolanus saying goodbye to his family and thereby becoming the vulnerable man that his warrior heart has fought to keep unexposed; a depressed Tony Soprano in the therapy sessions where he is the vulnerable patient rather than mafiosa crime boss.

➤ The final CLIMAX – or CRISIS – is where the inciting incident will ultimately take the story. CRISIS scenes can also happen at other stages in a story – at sequence, act, episode and series level. In *Life on Mars*, the climax of the opening sequence of episode one is Sam being forced to let the prime suspect go. The climax of the opening act is Sam meeting his new boss, Gene Hunt. The climax of episode one, series one, is Sam cracking the case, indirectly saving his girlfriend back in the present and accepting that he is still stuck in the past. The final climax near the end of series two, and the end of the show, is Sam returning to the present. The climaxes are what you and the story are always working and building towards.

➤ CLIFFHANGER scenes sustain tension by cutting away from a crisis and deferring conclusion, clarity or satisfaction. The classic example of this is in soap opera, where we must tune in next time to find out what happens. Many scenes contain an element of cliff-hanger in them to keep up the tension and momentum. You should never finally end a drama on a cliffhanger because it is cheating the audience of final satisfaction. *The Green Wing* ended series one literally on a cliffhanger – but this was a comedy series that revelled in just such self-conscious irony, and it did return for a second series (which likewise ended on a cliffhanger).

➤ DELIVERY scenes are the natural successor to the cliffhanger – where you stop deferring the conclusion and satisfy the audience.

➤ SCENES THAT DO EVERYTHING almost never appear in film or TV, they are unusual on radio, but are less unusual in theatre in the form of one-act plays that are essentially one unbroken, real-time scene. Beckett was the master of this form. Ironically, a real-time experience in a single setting has become something of a preserve for absurdist theatre – where 'real' means something very different from realistic or naturalistic.

THE THEATRICAL SCENE

In theatre, where the concept of literally setting a scene was born, there is always a necessary leap of imaginative faith – a willing suspension of disbelief – in the notion that we are live observers of a fiction. Classically, theatre has always had the freedom to manipulate the space in a non-realistic way. More recently – and with the proliferation of smaller, studio theatres – that imagination has become confined (some would say strangled) in the revolution of realism, naturalism, the 'fourth-wall' principle (Strindberg, Ibsen) and the kitchen sink (John Osborne).

Stage plays can be a single scene in a single setting (Beckett's *Endgame*, *Krapp's Last Tape*) or they can have the scope of a Hollywood action movie (Shakespeare's *Coriolanus*). If your scene is designed to represent an authentic, naturalistic reality, then you set yourself a practical challenge with changing the setting from scene to scene. If not, then the freer you are with your proposed scene setting, the freer your storytelling can be.

However, theatre also has the remarkable ability to take an audience into an enclosed, even claustrophobic space (Genet, Osborne, Pinter) in a way that you can never physicalise with such intensity for any other medium – because in theatre the audience can be up close with the actors and feel as though they are in the scene. In promenade theatre – where the audience literally is in the scene as the action moves around them – this can be even more sharply realised.

The choices you make about how you set the scene in your script will be inextricably linked to the kind of story you are telling, the kind of physical experience you wish to create, and the kind of space in which you imagine your play will be performed. The question you need to ask yourself is: can the scene be produced and performed? Try not to be hemmed in by realism unless it is an integral part of your play; you will be amazed by what imaginative directors, designers, sound and lighting technicians, and actors can achieve.

THE RADIO SCENE

Some would argue that in radio there are no scenes – and formally, they would be right. You do not set a visual scene that an audience observes – you frame an audio experience that only has a setting as evoked by acoustic clues and signals, and that at its best will allow and inspire the audience to imagine the scene in their mind visually. (The exception to this is if you record on location rather than in studio, since you may well be recording in an actual place – for example, Jeff Young's *Carandiru* was recorded on location in Carandiru prison in Brazil.)

For this reason, radio potentially has a greater fluidity and fewer formal, technical and logistical hurdles to leap. In theatre, you physically demarcate a new scene. In film and TV, the camera will literally set up somewhere new for a new scene. In radio, you can to a large extent do what you like in production and editing; and you will be amazed by what producers and sound engineers can do.

As a writer, however, you can't really do what you like. Your script must still be usable and recordable for an actor and producer. You should indicate place/environment wherever possible in your script. And because the audience does not have their eyes to rely on – which can easily tell us, for example, when a character has aged – it is difficult to make non-linear scenes and narrative work clearly and coherently for an audience. *Memento* and *The Singing Detective* would be a nightmare to adapt for radio.

One crucial benefit in radio is that locations and set-ups are essentially cheap. Big crowd or battle scenes are not necessarily easy to do well, but they are less expensive because you only need to provide sound. Therefore the scale and imaginative ambition of your scene setting can be unlimited – your character can be in a black hole in space, on top of the

Eiffel Tower, at the centre of the earth, at the centre of a brain or even a dream. In radio, you can truly let your imagination fly – if, of course, it is right for your story.

Radio can also be devastatingly simple. Two characters in one location. Even one character alone in monologue. Don't go wild with imagination for the sake of it. The crucial thing is to make clear and meaningful use of acoustic storytelling. Make your drama, conflict and scene setting work together to enhance what is at the heart of the story. Don't rely on endless sound effects, think instead about acoustic environment. Be clear, simple and unfussy in your script. If the scene is set in a café or library or tube train, then simply say so at the start of the scene rather than attempt to detail exhaustively every small sound that contributes to that essential soundscape. Leave the producer and engineer something to play with.

THE SCREEN SCENE

In film and TV, setting a scene is extremely expensive. The cost of filming drama is so prohibitive that producers will need to feel convinced that the scene is absolutely and unequivocally indispensable to your story. It isn't a writer's primary job to worry about money and budgets – but it is the writer's job to convince the reader that every scene is necessary in your story and therefore worth the expense.

In film and TV, scenes can be as little as a moment in which the character is present. However, a shot in which nothing really happens is not really a scene – it doesn't frame action, it frames a static picture. So distinguish in your mind between shots and scenes. A scene is where some form of action or dramatic development occurs. It might be brief, small, almost imperceptible even – and this momentary, minute quality in some ways characterises precisely what a camera can uniquely achieve.

TV is a more relentless medium for dramatic storytelling than film. The space you might carve out for your story in theatre, radio and even film will not be so readily available in TV. Concision, focus and a remorseless ability to pare down your work is key. Relentless doesn't necessarily mean at a fast pace (though it might) – rather, it means that the domino effect will be given its ultimate and most streamlined expression on TV. But this is also true of certain genres of films – such as action-thrillers. There isn't a great fundamental difference between the scenes you might see in *24* or

Children of Men. The narrative construction and shape will feel very different, but the way the camera captures the story is essentially the same.

The thing to remember is that you can go in close, pull back wide or be anywhere in between. Film and TV scenes are not just about what you show and what we see, but about how up close to the action we are and what angle or perspective we see it from. But remember, you shouldn't direct the camera in scenes; direct the action, and the director will be able to work out the best way to capture it. What you can do, though, is give a sense of how intimately close or panoramically wide the scene is, and you should do that as simply and clearly as you possibly can.

FROM PLAN TO ACTION

'Most of my stuff has to come quite quickly, mostly as shorter plays that can become longer, otherwise I get stuck in over-thinking. In fact, any time I've ever tried to give myself "time" to write a "full-length play", I've always – without fail – screwed it up. Scripting for film and TV is different, but with theatre all my plays have come from something shorter.'

Jack Thorne

There is a real danger in spending too long thinking about your idea rather than actually writing it. Some writers spend for ever researching and planning and stewing and ruminating and ultimately prevaricating. Like Hamlet, you can spend for ever deciding what is the best and right way forward. At some point you just have to kill the king.

With stage and radio plays, the actual script part can happen quickly once you are ready to write. But with TV and film, generally speaking, the complexity of narrative and the format of plotting that narrative for a camera to capture mean it's easier to get tangled and knotted in plot, and harder to see the story forest for the narrative trees.

But at this point, whatever the medium, you should be ready to write SOMETHING.

READY TO WRITE

Once you've got to the stage of working out how the middle will carry you through to the end, then you are ready to write something. If your characters have deepened and developed, and if your story is clear and coherent in your mind, your idea is already being realised. It is still in a state of becoming, but it is also taking real, tangible shape.

Cast back to the start – idea and premise, putting distinct flesh on archetypal bones, starting out on a journey of movement and change, creating characters that drive that journey. There's no guarantee that your well-meaning hard work will get you to the point where your idea is being truly and successfully realised. But it will help – it really will. And without the legwork, you'll most likely hit a wall soon, even if you come out of the starting blocks with what seems to be a cracking pace in the opening pages. Those first pages of draft one can be deceptive. They can come thick and fast and you will feel like you have got this thing sussed. Beware that feeling. Nobody ever has this thing sussed. They are just more prepared and more experienced than they once were.

REFER TO THE BLUEPRINT

Dig out the blueprint (or road map, or plan) you put together at the end of 'the beginning'. (Strictly speaking, it should never have been put away . . .) And dig out the synopsis, if you wrote one. Look again at what you wrote. With everything you've since learned and created in the middle, do they still stand up? Is there anything about them that could/should change? Ask yourself the same questions about the big picture:

➤ Does the story work?
➤ Is it the one you wanted to tell?
➤ Would someone else who doesn't have access to your brain get it?
➤ Does it hang together as a coherent whole?
➤ Does it have the right form and shape?
➤ Is the tone unified?
➤ Are you trying to do too much in your story?
➤ Is it focused enough?
➤ Does it feel original?

> What is distinctive about it?
> Does it have strong characters and strength of character?
> Is it what you wanted it to be?

And then ask some new ones:

> Does the middle take the characters inexorably towards the ending?
> Do the characters and story develop engagingly through the muddle in the middle?
> Is the approaching ending an as-yet-elusive but somehow utterly inevitable consequence of all that has gone before?

DEVELOP THE BLUEPRINT

If the plan of the beginning still works and you still feel confident about the ending all this has been leading towards, then set down your plan of the middle. Take the muddle and the consequential complexity of the middle, and plot the physical, emotional and psychological peaks and troughs that sequentially build towards the ending.

What does it look like? Does it look and feel like the story should look and feel? Remember that your blueprint is a malleable, working document. It's not there for posterity but to help you as you go. Use it to organise and clarify and shape and test the story.

STEP OUTLINE

If you think the big picture blueprint is working for you but want a more detailed template to work from, the next stage is a step outline. How detailed that next step will be is really up to you.

In theatre and radio, it may well not be very detailed. Many don't bother with one at all. The difference with theatre scripts in particular is that a step outline won't detail all the many and various scenes, as in a screenplay, because they usually do not have anything like so many. Rather, it might detail the 'steps' (or sections, or sequences) within larger, longer scenes (or acts). So it's still a step outline – but the steps will not look and roll out exactly like those in a screenplay.

In film and TV, step outlines are more likely and common – not simply in heavily story-lined TV shows (where a script editor must keep an arch eye over how the narrative fits with what goes before and beyond the episode), but in any script because the visual medium tends towards numerous scenes and is therefore a potential maze of complication. For some, a screenplay step outline is there to clarify the core actions and events of the scene and how these juxtapose across the narrative. For some, it also means a detailed version of the scene written more or less in screenplay format – almost like an overwritten script without dialogue.

The thing about step outlines, as opposed to treatments and even blueprints and maps, is that you can get a more detailed feel for how big and long or small and short any given scene might be and how they flow from the one to the other through sequences.

It's up to you to work out what works for you. If your instincts scream 'No detailed step outline!' then fine, don't do one. But if so, make sure your blueprint is a really strong one. It's better to get the story wrong (and then resolve the problem) in an outline than in the script. Once scenes and dialogue are committed to a play format, whether for stage or radio or screen, you can get attached to them, and they become harder to trim down (or kill off altogether).

WILD DRAFTS

Even though nothing yet is set in stone and the ending isn't necessarily worked out in full and fine detail, at this stage you are probably itching to just write the thing. If you really can't bear to plan any more, a way of scratching that itch is to write a wild draft (rather than the first 'proper' draft).

However, wild drafts don't work for everything or everybody. In theatre and radio, a wild draft is do-able and there's a case to be made that too much time spent planning can be counter-productive and sap life and voice out of the process.

Film and TV scripts are very different things. I think it's likely to be counter-productive to do wild screenplay drafts. I've seen too many writers tie themselves in terrible narrative knots by writing a draft before the story (or the writer) are ready. So if your idea is for a 60-minute TV or 90-minute film then I'd advise against a wild draft – it's something you could come to regret sorely when you find yourself lost and stuck trying to undo something that is already committed to paper.

The point about a wild draft is that you need to be prepared to ditch it altogether. Little might remain in the finished script. Or you might just find yourself with the bulk of what you need. It can go either way. What's trickier is when it's somewhere between these two extremes, because then you get into the knottier tangle of working out which bits to keep and which to cut. The choice, as they say, is yours.

WRITE THE BEGINNING

There is perhaps a better, more sane and more pragmatic option. Rather than commit to a full wild draft, write the beginning instead – and give your plans some concrete expression without necessarily getting bogged down with too much volume and complexity.

It's useful to see whether or not what you have planned does actually work in practice – to see whether or not the tone and feel and shape and choices you made for the beginning do what you hoped they would. But it's important not to do this before you have a clear sense of how the middle will get to the ending. Don't write the beginning too soon. Script departments are littered with stories that start well but get lost in the middle.

Hopefully this way the itch will be scratched without you breaking the skin, drawing blood and leaving a scar.

4
The End

AN ENDING IN SIGHT

So here it is. This thing I've been going on about since the start: the ending. And these are the dualities that have become evident about endings.

First:

➢ Great endings are utterly crucial in the story – integral and fundamental to how it begins and how it develops through the middle.

➢ Yet great stories aren't all about the ending, they are about how the characters get there – how they journey towards it, earn it, fight for it, struggle to avoid it, as a consequence of their desires and needs and decisions and actions.

Second:

➢ Great endings feel inevitable – a necessary consequence not simply of everything that has gone before but of where the story is taking us from the beginning.

➢ Yet great endings are not predictable or clichéd – the inevitability must still surprise and grab us with its force or intensity or wonder or depth or completeness (rather than with just cheap twists and turns).

Since these have been key, irreducible elements throughout this book, they should come as no surprise to you. And hopefully the work you have done through beginning and middle will be driving towards them rather than trying to avoid them in the hope they will go away and bother somebody else – because they won't.

FUNDAMENTALS

Again, a fundamental necessity about the ending:

➢ You did not need to know all the fine and exact details of the ending in order to get here – you just needed a strong, compelling sense of what that ending must fundamentally, essentially, necessarily be at its heart.

Or another way of putting it:

➤   The ending is the answer to all the questions you have posed the characters, and the characters have posed themselves, throughout – it is the fundamental answer to the question of the story.

Or even this:

➤   The ending is the final, cohering expression of the whole story.

SOME ENDINGS

Put this way, here is what the ending fundamentally means in some of the examples discussed so far.

Life on Mars: Will Sam Tyler solve the case and get himself back to the future?

Hamlet: Will Hamlet take revenge and pay the ultimate price that all avengers pay for their 'satisfaction'?

Merlin: Will young Merlin protect Prince Arthur and Camelot while concealing the outlawed magic that gives him his strength?

Fish Tank: Will Mia realise her dream to dance and so escape the prison of the estate and her anger at the world and people around her?

Criminal Justice II: Can Juliet Miller prove she is innocent of 'murder' and protect her estranged daughter without revealing the awful truth behind her decision to kill her husband?

Bodies: Can Rob Lake become the doctor he wants to be without compromising his integrity, his colleagues and his patients along the way?

Closer: Will any of the characters find the unsullied love and intimacy they really need or will the other things they think they want always get in the way?

State of Play: Will Cal McCaffrey get his story and find out the truth without it destroying his relationships and damaging those around him?

Billy Elliot: Will Billy realise his dream of dancing not in the shadows of secrecy but under the bright stage lights he deserves without it ruining his relationship with father and brother?

Moon: Will Sams 1 or 2 ever get home? And what will 'home' really be or mean if they do get there?

'THE END'

Don't assume the 'ending' means the final scene or moment followed by a fade to black. The ending isn't so much the final conclusion and parting glimpse as the final conflict and climax and crisis – the moment of truth that is the culmination of everything that has gone before. The ending is not the last look into the cinematic sunset before the credits, or the concluding TV close-up before the theme music kicks in, or the parting emotion of a play before the lights change and the applause starts, or the final noise/silence before radio credits are read. Rather, it is the final events and actions and decisions and outcomes and fallout that follow on from what has gone before.

Shakespeare's *Hamlet* exists in different versions – probably evidence that he rewrote the play after having seen it in production – that offer significantly different codas, but where reaching the ending is fundamentally the same for the central characters. In one version, Fortinbras arrives to seize power at the end; in the other, he doesn't, and Horatio has the final words of the play. The excision of Fortinbras in the latter version means cutting earlier scenes, dialogue and references, including one of Hamlet's famous monologues, 'How all occasions do inform against me . . .' Yet Hamlet's journey going forward is not fundamentally or substantively different – though it is tighter, more focused, more dynamic. Even after the significant rewriting of narrative and the cutting of characters, scenes and strands, the ending is still fundamentally where the story was always trying to get to from scene one – Hamlet at long last carrying out his revenge.

SIMPLE VERSUS COMPLEX

The fundamental qualities of the various examples above do not mean endings must therefore be simplistic and singular – saying only one thing about one character. Endings are relative to the number and prominence of the characters whose stories require and deserve a conclusion. So in films like *Gosford Park*, *Crash*, *Short Cuts*, *Magnolia*, and in any serialised drama, it is necessarily a more complex, many-headed thing. And in the case of those epic tales that span multiple 'single' instalments, final endings can become mini-epics in themselves – part three of *The Lord of the Rings* trilogy goes through ending after ending after ending. Or rather, coda after coda after coda. The ending is Frodo's. The rest is the tying of loose ends for all those who have helped him on his way.

You need to look back at where the POVs have been throughout. Whose story is it primarily? Who else's story is it? Do they conclude together? Shakespeare was a master of pulling together numerous conclusions into one big final scene. But it's much, much harder to do this for radio and screen because that intrinsic theatricality is much less convincing in any other medium.

The point is that your ending must fit with everything else. Not simply all the narrative, plot and consequences of actions that have gone before, but with medium, form, format, idea, concept, premise, genre(s), tone, feel, scale and, most importantly, *character*. However much of the 'arrival' at the story destination and the *anagnorisis* you choose to show, the ending is where you take the characters, where we go with the characters – where the characters take themselves.

IS THAT IT?

We have all experienced that cruel moment sitting in the theatre, the cinema or at home, when the final moment comes and we say: 'Is that *it*?' Where the ending just doesn't sit right. Where we feel short-changed by an incomplete story. There is sometimes a curious pause just before the lights fade or credits roll where we feel this cutting question already falling from our lips. Sometimes a quick cutaway attempts to prevent the question from forming immediately. But if the ending doesn't deliver, the question will come pretty quick anyway and empty tricks of production won't stop us asking it.

The very last thing you want your audience to experience is the detached feeling of 'Is that it?' They can come away as hurt, upset, despairing, drained, challenged and shocked as they can sated, smiling and with a spring in their step. But dissatisfaction means your story hasn't worked for them.

ENDING IS EMOTION

Of course, you can't and won't 'satisfy' everyone. What works for some will not work for others, and audiences can violently disagree about endings – but that's fine so long as it's an involved, engaged, impassioned response. For some, the final shots of the real survivors of Auschwitz in *Schindler's List* was an extremely fitting and moving coda; for others, it was an unnecessary, sentimental adjunct that eclipsed the integrity of an otherwise powerful film. But I doubt anyone has ever come away from the story feeling nothing at all.

Your ending must make your audience *feel* something – the thing that your story was always about, the idea that was always at the heart of it.

A FITTING END

Ultimately, you need an end that fits. That coheres. That concludes. That delivers. That tells the story, expresses the characters and literally realises the idea.

All great tales need a fitting end that makes the story ultimately cohere, no matter how obvious or strange that might appear to be. If it's a fitting end, whether it's for the most heart-warming of comedies or the most heartbreaking of tragedies, it should satisfy the audience.

SATISFACTION

What is satisfaction? Is it simply getting what you wanted? What you hoped for and expected? What you needed? Or is it more than that?

ENTERTAINMENT

To some, entertainment is a dirty word. To their mind, it means generic and cheap, slavishly serving up what an audience wants, meaningless, without lasting worth and value, just 'fun' or 'funny' with no deeper resonance or meaning. And it's true that much poor or just half-decent work across mediums will be these things and nothing more. But they won't *necessarily* be so – in just the same way that all stories in which the writer is trying to be serious, deep, meaningful, worthy, genre-bending or audience-challenging won't *necessarily* be great drama.

Entertainment is a form of satisfaction and it is only a bad thing when it is done badly – just as 'serious drama' is only good if it is done well. I would rather come away from a light romantic comedy satisfied and entertained than come away from a purportedly deep and meaningful drama unsatisfied and annoyed. Entertainment is not really or necessarily just the preserve of the happy, hopeful and comic. In a way, it is anything that satisfies. Yes, synonyms for entertainment do include: amusement, distraction, diversion. But they also include: activity, pursuit. If we engage with something from beginning to end, then it is 'entertainment'. Don't be thrown by or afraid of the 'e' word. Seek to satisfy by telling your story as well as you can, no matter how genre-driven and light, or dark and strange, it might be.

FOLLOW THROUGH

Satisfaction doesn't mean that nothing exists beyond endings or that they can't be fraught and difficult. Rather, that they follow through on everything you promised at the start and all the way through.

This is at the heart of why Robert Towne's original conclusion for *Chinatown* wasn't the right one. For Jake Gittes, 'Chinatown' is a place where only bad things can happen. For Evelyn, it's hard to see how an emotional life so damaged by the childhood abuse at the hands of her father could end positively. In the corrupt world of 1950s Los Angeles, people like Noah Cross get away with very bad things. It isn't a glorious heroic tale of good winning out against evil. It is a sullied tale of anti-heroism where realising the truth and trying to fight it simply comes too late. Jake helping Evelyn and her daughter escape remains a possibility in the story, a real enough hope to make them try at the end. But if it was a truly realistic hope then that's where the story would have started and would have always been heading. It would have been Evelyn's story of recruiting a shady private detective to help her. But it's not. It's Jake's story of realising too late that he has the potential to do the right thing, no matter how wrong he gets it along the way or how wrong he has got it in the past. Polanski's ending follows through on everything that Towne's story has promised all the way through. It took him a long time and a disagreement with Polanski to come to realise what the right ending and coda was for his story.

If your idea and story and characters are strong, then even if it takes a long time to get to the right conclusion or coda, you should never need to 'come up with an ending'. Writers do try to come up with endings – to tack on a twist of events or a major catastrophe or a revelation of information. But if the ending doesn't follow through, the audience will be able to see the join and the glue and the sleight of hand. It's pointless. Don't make it hard for yourself – do the hard work at the start and the ending will necessarily come, as it necessarily did for *Chinatown*.

THE STORY BEYOND

The contradiction about the endings of many a great story is that the fictional world does not necessarily stop turning once the story ends. The power of great characters and stories is that in our engaged mind and heart they have a life beyond the curtain call or credits. I'm not talking about sequels. I'm talking about what we don't see. All the way through the story, there are things we don't see – the rest of the life from which the story elements are drawn and selected. Great characters make us feel that this unseen life still exists even though we don't see it and don't need to see it (and, of course, even though it is a fiction). Likewise, great characters make us feel that this unseen life will continue on after the ending.

The exception to this is absurdist and surrealist drama, in which the events of the play are the *only* reality – or the events play out again and again as a repeated reality, a dramatic nightmare in which the characters are trapped. These are few and far between – usually either plays from a particular movement/era of twentieth century theatre, or the preserve of TV anthology shows such as *The Twilight Zone* or *Tales of the Unexpected*. (Many would say the truly absurd and surreal has had its day – or rather, the seismic times that inspired them have long since passed.) Even in the very strange worlds of Charlie Kaufman, the characters absolutely have a life and story beyond – in fact, that *is* the story of *Eternal Sunshine of the Spotless Mind*.

OPEN ENDINGS

If satisfaction is delivering, following through and (God forbid) entertaining, then what is the opposite of satisfaction? An open ending?

Aspiring writers often presume the 'story beyond' means the same thing as an open ending. But it doesn't. If what we have seen in the story has had a meaningful effect on characters – if it has been momentous rather than momentary – then we will guess and presume and hope and maybe fear for what will come after the story has finished. This does not mean the ending is open – rather that it concludes one stage and precedes the start of the next stage, the next journey, the next story for the characters.

Open endings are where there is no closure, no clarity, no completeness, no follow through. Open endings are a poor excuse for not telling the story properly. They are unsatisfying. I don't really know of any truly great works with truly open endings.

OK, so there's *The Sopranos*. Theories abound about the final scene, the way it cut short and didn't follow through a final, ultimate conclusion. But the final scene wasn't the ending – it was the final scene. The ending isn't open. The coda was a blank, black screen. The conclusion, in one sense, is Tony, his wife and his son (his daughter is outside, trying and failing to park her car) sitting together in a diner about to order food. Which says a lot about the whole show. It's not just a gangster show about mobsters getting whacked. It's a show about Tony, about his family, about the semblance of normality in a world where extreme things happen. It's not an open ending. It just doesn't deliver a neat conclusion.

OK, so there's also *Twin Peaks*. At the end of season two, we think we're going to find out who killed Laura Palmer. Yet we don't. But maybe that's because the show is not about who killed Laura Palmer – maybe it's about 'what' killed Laura Palmer. And we do see what killed her in all its dark, twisted mania in the final scene.

The point about these two examples is that they are the final scenes from TV shows, one lasting two seasons and the other lasting six seasons. They are not single, finite, closed stories. But they are also not 'open endings'. They are just not easy endings or simple endings or neat endings. They are complex conclusions to complex stories, and in both it is clear there is a life and story beyond the ending – whether or not Tony Soprano is whacked in the blackout, and whether or not Dale Cooper is really possessed by Bob.

AMBIGUITY

Both these final scenes seem to have a sense of ambiguity about them as we ask ourselves what really happened and what the ending really is. However, 'ambiguity' is a much overused and misused term, in particular by inexperienced writers trying hard to justify a lack of clarity in their story.

Ambiguity is not a lack of clarity – on the contrary, it is the possibility of more than one clear meaning. Take the sentence: 'They are cooking apples.' This can mean either a reference to the kind of apples used for cooking, or a reference to some people in the act of cooking some apples. Both meanings are perfectly clear – they just happen to be equally possible given the way that particular sentence is phrased. Without more information and context for the sentence, both meanings stand.

The problem with 'ambiguity' is that it is too often inaccurately used to explain away vagueness of meaning, extreme obscurity – and, in the end, a lack of meaning. If you want your ending to express ambiguity, then you need to think very clearly and carefully about what the alternate but clear possible meanings are. This is a *lot* harder than it sounds and than you would think. There aren't many stories that truly manage to do this. You might say that in the blackout ending of *The Sopranos*, there are two basic possibilities – either Tony dies or he lives. We don't know. Both are possible and both follow through from everything we have seen over six seasons.

A brilliant ambiguous ending is that in *Memento*. Having been told that his apparent mission to avenge his wife's murder is a fallacy and that he is in effect being utilised as a hit man, the hero wakes up in a new scene and appears to continue as before. We do not know whether or not it is indeed a fallacy. Both possibilities are clear and, in the story, logical. But by the time he reaches the next (final) scene, the hero who cannot form new memories appears to have forgotten this bombshell. He does not know the truth. He will never know the truth. The ending is a true ambiguity, and in that ambiguity is contained the brilliant poignancy of the story. Which is better or worse: the unbearably painful vengeance that spurs him on or the unbearable truth that his vengeance has been devised to give meaning to an otherwise meaningless life? And in a final, brilliant dramatic irony, the character carries on having forgotten the question, while we are left with the bombshell of ambiguity, fully conscious of its meaning and fully aware of how painful both possibilities are.

Ambiguity is not for the faint-hearted or muddy-minded. It is for those who are absolutely clear about what they are trying to say and show.

TWISTS

Concluding twists are a regular feature of the thriller, detective and horror genres. The audience for these genres expects the story to try to hoodwink them and surprise them at the end. When twists are done well, they are about the revelation of important information that we just haven't quite worked out for ourselves. Done badly, they are tricks thrown in that don't follow through or make any sense of what has gone before.

Some kinds of twists are about the moment of *anagnorisis* – realisation – for the character about who (and what) they really are. They are often supernatural, as in *The Sixth Sense*, *Angel Heart*, *The Others*, or for Annie in the pilot of *Being Human*. Or they can be psychological, as in *The Machinist*.

Other kinds of twists are about the moment of realisation by the hero about the truth of who (or what) another character really is, as in *State of Play*, *My Summer of Love*, *Chinatown*, *Unbreakable* or any number of whodunit, mystery and detective stories.

Once in a blue moon they are revelations by the hero of something fundamental they have kept secret from the audience, as in *No Way Out*, where the naval officer in pursuit of a Russian spy turns out to be precisely the double agent he is meant to be pursuing. This one is a dangerous game to play with your audience – you risk alienating them at the end by saying that the character is not the person they have been rooting for.

The late revelation of information comes in all kinds of stories, in particular comedies where a character's attempt to hide or cover up something fails to comic effect – from Basil Fawlty pretending Sybil is ill or hiding the rat from the hotel inspector, to the revelatory resolutions of Shakespeare's *Comedy of Errors*, *Much Ado*, *Twelfth Night* et al. But these aren't twists. Usually we can see the secret or truth being suppressed and our comic delight is in seeing how badly the characters do so and in the irony of knowing it will come out in the end. Real twists are where the audience is as surprised as the characters by the revelation.

Audiences for genre-driven stories take a delight in trying to guess the reveal before it comes. And the reveal only works the first time they see the story, so if you are going to make one then it needs to be impactful, fundamental, coherent and the true completion of the story. If it's a cheap trick then it's a cheap story. If it's a meaningful revelation, you can satisfy both story and audience alike.

DEUS EX MACHINA

I have already talked about this – the turn of events that comes from no-where and hijacks the story. The chariot descending from the heavens for Medea resonated in the themes and the world of the play. But without that true resonance, agants from outside the world of your story thus far step-ping in and changing events fundamentally or irrevocably are a problem.

What it really means is a failure of story – a desperate attempt to salvage a story that has no ending. The ending must follow on. If at the end you reinvent the rules of the universe you created at beginning, then what was the point of watching everything that came between the two?

The difference between a twist and a deus ex machina is that one is the character-driven revelation of meaningful information at a crucial point in the story, while the other is a conveniently thrown-in change of direction that reveals nothing meaningful and does not conclude the story.

ANAGNORISIS

The point about great twists is that they are not really 'twists' at all – they are a revelation or realisation of something we didn't yet know or hadn't yet worked out. In all the examples above, with the exception of *No Way Out*, the twist is the *anagnorisis* – the realisation and revelation of a crucial truth in the story and for the characters. Dr Malcolm Crowe and Grace Stewart and Annie realise they are ghosts in *The Sixth Sense*, *The Others* and *Being Human*. Harry Angel realises he is the killer and has sold his soul to the devil in *Angel Heart*. Trevor Reznick realises he isn't being haunted or stalked by anything other than his own sense of guilt in *The Machinist*. Cal McCaffrey realises his old friend is at the heart of the conspiracy in *State of Play*. Jake Gittes realises the truth of Evelyn's relationship with her daughter and father in *Chinatown*. Mona realises that her relationship with Tamsin was founded on lies in *My Summer of Love*. They are all realisations and most are (unless we've already guessed them) also revelations. They are the *anagnorisis* – a crucial part of the end of the journey.

Anagnorisis is not about sudden clarity that comes from nowhere. It is earned, fought for, pursued – even if the character does not realise until the final moment that is what they have been doing. It may be a surprise to them – but it shouldn't be a non-consequential, random shock because this means the muddle in the middle has simply been a meaningless mess, rather than a mess with a purpose and a point. Utter villains need not make this journey – but the heroes simply must. And so will the other characters to greater or lesser degrees.

Realisations and revelations are not necessarily sudden twists. With most characters, it is a more slowly dawning realisation or understanding or appreciation of the journey they have been on and who they really are after travelling down that road. For Oedipus it is a sudden tragic understanding that his hubris and arrogance have taken him down a very wrong road indeed. But for Sam Tyler in *Life on Mars*, the end of episode one is a dawning realisation that solving the Raimes case won't get him home, while the end of series two is an eventual realisation that he is ultimately more himself and at home in the 1970s than he ever could have thought. For Mia in *Fish Tank* it is the realisation that her dancing dream turns out to be a grubby sordid reality, but that she has the pride and strength of personality and intelligence to walk away and readjust her desires. For Schmidt in *About Schmidt*, it is the realisation that he has the choice of whether or not to speak the truth at his daughter's wedding, and that if he does do so then it will have consequences.

For Hamlet it is any number of things – one of which is that having set in motion a chain of events at the beginning, the end is inevitable and he must simply accept that what will be will be (even though all he has done and not done throughout makes the ending come about, so 'what will be' is of his own actions). It is a realisation that he must take responsibility for all the tragic, messy, unwanted consequences of those events – the deaths of Polonius, Ophelia, Rosencrantz, Guildenstern, Gertrude, Laertes. It's also a realisation that he has come to some kind of terms with the grief and anger and angst and confusion of the beginning – so that the 'rest is peace'.

Not every *anagnorisis* is clear-sighted or even fully conscious. For Stanley, a dumbstruck silence the morning after is a kind of *anagnorisis* in *The Birthday Party*. For Babak Beiruty in *The Incomplete Recorded Works* the realisation is a very weird, warped understanding that he must cut out the cancer from his body – and by extension, his obsession with a girl he will never see again – and that this must surely kill him. For Leonard Shelby in *Memento*, the moment of realisation comes and goes, and it is our job to carry the poignant ambiguity of his life with us as he fails to remember the possible truth that has just been revealed to him.

There are only a small number of 'successful' stories I can think of that really challenge this. In Mike Leigh's *Naked* it isn't clear at the end, when Johnny limps away down the road refusing to accept any form of closure, pause or empathy, whether he clearly understands his alienation from everyone around him and decides to embrace it or whether he does not reach that realisation and so is stubbornly continuing as he always has. This ambiguity, for me, casts an unsatisfying cloud across the story. He is a brilliant character and creation, but I'm not sure whether the random quality of his encounters through the main body of the story lead him to a point of change, a point where he sees himself and/or the world differently enough to make the story we have seen truly meaningful.

Anagnorisis can come in many shapes and forms, but if it doesn't come in some way, at some point, to some degree, no matter how momentarily, then there can be no real and true satisfaction – no ending to the journey your characters have gone through to try to satisfy their wants and needs at the start and throughout the story. This is the difference between dramatic stories and pure comedies. In pure comedies, the characters never quite self-consciously realise who or what they are and therefore are never quite capable of change. In drama, characters can realise and can change; whether or not they do so, or do so successfully, or do so in time, is the subject of your story.

IMPACT

Dramatic satisfaction isn't about the temporarily bloated 'fast food' feeling of fullness in your stomach. It is about the immediate impact and then the lasting completeness of an experience.

Rather than a bloated fullness, I think the best and most satisfying endings do deliver a kind of sucker punch. They hit you. They have an impact. They affect you – whether that's an immediate, winding blow or a delayed response that gets you later. If you feel nothing, then what was it all for? Don't make it just a chuckle – make it an infectious belly laugh that gives you a stitch. Don't make it just a bit sad – make it heartbreaking. Don't make it just diverting – make it overwhelming. Don't make it quite clever – make it fiercely intelligent. Don't make it melodramatic – make it dramatic. Don't make it just OK – make it great. Make it satisfy.

STRUCTURE AND THE ENDING

If the beginning means setting characters out on a journey, and the middle means driving them through the peaks and troughs of the difficult road ahead, then the end is ultimately the arrival. It is the distant point that the characters wanted, needed, necessitated, whether or not they knew it – and that in some cases they have always been gazing towards longingly. Structurally, it is the point that all roads either do or pointedly do not lead to.

Picturing this as a physical journey – roads, routes, terrains, destinations – is useful but don't let it confuse you or what you are doing. If your story is of characters in one room, or a character trapped inside their own head; then the structure will still be a journey – but it won't look or feel like a physical one. Rather, the physical journey is a metaphor. The road from doubt to faith, or faith to doubt, is a journey. The road from psychological confusion to clarity or vice versa: from social acceptance to alienation or vice versa; from feeling nothing to feeling something; political or philosophical disenchantment to conviction; professional failure to success.

The road from any state of being to another, just as much as from one physical place to another, is a journey.

CLIMAX AND CRISIS

Key structural elements in this journey at the end are the climax and the crisis. The climax is the big peak, the final culmination of waves of increasing intensity that must then ultimately break in some form of resolution or conclusion. It is the metaphorical wall of water that only stops when it hits the shoreline.

The shoreline is the crisis – the make-or-break point where events can no longer be deferred or avoided. It is the point beyond which things will have changed, for better or worse. It is the final big battle or confrontation for the characters. It is the critical dilemma and choice and decision for the characters. It is their moment of truth, the deciding factor about what happens next in this world. It is the point at which they either will or will not get what they want, or need, or deserve. It will be life-changing for the characters whose story this is, whether that is in the quiet measured world of personal stories in *The Station Agent* or is about the future of humankind in *Children of Men*.

In *The Station Agent*, the climax is the awkward falling apart of the two relationships that Fin has cautiously developed with Olivia and Joe, culminating in his angry drunkenness in front of half of the small town in the bar. The crisis is his subsequent decision over whether to withdraw completely and revert to the isolated shell in which he started out, or not to let go and persist with Olivia despite her apparent rejection of his friendship. He decides to persist because too much has already changed and it means too much to him.

In *Children of Men*, the climax is Theo trapped inside the horrendous prison of Portsmouth with the pregnant woman he is trying to protect en route to her escape. To complicate matters, she now gives birth to the first baby born in the world for eighteen years. The crisis is finding a way of leading her and her baby to safety in the middle of a pitched battle. There is a moment, where they are separated, when he could just give up, walk away, unable to do any more. But he persists, even though it means coming away with a fatal wound.

You don't get a much greater contrast than between the scale of these two kinds of stories – between quietness and noise, personal story and global impact, intimate character drama and high-concept action thriller. But despite the very different worlds, the intensity, power and dramatic impact of climax and crisis are of equivalent dramatic value in their respective worlds.

CHANGE

Change is crucial. At least one significant thing must change. If everything remains the same then the journey is meaningless. Your hero may fail to prevent the terrible disaster or tragedy that they have fought to avert throughout, but if something about them or the world around them is somehow meaningfully different as a consequence, then it will have been worth the sacrifice. Fin ultimately chooses not to hide away from the world, a far cry from his desire to escape at the beginning. Theo ultimately sacrifices himself for the sake of humankind, a far cry from his dismissive cynicism at the beginning.

Despite his anguish at the end and the extremely bleak conclusion and coda of *Chinatown*, Jake Gittes has managed to show and realise that he's more than just the hackneyed private detective he had allowed himself to become. He may not recover from what the ending has done to him and he may not have been able to help Evelyn or her daughter escape, but he is a better person than he was and he is a better person than just about anyone else around him at the end.

RESOLUTION

The point where climax and crisis effect a change – an outcome, a culminating consequence – is the point at which the story reaches a resolution. Resolution is where the wave has broken and we see a landscape that looks somehow different – the plateau of a somehow new world that is the consequence of the intensifying peaks and troughs that have gone before.

Don't mistake 'resolution' for a happy ending. The resolution is the outcome – whether good or bad, happy or sad, fulfilling or unfulfilling for the characters. Resolution means dramatic satisfaction. It's the necessity of all that has gone before. And with resolution comes some form of acceptance. Whether or not the characters like it, there is a realisation or understanding that this is how it is. Characters may not accept it for long, and the coda or 'story beyond' may be their continued fight against the outcome, but the resolution is a point of acceptance and acknowledgement that the outcome in this story as we see it is real.

The resolution for Shaun in *This is England* is reconciliation with his mum, and simply being able to talk about the dad/husband they have both lost and miss so much without it necessarily provoking a raw, painful, angry emotion in him.

In *Blue/Orange* the resolution for sectioned patient Christopher is that he is discharged but with an anxious sense of how he will cope, while for his doctor Bruce it is that he has screwed things up by meaning well, and for consultant Robert it is that he has got his way but not without casting something of a shadow over his professionalism. It's a play about three people with three intertwined resolutions.

In *Hamlet*, the resolution is that the truth about Claudius's guilt comes out and Hamlet is able to take his revenge; but he, along with Gertrude and Laertes, will pay with their lives and Denmark will lose a King, a Queen and a Prince in one fell swoop.

In *Moon*, the resolution is that although Sam 1 cannot survive, he can help Sam 2 escape before the 'repair' shuttle arrives, so that one clone at least will live to tell the tale of their manufactured lives.

CONCLUSION

The conclusion is the drawing to a close of the story and it isn't necessarily the same thing as the resolution. In *This is England* it is Shaun's 'goodbye' to his father, as he throws the flag of St George (tainted by his close brush with the far right) into the sea. In *Hamlet* it is Horatio (or Fortinbras, depending on the version) lamenting how such tragic events could come about. In *The Station Agent* it is the three friends sitting together, relaxed, enjoying a cigarette and a joke and comfortable silence. In *Children of Men* it is the ship *Tomorrow* appearing through the mist to rescue mother and child when all appeared to be lost. In *The Incomplete Recorded Works of a Dead Body* it is the 'narrator' of this faux-documentary providing a conclusion to the final recording of Babak performing fatal surgery on himself.

The thing about conclusions is that they give the audience the opportunity to take a breath, to reflect, to prepare for the light fading, the sound fading or the theme music to kick in. They don't answer all the questions that have been raised but they bring a moment of identifiable closure.

CODA

The coda is where the story is self-consciously drawn to a close – as in the concluding voice-over in *American Beauty* – or where we glimpse ahead to the future of the characters – as in the 'photo album' in *Four Weddings and a Funeral*. It is a brief, even momentary expression of the 'story beyond'.

Most stories have a kind of unspoken coda – an implied nod forward to the future. In *The Station Agent* the conclusion is also a nod to how life can and hopefully will be for the friends now.

Some codas are much more oblique and unexplained, like the final credit sequence of *Hidden*, where the camera rolls, watching students come and go from a school. What you see if you look hard enough is that the son of the dead man suspected of the stalking and the son of the couple being stalked meet on the steps of the school. We don't know if they concocted the whole thing together all along, or if Majid's son has ominous plans for Pierrot, or if the as yet unidentified stalker is making a new tape and the cycle will continue, or if they just know one another and there is no ulterior meaning. So it's an ambiguous coda – which befits a film that never really gave up obvious, neat, simplistic answers to what was going on from the start. Because it's not about 'what's going on', it's about what people do, how they react, how they change, how they cope when the bubble of middle-class security around them is burst.

ABSURD ENDINGS

The exception that proves the rule is truly absurd and surreal drama, in particular where characters are trapped in a recurring reality or nightmare. At the end of Ionesco's *The Lesson*, the pupil and professor are left at the end of their tethers. And then, once the pupil has departed and the professor is left to face his failure, the doorbell rings and the same pupil is shown into the classroom to begin her lesson – again. There is ultimately no real conclusion or resolution – because it is a repeating pattern – except that the lesson is always doomed to failure and that professor and pupil alike are trapped within this failure, forced to endure it again and again (like Sisyphus interminably pushing the boulder up the hill).

Absurd and surreal endings only really work and satisfy if they are the expression of a fundamental existential quandary, one that has resonance even though it defies change and meaning. If you plan to go down the absurd road, then don't do it for its own sake or for the 'effect' of it – do it because the only inevitable conclusion in the world you have created is one that necessarily defies conclusion. In *Memento*, there is an absurd quality to the fact that Leonard can never really change because he can't really form new memories – but it is a truly poignant expression of his unique life rather than an empty trick of the plot.

SERIES AND SERIAL HOOKS

All these things are well and good for single dramas, but series and serial episodes must conclude a stretch of the story while propelling the character and audience into the next. Until you reach the last ever episode, there is never a complete ending and so never quite a conclusion.

In soaps, unless your episode is the culmination of a major storyline or multiple storylines – such as the twenty-fifth anniversary episode of *EastEnders* – then there will always be some kind of hook or cliffhanger for the next episode. There should be a sense of climax, crisis and resolution for the story of that episode, but instead of a conclusion there will be an unanswered question or intrigue, or the sure knowledge that what has just happened in this episode must have necessary consequences in another – the classic 'out on so-and-so's face' shot before the 'dum-dum-dum' intro to the *EastEnders* theme music. Satisfying with an ending while keeping the show moving across week, month and year is one of the defining factors of what makes a great soap writer.

But if your calling card is for a series then it shouldn't be for a continuing series, it should be for a returning series or serial. Most returning series, especially those with a strong precinct, will necessarily have a story-of-the-week format at their heart and so you will probably not need a major cliffhanger, just a promise that there will be another fantastic story-of-the-week next time round. So the end of episode one of *Hustle* is Danny stylishly winning a hand of cards having got himself into the gang – all the detail you need to know about the show and what it will promise for the future of this series.

Those returning series with a wider serial arcs – *Being Human*, *Bodies*, *Skins* – will probably have a cliffhanging element, even though there is a story-of-the-week that comes to some form of conclusion. So in series one, episode one, of *Being Human*, after the crisis in which Mitchell chooses his friends (and humanity) over the rallying vampires, and the resolution that the three flatmates have a solid bond and security in one another, we cut outside to the conclusion of a man watching George through the kitchen window from the shadows. This man will come back in the next episode and be a pivotal influence in George's developing relationship with his werewolf self.

In serials which reach a finite ending – whether they are three episodes over three weeks, or six over six, or five episodes over five nights in one week – the story of that episode will be less conclusive and the cliff-hanging element will probably contain a major turn of events. Just when we thought the episode was coming to a neat resolution, a major new element or turn on an element will be the conclusion, and we will hopefully come away both satisfied by what we've seen and greedy for what we think is to come. So, at the end of episode one of *Criminal Justice II*, stabbed and critically injured, Joe's eyes flicker open with the promise of something, while the senior police detective dampens the spirits of his juniors having nailed their suspect by asking 'why' she did it. This, of course, is what the whole series is about. Will anyone find out why she did it? We know why. But will the truth come out in time to prevent a miscarriage of justice? In the extremely measured pace of this series and first episode, the fact that this question comes out of the mouth of a policeman is something of a turn or surprise and will impact not just the killer Juliet, but the junior detectives Sexton and Flo, whose own relationship will ultimately not survive this difficult case.

CLIFFHANGERS

You can only really get away with a cliffhanger in a single finite story if it's done with a sense of humour and a lot of comedic skill. In *The Italian Job*, the literal cliffhanger at the end seems to break all the 'rules' about following through. But does it? At the end of a comic heist caper, what should we expect? The final killer line from Michael Caine's character rescues the film from an open ending – because he always has a new idea, he always has a new plan. In a way it doesn't matter whether they save the loot or see it disappear over the cliff – because there will always be the next 'job'. There's something about this ending that says everything about the whole film. (I don't think the same can be said about *Lock, Stock and Two Smoking Barrels*, when the antique guns teeter on the verge at the end; it's a self-conscious nod towards *The Italian Job* but it doesn't express the whole film, it's really just a trick.)

Cliffhangers at the end of a series are rather different – after all, the job of any show that has returnable potential is to hook an audience to want to come back again later. But true cliffhangers are rarely used like this. The best was at the end of series one of *The Green Wing* – three characters sitting in a van literally hanging over a cliff edge. In a show that was smart, intelligent, knowing and unique comedy, that series ending really, truly worked.

Cliffhangers at the end of each series or serial episode (but not concluding ones) are another thing altogether. You need the audience to come back to pick up the story next time. But remember that the cliffhanger isn't necessarily the climax of the events of the episode. Often it is the twist or turn just around the corner from the climax – it is the start of the next stage of the ongoing story.

Some series and serials are more extreme in how they cut away at the end of an episode. *True Blood* episodes have a habit of stopping mid-climax or mid-event, and picking it up again in the next episode (a week later) at pretty much the same place. But with your calling card script, it's crucial that you demonstrate you can conclude an episode story. So while a hook is necessary, you need to be wary of a true cliffhanger. Because there's always the danger that it will necessarily leave a reader unsatisfied precisely because it doesn't deliver a definitive conclusion.

THE NATURAL ORDER

It's hard to get away with reinventing the 'natural order of things' in an ending because it naturally follows that events will climax in a crisis in order to reach a resolution and so a conclusion. It's telling that while much of *Memento* has run concurrently backwards and forwards, at the end of the narrative we see the two converge and the final events play out in a linear way and a more natural order for the story to have its meaning.

NO PAUSE FOR BREATH

In some stories the events of the end run so rapidly that climax, conclusion, resolution, coda can merge into one scene or sequence.

In *My Summer of Love*, the climactic revelation that Tamsin has been lying about her life all along leads straight into the final crisis, resolution and conclusion where Mona confronts Tamsin, teeters on the edge but pulls back from the brink of a violent, vengeful act, and walks away. That final sequence from crisis through to conclusion happens very quickly.

In *The Seagull*, after the crisis of Konstantin accepting the loss of Nina and tidying away his papers, the resolution of his off-stage suicide and the final conclusion of this being confirmed for us happens very quickly. In fact, when it finally comes, it is sudden and stunning.

A MEANS TO AN END

For some stories, whatever the medium, the ending is a brief affair. For others, it stretches much further across the narrative. There are no rules about how long it should be. But without that sense of climax, crisis, resolution and conclusion there's a real chance that it won't follow through or satisfy in terms of story structure. Because although story and structure are in a way indivisible, structure is still a means to serve the telling of the story, not the other way round. So whatever you choose to do, the way the events play out at the end must fit and tell and express and complete the whole story. This is nothing less than crucial and fundamental – which is why it is so hard to get right.

THE CHARACTER'S VOICE

Why does the character's voice come so late in this book? Because for most kinds and forms of scripts it is in a way the last element that you should commit to paper – and because I'm encouraging you to wait. You will be 'writing the character's voice' throughout – in preparation and in your head. But the character's voice is a fundamental means by which you express character and move your story forward. So you can write innumerable variations on plans, blueprints, outlines, treatments, yet once the characters start speaking there becomes something more permanent about the script – more finished – whether you like it or not.

You need words, but words can take over and take on a life of their own. They can be hard to trim, painful to cut, a headache to rearrange. It can be hard enough to make the things characters say ring true in the first place, never mind change them no sooner than they are said. Spoken words are the final link in the chain, yet also a potential dead weight. But while you need to tread carefully with the character's voice, you also need to be bold.

MOUTHPIECES

The biggest problem with some scripts is that the characters and the things they say become a mouthpiece for the writer, or the mouthpiece for a position in a debate between opposing views. In both, they stop being a dramatic character and become something else – something less. They express a standpoint but they have no real personality, no real voice.

Some writers are overtly political and dialectical and want their work to discuss and debate – but they are able to make their characters express and explore an issue rather than allow the issue to define and voice the characters in a monotone way. Trevor Griffiths' *Comedians* is a brilliantly dialectical play about the politics of comedy and the lives of a group of men trying to learn to be 'funny'. But Gethin Price, Eddie and all the characters are not simply (or even remotely) mouthpieces for sides in the debate, but the driving forces behind an emotive, intense, dialectical drama in which comedy itself is about much more than just telling jokes and 'being funny'.

DIALECTIC

Dialectic is about argument. Not rows and shouting matches, but real argument – a disputation or debate, a method of trying to resolve the differences between conflicting views. Dialectic isn't necessarily about identifying one side as 'true' or 'right' or 'better' – it is about the need to reconcile a contradiction. It is about conflict and movement.

This doesn't mean that 'arguments' in scripts should sound like a philosophical or political debate. They might – but only so long as the debate is between characters with strong beliefs who are trying to achieve something, rather than strong beliefs shoehorned into the mouths of characters whose only purpose is to represent one side in the debate.

Even if the dialogue is not overtly political or 'argumentative', in great writing there is always a kind of dialectic because dialectic can be about any kind of conflict, any kind of argument. The point is that meaningful argument isn't just about characters shouting at or disagreeing with one another – it is about characters refusing to accept and trying to reconcile a problem, a conflict, a situation in their life.

DIALOGUE IS NOT CONVERSATION

A mistake many scripts make is in the assumption that dialogue is the same thing as conversation, with characters rambling inanely, without purpose, as we might do in 'real life'. A dialogue is of course where two or more people 'converse'. But it also means a discussion, an informal exchange of ideas or opinions, or a formal political discussion between two groups.

Conversation can be casual. But dramatic dialogue should presume a sense that the voices are speaking for a reason – not just to fill empty space or time, but with purpose. In the real world, anyone can 'chat'. But when we refer to having had 'a dialogue' with somebody it is loaded with a sense that matters of import and significance were discussed.

Dramatic dialogue is not casual. It should say, mean, signify, imply, express something to moment, character and story, no matter how casual it might appear to be on the surface. It may not be clearly stated what that something is, but it should be there.

MONOLOGUE

Monologue is, I suppose, the alternative to dialogue. It's a singular voice communicating with us. It's not the same thing as soliloquy – which is a theatrical device to allow characters in a dialogic play to speak when only the audience can hear. 'A monologue' can also mean any character veering off into a big speech. But monologue as a form of voice and story is very, very, very hard to write well. I've seen many scripts for radio that say they are a monologue when in fact they are a short story to be read aloud by an actor, and even more scripts for theatre and radio that say they are a monologue when really they are just a character relating a story. I've also seen many scripts for radio which purport to be like Alan Bennett's brilliant *Talking Heads* – but which don't seem to notice that Bennett's plays were actually dramatic narratives over time that were written for TV (not radio), and this is what made them utterly unique. These 'talking heads for radio' are almost always big chunks of a character talking, and without a present-tense dramatic and temporal narrative for the character.

This is crucial. Dramatic monologues are not a character relating the story to us; they are a present-tense narrative in which a character is alone rather than in direct dialogue with another character. They are two entirely different things. So in Bennett's monologues, *A Lady of Letters* is the story of a woman who writes accusing letters, so much so that it finally lands her in prison – where she discovers an ironic sense of freedom. *A Bed Among the Lentils* is the story of an alcoholic vicar's wife having an affair with her local Asian grocer and rediscovering herself in the process. *A Cream Cracker Under the Sofa* is the poignant story of an old woman who has a debilitating fall and, while hoping that someone will knock on the door and help, reasons whether it is better to die now than waste away in a care home. Each of these is a dramatic situation, a present-tense story, a character on a journey – a character in some kind of danger.

The form of monologue can come in many shapes and sizes. Usually they occupy a curious space in which the character can communicate with us in a direct address, as in Lee Hall's *Spoonface Steinberg*, Beckett's *Happy Days* or Sarah Daniels' *Sound Barriers*. In Jack Thorne's stage play *Stacey* it is a curious address to the audience using a photo slideshow. In Ed Hime's radio play *The Incomplete Recorded Works* it is a fragmented series of recordings made by a sound artist. In Dennis Kelly's radio play *Twelve Shares* it is those parts spoken by a woman in a twelve-step programme to a group of people on the programme with her. In Hugo Blick's exquisite TV comedy drama *Marion and Geoff*, it is a series of moments just before and just after something significant happens while sitting with Keith Barret in his car. And in a one-off episode of *EastEnders*, it is Dot Cotton recording herself saying to husband Jim all the things she couldn't bring herself to say to his face.

In every example here it is a story, a dramatic narrative, a way of communicating with us while the story is still going on. The key to single voices in monologue is remembering that they need to be dramatic – the voicing of the character in a story, rather than the relation of the narrative by a character sitting outside the story. If you are writing a monologue or monologue scene, ask yourself a few simple questions:

➤   When and where is the character as they speak?
➤   What, if anything, are they doing?
➤   What will happen if what they are telling us does or does not come to pass?
➤   What is the difference between how they speak in this moment and how they spoke yesterday or might speak tomorrow?

THEATRICAL SOLILOQUY

One thing that is unique to theatrical voice is the soliloquy – where character and audience can communicate directly without any other character knowing. In great drama, it is a way into the character's mind and heart – through their voice. In great comedy, the 'aside' is a means by which a character can entertain us at the expense of other characters. It isn't something you tend to get so much in modern theatre – not with the same frequency and brilliance as in Renaissance drama. Once in a blue moon it is employed for the screen, as in TV adaptations of *Moll Flanders* and *House of Cards*, and to brilliant effect. But it is a fundamentally theatrical sleight of hand.

'INNER' AND 'CLOSE' FOR RADIO

There are two unique things you can do with voice for radio. One is to bring the voice 'close' – to a space perhaps equivalent to (but not the same as) theatrical soliloquy, where it is literally close to the microphone and metaphorically close to the audience. The second is to express the 'inner' voice, to offer the audience a direct line into the character's head and thoughts – not a stream-of-consciousness reflection of the mind thinking, but a direct communication with the listener.

These are both frequently used in radio – and although they aren't necessary, and you would never get them in *The Archers*, they are a way of expressing voice unique to radio.

THE CINEMATIC VOICE-OVER

In film, they say 'Show don't tell,' That is, unless you are writing a voice-over. There are two kinds of VO. The poor ones, which relate information, offer a commentary, fill in the blanks in the narrative. And the good ones, which aren't about information but about mood, tone, voice, personality – expression. The former can be found in any number of films, assisting the narrative. The latter is the preserve of the rare few, such as *Taxi Driver*, where it is a fundamental part of who and what the character is, and the relationship we have with them. Great VOs don't assist the narrative conveniently – they express the character fundamentally.

TV CATCHPHRASES

Although they can seem like a blunt tool, catchphrases in TV drama can really resonate. From Bianca's 'Rickyyyyy!' to The Doctor's '*Allons-y*' (in the David Tennant incarnation) to Gene Hunt's 'Fire up the Quattro', catch-phrases are a Dickensian trick of instant characterisation. This does not mean the catchphrase is all that there is to them, but it can be a handy start. They are obviously much more common in sitcom and sketch shows, and in drama they are more the preserve of soaps and shows with a tang of adventure about them. But in a medium where characters need to be big on a small screen and grab the attention of a potentially distracted audience, they can work wonders.

CAN YOU HEAR IT?

Great voice-writing is a talent and I don't think it is something that can be simply taught or acquired. You can learn to focus it, to sculpt it, to make it more dynamic, to make it less overstated – but I tend to think you can either write it or you can't. I have read scripts in which the idea, world, story, narrative and so on are all clear, strong, even powerful – but where the dialogue is awkward, wooden, on the nose, overstated, where it doesn't ring true and sound like a person speaking.

Essentially, it is less about whether you can write voices as whether you can hear them. I can't show you how to hear them. Nobody can. But listening obviously helps. It doesn't guarantee you will really truly hear, but if you don't listen hard then you will never hear. Not just listening to how different people differently speak but also metaphorically listening to who your characters are so that you can voice them authentically.

CAN YOU SAY IT?

Another problem for many writers is that although they can happily write down the words, they never actually voice them physically. At the risk of your family, friends or neighbours suspecting you are going mad, you need to voice words physically to see whether they can be said. If you find a line comes out garbled or awkward or without a sense of rhythm then the actor will find the same problem. Actors are not just there to say lines – their skill is inhabiting characters so that when they say the line we believe it is the character speaking rather than just an act of ventriloquism.

Can you say the line? Is it sayable? Does it sound right? Does it sit right?

DIALOGUE IS NOT LOGICAL

Just as dialogue is not conversation, so too dialogue is not necessarily logical. Although it should be dramatic and not just casual, generally speaking unless something is carefully rehearsed then real people do not necessarily interact and communicate in clear, organised, logical ways. People misunderstand, mishear, mistake, fail to express, ignore, cling on to, refuse to accept things that are said. The clearer the character and the conflict in your story, the more capable you will be of disorganising the logical movement of their dialogue. Debates and discussions progress, but not necessarily in smooth sequential order. Life and people just aren't like that. You need to be open to the muddle in the dialogue and dialectic as well as the purpose in it.

THE NON SEQUITUR

The logical consequence of non-logical expression is the non sequitur – the line that doesn't follow from what has just been said. One character asks a direct question; another's answer bears no clear relation to the question.

A play such as Caryl Churchill's *A Number* is a great example of characters failing to speak in logical ways. In scene 3 Salter asks if Bernard 1 hit Bernard 2 – but Bernard 2 rejects this as unthinkable. Then at the end of a circuitous scene and dialogue about the fractious first meeting between Bernard 1 and his clone Bernard 2, the latter finally admits he's afraid that Bernard 1 will try to kill him. If Bernard 1 had answered Salter's question fully and logically in the first place, there would be no scene – no dialogue, no discussion, no working through of what realising he is a clone is doing to Bernard 2. The seemingly illogical dialogue *is* the story.

Ultimately, people don't normally or naturally speak in 'speeches'. Rhetoric is a practised, applied skill, whereas dialogue is usually an imperfect, illogical means of expression.

VOICE IS EXPRESSION

Whatever the scene or moment, whatever the context, whatever the point in the story, dialogue will be an expression of the character in that moment. Dialogue isn't just a trading of words – it's an exchange of voices, an expression of personality, a voicing of desire, need, intent, feeling, belief, whether or not that is deliberate, accidental or even conscious. If a character is lying through their teeth and doing so convincingly, then it's an expression of who they are – a liar – whether we realise it or not in that moment.

What characters say won't necessarily be the truth or fact or right or wrong or good or bad or clear and coherent – it will be an expression of who they are at that point, in that moment, in that situation, and also of who they are fundamentally. If your characters are strong and compelling, unique and engaging, then their voice should express that somehow.

AUTHENTICITY

For voice to express character, it must feel authentic and appropriate for where the character comes from, how they have lived, the experiences that have shaped them, their education, their class – their personality. This doesn't mean there is a single voice for, say, a certain social class. Nor does it mean characters can't change, adapt and deliberately affect an accent and manner. But somewhere beneath what characters self-consciously do will remain the voice that belies who they are rather than who they wish to be.

Authenticity means listening, listening hard, and really hearing how people speak and what people say. If your play is about squaddies defending an outpost in rural Afghanistan then their voices will be affected by what brought them there and the necessities of being there – background, training, military language and slang. But a working-class teenage private from Essex on his first tour of duty will surely sound different from an experienced Captain who has been through Sandhurst, even though their technical shorthand may be precisely the same.

Unless your characters have a rare condition (such as Foreign Language Syndrome) then authenticity should mean ringing true with everything that we know about them and everything they know about themselves. It won't be the only thing that defines and characterises their voice – but it will be the fundament upon which it is based.

UNIQUENESS

As I said at the beginning, every human voice has a unique tone defined by the unique physiology. But uniqueness isn't just about a tone of voice – high, low, soft, harsh, resonant, thin, nasal, monotone, melodic.

Everybody has their own individual grammar. Even those who can execute perfect RP in perfect grammatical constructs will still have their own grammar – their own natural way of ordering and juxtaposing what they say. Everyone has their own rhythm and pace, their own way of phrasing, of emphasising, repeating, stumbling, pausing, or even gliding forward melodiously.

No matter how much they manipulate, practice and mask it, everyone has an individual grammar – and it usually exposes itself at times of crisis, when the mask slips.

Spoonface Steinberg speaks in a curiously forthright, matter-of-fact way, yet with a unique vocabulary and sense of phrasing that is a consequence of her autism.

Frank Gallagher speaks with a wild, ranting rhetoric when in one of the drunken or drugged reveries where he sets the world to rights.

Little Voice doesn't speak at all. She communicates through the songs of Judy Garland, Edith Piaf and Shirley Bassey until the climactic, critical moment where everything she feels and has wanted to say to her mother tumbles out.

Withnail speaks with the theatrical hyperbole of a failing actor who wants everyone to know that although he is mostly off his face, he is still more interesting and talented than they are. He doesn't just ask for a drink, he demands the finest wines known to man.

Malcolm Tucker in *The Thick of It* and *In the Loop* speaks in expletive-ridden but infectious and quite brilliant invective against anyone who crosses his path. His vitriolic tongue appears to know no bounds – yet despite his apparent rage, annoyance, dismissiveness and sheer offensiveness, he is normally in complete cutting control of what he says and how he says it.

TICS

It's as easy to give a character's voice a tic as it is to give that character a pronounced limp or quiff or mannerism – a stutter or stammer, a speech impediment such as a lisp or an unpronounceable 'r' or 'l'. Impediments can say something about character, but even a debilitating stammer will only go so far towards voicing who your characters are. Tics are really only surface – the first, main thing we see or hear. Using them to characterise voice alone will render your characters into clichés or solely comic creations. For dramatic characters, a tic can be an ingredient – but not the whole recipe.

ACCENTS

The same goes for accents. You don't need to 'write' accents literally. An indication the first time a character speaks is enough to establish the manner of their pronunciation. And remember, accent is not the same thing as dialect or grammar. A character can speak with a Liverpool accent and with a heavy use of Scouse dialect – but they can also speak with a Liverpool accent yet use non-region-specific grammar and vocabulary.

Accent is a way of colouring a character's voice – but it is potentially only as skin-deep as a tic.

DIALECT AND SLANG

Dialect is more complex and potentially more problematic. Dialect is a region- or class- or occupation- or experience-specific grammar and vocabulary. The issue is that not all readers or audiences will understand it. This is less of a worry for audiences because it's only one part of their immersion in the world and they potentially have other means of understanding what the characters say or mean. But trying to read a script written in dense, heavy, indecipherable dialect is a nightmare. It's not a novel – as with Irvine Welsh's books, where you can soak up the dialect and take your time. Scripts are written to be played, so reading them at a perplexed snail's pace is a fundamental block to knowing whether or not the storytelling for the medium really works.

For me, the rule of thumb is to be sparing and precise with dialect. Don't write the accent in a phonetic transcription of how you think it sounds. Just tell us what the accent is and allow the reader's brain and the actor to give it voice. Then use dialect when the word or term bears no real relation to vocabulary that might ordinarily be used.

Take the sentence: 'Do you understand?' In many regions the words are the same though the accent will vary. Some might say: 'Do you get me?' But this isn't really a dialect, more a re-phrasing that might happen in Liverpool as much as Brixton. But in parts of Scotland the dialect would be: 'Do you ken?' And this would not be used anywhere else. Certain circles, such as gangsters aping the Mafia they see in the movies or smart-arsed blue-collar professionals, might say *'Capiche?'* Which tells you something about who they are, what they do, how they think.

Not all use of dialect means replacing words, it might just mean additional texture. So when a character greets another with 'Alright', in Liverpool it might be 'Alright kidda', in Derby it might be 'Alright me duck', in Barnsley it might be 'Alright flower', in Glasgow it might be 'Alright hen or 'Alright pal', in Newcastle it might be 'Alright pet', in Afro-Caribbean communities it might be 'Alright blood', in the unreconstructed East End of London it might be 'Alright geezer'. And it might be none of these things. Your character might have their own unique way. Dialect is about variations in language and grammar, not the transliteration of accent. So keep it simple and sparing to keep it effective.

Slang, or jargon, isn't quite the same as dialect. It is less to do with where people are from and live as with the arena in which they converse. So soldiers use slang. Gang members use it. City traders. Policemen. Builders. Management consultants. Drug dealers. Bloggers. Slang is about using language in niche ways, ways that make sense usually only to those who understand the language, whether it's for their convenience or to obscure it for anyone else listening.

The problem with slang – as encountered by any writer trying to catch authentic 'street' dialogue for teenagers – is that it can shift and change and date quickly. So again, use it meaningfully and purposefully, not casually – because as a token or over-used or under-researched gesture, it will stick out like a sore thumb.

NATURALISM

In stories, naturalism and realism are not the same thing. Realism is the unflinching portrayal of life as it can be at its lowest ebb and in the absence of fairy-tale endings. Realism isn't the style of the telling, it is the portrayal of subject and world.

Naturalism is more to do with style – the natural manner in which the world is presented, and which we recognise. Many elements of *La Haine* are naturalistic – such as the dialect the teenage characters use – but the story is realism. It is an almost operatic expression of a ghetto in Paris with glorious shades of black, white and grey (when colour would be more naturalistic).

In dialogue, naturalism is a more useful term than realism. Naturalistic dialogue doesn't feel arch, artificial, theatrical or filmic, sculpted, manipulated, but sounds like something any person would say. Ken Loach's films are naturalistic, while Mike Leigh's are not. Both often explore the lives of ordinary people. But Loach's characters (or rather, those of the scriptwriters he has worked with such as Paul Laverty) speak naturalistically.

But a naturalistic style does not necessarily mean great dialogue and it can be a badge of false honour proudly worn by some writers – false because it only really tells us that the characters speak and the world is presented in a certain manner, not that the story is good. Just because it is naturalistic doesn't mean it is therefore more worthy or meaningful or interesting or expressive. It is only these things if it is the authentic expression of an engaging character in a dramatic situation – in a strong story. Don't be hoodwinked by the allures of naturalism – it's a choice you make about world, character and style, but it won't make your script better or have more intrinsic value by itself.

Also, don't presume convincing naturalism is easy to write. It isn't. It requires an intense, deep understanding and awareness and receptiveness to what 'naturalistic' and 'natural' means when people express themselves.

STYLISATION

The opposite of the naturalistic is the stylised. Stylised dialogue – and overall style – is self-conscious, deliberate, not an attempt to reflect what appears to be natural but a desire to create and control a style and tone and timbre and manner. (Ironically, the more self-conscious you become about making your characters sound naturalistic, the more likely it is they will become a stylised version of natural – and so not natural at all.) In a way, since all scripts are a fiction, all dialogue is stylised. It doesn't come from nowhere, and it is styled as much by medium, tone and format as by the writer's hand. There are infinite variations on what this non-naturalism might look, sound and feel like.

A Number is a play in which the deliberate, constant, repeated non-finishing of lines, non-answering of questions, disorganisation of expression and non sequitur is a key characterising feature. For an outlandish world in which a man discovers there are 'a number' of cloned versions of himself in existence, and which explores the existential meaning of being yourself when there are a number of 'you', it perhaps makes complete sense that the dialogue is by turns awkward, dense, strained, elliptical, incoherent, yet also at times startlingly clear and unambiguous.

So what about *Moon*? In another (literally) outlandish world where clones realise they are clones, the style is far more naturalistic. There's no necessity that a certain kind of idea or subject or story will require or derive a certain style of dialogue and storytelling. In both examples the style and tone feel like they fit and work.

Caryl Churchill's style in her play is brilliantly spare, uncompromising, perplexing, frustrating, yet expressive and in a way strident. In the end, it isn't overdone or overplayed. Those moments where characters do clearly express what they mean – and are realising what it is they think and feel – make perfect sense of the ellipses elsewhere. It doesn't explain them away or simply clarify them, but it does make sense of why they are the way they are. One of the journeys of scene three is for Bernard 2 to realise and admit that he is truly frightened of Bernard 1. The dialogue takes him on that journey in all its circumlocutory glory.

In the indie movie *Brick*, the world of the contemporary American high school is expressed and turned inside out by the highly affected film noir gangster dialogue that the characters use. It isn't just the dialogue, it is in elements of the action and story too. But while it looks like any modern American high school, it sounds like a movie from the 1950s. It's a masterstroke that you either do or don't buy into. Here, the writer uses a very specific genre-infused self-conscious style in order to tell the story of contemporary kids in a unique way.

Much is said about Pinteresque dialogue. But Pinter's best characters all have a voice of their own. Meg, Petey, Stanley, McCann, Goldberg and Lulu all sound different, unique. What perhaps characterises the 'Pinteresque' is the style and tone of the drama as a whole, and the moments where the action pressurises and changes how the characters speak – such as Goldberg and McCann's interrogation of Stanley in *The Birthday Party*. Here, they become an intimidating force with a sinister machine-gun style of bullying delivery to scare Stanley. If dialogue is a way of expressing the whole world, then Pinter's dialogue is Pinteresque because it expresses the whole world of his plays.

The danger with stylised dialogue – especially when writers are trying to be absurdist or surreal – is that it takes over, it replaces all voices with one voice, one tone, one register. Even if your story is an absurd, repetitive or fragmented nightmare, it doesn't mean the characters should not have a unique voice. On the contrary, if they don't have one, then your idea will feel more like a trick, a single statement, a play about an idea rather than about the characters.

RHETORIC

Rhetoric is the artful technique of manipulating language with the intent of persuading the listener to agree with the speaker – whether or not what is said is truthful, rightful or justifiable. Rhetoric is a series of tropes and tricks and constructions that are employed towards an effect. It does not come naturally, although the more a person uses it, the more second nature it can become. But it is ultimately an applied technique.

It is the domain of kings and queens, presidents and prime ministers, politicians, preachers, agitators, lecturers, lawyers, poets, seducers, salesmen, advertising copywriters. Think about the effect of the great speeches in history – Marc Antony in Rome, Jesus Christ's Sermon on the Mount, Henry V to the troops at Agincourt and Elizabeth I at Tilbury, William Wilberforce on abolishing slavery to Parliament, Abraham Lincoln's Gettysburg Address, Churchill's wartime speeches, John F. Kennedy's inaugural address, Martin Luther King's 'I Have a Dream', Enoch Powell's 'Rivers of Blood', Barack Obama's election campaign and inaugural speeches. Rhetoric is the art of making a great speech, such as those in *Henry V*, *Independence Day*, *Julius Caesar*, *Wall Street*, *Cyrano de Bergerac*, *Romeo and Juliet*, *Murder in the Cathedral* – or as delivered by the barrister in any number of TV legal dramas.

Rhetoric isn't solely for the formal purpose of delivering a persuasive speech. It can be anywhere that a character seeks to persuade another, but it will necessarily be identifiable in the way he or she organises, juxtaposes, inverts, repeats, compares, contrasts, exaggerates and alliterates to get a point across.

The danger is that it becomes an empty trick, impressive to hear but without true substance or meaning. So you need to decide for any given moment where exactly a character's rhetorical words sit on the scale between powerful persuasion and empty outpouring.

LYRICAL

A 'lyrical drama' is a particular kind of species – not really a play, but a lyrical poem with a narrative structure, such as Shelley's *Prometheus Unbound*. Lyricism in dramatic writing – beautiful, resonant, emotional, songlike expression – can be a truly defining quality, but it's not normally achieved when the writer is consciously trying to 'be poetic'. What you tend to get there is sentimentality, indulgence or (sin of all sins) bad rhyming. Lyrical dialogue and monologue does not need to rhyme and does not need to 'be poetic'. It needs to sing a kind of song that expresses the voice of the character. So it can be restrained and elliptical while being lyrical. It can be menacing and febrile. It can be contemporary and slang-laden. It can express a complex, difficult emotion. It is a kind of song that the characters and the play sing – not necessarily a literal song (as in a musical), but an emotional expression that isn't 'naturalism', isn't conversation, isn't just dialogue.

The plays and characters of debbie tucker green have that unique lyrical quality. Jim Cartwright's *Road* has a lyricism as it journeys through disjointed lives. Sarah Kane's *Crave* feels (in production rather than on the page) musically hypnotic. *Under Milk Wood* is perhaps the most famous example of lyricism – not surprising, since it was written by a poet rather than a dramatist. But people too often try to ape Dylan Thomas's piece for radio, saying they have written a modern, fresh, unusual take on it or a play inspired by it when in fact all they have done is lazily copy the form in the hope that it will mask not really having a story. *Under Milk Wood* was utterly unique; don't try to copy it, create your own lyricism. But do it through the expression of character and story, not through an attempt to 'be lyrical' or 'poetical' for the seductive sake of it.

ON THE NOSE

The big problem with a great deal of the dialogue (and monologue) written for any medium is that it is 'on the nose' – a straightforward statement with nothing beyond what is straightforwardly stated. It is extremely easy to write this way or to rewrite out the more on-the-nose parts. Ultimately, if you have dialogue that is only there to state obvious things in obvious ways, then look again to see if what is stated could be put another way, explored another way, or expressed through a conflict and dramatic moment.

EXPOSITION AND INFORMATION

The reason people write on the nose is because they have information they need to get across and take the path of least resistance towards that exposition. The clumsiness with which writers state information through their characters truly knows no bounds. But although it's easy enough to spot in another's script, it's rather harder to avoid in your own.

The first check you need to make is this: people do not tell each other things they already know in obvious ways, and neither should characters. So at the dinner table, hubbie says, 'Darling, do you remember the holiday to Italy we took just after I got promoted and just before you became pregnant with little Bobby?' Well, of course she remembers it – it was just after he got promoted and just before she fell pregnant. Unless there's a good reason why the character should have to explain it in such a way (perhaps his wife is an amnesiac?) then you need to find another way. Because this isn't dialogue – it is backstory crowbarred into the conversation for the sole benefit of informing the audience.

It's important to put the exposition of information at the heart of the drama, story and conflict in the scene. One of the best examples is Evelyn's dramatic revelation in the climax of *Chinatown*. At this point, Jake has had enough of her games, he's willing to turn her over for the cops to deal with. All he really wants to know now is the truth about the young woman she has been keeping secret.

So Evelyn tells him. Katharine is her sister. And her daughter. With each seemingly contradictory statement, Jake tries to slap the real truth out of her. Until she says 'She's my sister and my daughter! ... My father and I, understand, or is it too tough for you?' This gut-wrenching revelation is a pivotal moment at a critical point in the story, and it is made without actually stating the 'fact' or 'truth' overtly. Some things do not need stating. The information is all there. And it had to be beaten out of Evelyn at a point of crisis. In this scene, the exposition is at the very heart of the drama and the story.

'BAD LANGUAGE'

It's not a major point, and the level of 'bad language' you use is dependent on the kind and genre and tone and audience of your story; but I think that as a general rule of thumb, less is more. Not because I'm prudish, but because the more you use something the more you reduce its impact. The more expletive-laden your script, the less power and effect that language may have within the story and on the audience. We eventually become immune to it.

On radio there isn't, as in TV, a strict 'watershed' hour before which language and subject matter must adhere to guidelines about what is acceptable for certain audiences. But there will still be a strict scrutiny over what is and is not acceptable. On radio, words that are deemed questionable in terms of race, gender, age, religion or disability are likely to offend as much (if not more) than extreme expletives. But interesting tales abound about producers trading five 'shits' for one 'fuck' in order to get the right effect in their play – because they know that sparing use is worth much more than repeated use.

Writers sometimes justify a constant stream of expletives by asserting, 'Well, that's how these people talk, it's authentic.' Which is fair enough. But remember, dialogue is not conversation. Dramatic language needs to have an effect and be effective, therefore you need to control it, use it, manipulate it, sculpt it. If the audience becomes inured to 'how these people talk' through overuse, surely you have failed to express the character and depict their world authentically?

(PREFACING)

The prefacing of a line of dialogue in (brackets) to indicate how you think it should be said is one of the most irritating things known to script editor, director and actor. It suggests a lack of faith in your words – and in their ability. It suggests that when you say '(*angrily*)' or '(*firmly*)' or '(*sadly*)' or '(*wistfully*)' that there is only one possible way and one possible meaning in the character's words. That there's no possible subtext or shading or ambiguity or complexity of meaning that director and actor can bring to it. It is simply poor writing. If something needs to be stated about how a line is delivered, then what you should look at is the action, what the character is doing, the dramatic situation the character is in – and not the basest element of how they are saying it.

SHOUTING!

Again, not a major point – but the same thing goes for exclamation marks. I have read scripts where more or less every line of dialogue is followed by an exclamation mark. Then lines of extra emphasis have two. And extra special lines – usually melodramatic wails of tragic angst – have three or more.

Again, less is more. Only use exclamation marks on the rare occasions when the character is actually exclaiming. Only use them when you need them. I even think that putting lines of extraordinary emphasis ALL IN CAPITALS tends to be more effective than using endless exclamation marks. Sometimes words and lines have great import but they are not shouted or exclaimed, rather they are stated with gravity or firmness or absolute clarity or a sense of finality. In these instances, CAPITALS can work best.

TERSE VERSUS GLIB

On a different scale from that between the naturalistic and the stylised is that between the terse and the glib – or to use TV examples, between *24* and *Desperate Housewives*. In *24*, in keeping with the tense, fast-paced, action-thriller genre, the dialogue is terse, almost eloquently functional, used when absolutely necessary and not at any other time; it is not a show about language, it is a show about action. In *Desperate Housewives*, in keeping with the quirky, dramatic–comic suburban lives of neighbours whose paths intersect far too frequently, the dialogue is fluent and easy, often rapid-fire and witty, the first recourse for the characters in most given scenarios.

Scripts in any genre will tend to have a kind of core register, a core tone to them somewhere on this scale between the monosyllabic and the profuse. Neither is fundamentally better than the other, the key thing is that they suit the kind of story you are telling. An intense drama is unlikely to be glib, a bright comedy is unlikely to be terse. Sometimes the two can be straddled strangely – such as in *Dead Man's Shoes* (and many Shane Meadows films) where the avenger's scenes are terse, the gang scenes are glib, and putting both in the same scene means something curious in between. And this is in a way at the heart of what the film is doing – because it's not like any other revenge tragedy you have ever seen.

Where on this scale sits the core tone of your characters' voices and the world of your story?

WIT AND WORDPLAY

Glib is great if it's the right choice for your world. But be careful of overdoing wit and wordplay – of trying to make your characters sound as clever as you would like people to think *you* are. This happens all the time. It's not a crime. We want people to think that we're good at writing, that we're intelligent and clever and have a way with language. But be careful your characters don't become mouthpieces for cleverness, because this kind of thing wears very thin very quickly. It makes sense that Sir Humphrey is always superlatively clever in *Yes Minister* – just as it makes sense for Jim Hacker never in his wildest dreams to be so sharp or quick, and therefore to sound a bit dim in comparison. The more time you spend trying to be witty, the more often you will end up sounding like Polonius – making linguistic jokes that no one else finds as funny as you do.

SILENCE AND SPACE

The character's voice is obviously very much about words. But it's not only about words and action. It's also about silence – the space between words. When Pinter and Beckett meticulously write in their pauses and silences, this is what they are writing – the space of silence. The space where something other than words can exist. The space where no words are suitable or sufficient, the space where the voice is defined by its opposite state: the silence of not speaking. It is not just an empty space or pause; it is a full, pregnant, meaningful, expressive one.

There have been some great silences in drama. Shakespeare's Coriolanus is utterly lost for words when his mother and wife persuade him not to vent his fury on the Rome that exiled him. It is a turning point in the play and it is a moment that will ultimately kill him. Konstantin in *The Seagull* spends an aching silence methodically clearing up his papers before leaving the stage in order to kill himself; it is the resolution of the play. Samuel Beckett wrote whole short plays without words. Little Voice doesn't speak words unless she absolutely must and until she is absolutely pushed to the edge. Fin in *The Station Agent* barely speaks for much of the story and his desire to 'be left alone' is at the heart of the story. But silence is not always so critical. Silence is also a means by which what is done and what is said can be absorbed, taken on board, observed. Even in radio, the space of silence and the silence of space is crucial. It's easy to write lots of words. It's harder to demarcate the space around words. Great writing is also knowing when not to write anything at all.

SUBTEXT

It is impossible to 'write' subtext because subtext literally does not exist – it is what is not said, it is below or behind or beyond the text. Therefore it is not text and it can't be written down. But great dramatic writing has subtext, otherwise what is said would ultimately have no depth or complexity or subtlety and therefore be on the nose the whole time. So subtext is the single hardest thing to write well in drama, and not simply because it is logically impossible but, worse, because it requires your characters and story to have real, true, palpable depth.

Subtext is the secret life of the character's thoughts, feelings, instincts, intentions and fears. Subtext is the unspoken conversation that is held between characters when words and acts are not enough. Subtext is the part of us that we are unable, unwilling or afraid to openly express – that we may not even be aware is there to express. Subtext is the extra dimension that brings characters and scenes to fully-fledged life. You should explore the extra dimension in your characters – the thing that makes them a personality like no other as opposed to a stock or archetypal character.

Take any great scene from any great script and ask yourself what is the subtext? The great – and also the most frustrating – thing about it is that, because it isn't stated, it is utterly open to interpretation. And what you find may not be what the writer remotely intended or what anyone else can hear. And in this sense you also can't 'write' it. But the more you invest in your characters, the world and the story, the more subtext audiences will find and the more resonant will be your writing. There is no ongoing delight in discovering the same thing over and over and over again in a story – it is the new things, the new discoveries, the new insights, the new under-standings and depths and layers of character that make subtext. Great dramas get better with each viewing or hearing – not because the words are different but because what is not said can develop and deepen.

WRITING AND REWRITING

If you have been able to resist yourself and haven't already started plough-ing on with the script, then now is the time. If you have gathered together all your plans and materials and tools, if you have looked potential weak-nesses and problems in the eye along the way, if you have worked yourself to the point where you are just itching to write, then now is the time.

You've had ample opportunity to warm yourself up and gestate, nurture and grow your idea. In every script there must come a point where there is no more research, no more preparation – no more delay, no more excuses.

I have argued strongly against writing too soon and for doing the legwork properly. But you also have to learn to recognise when you have checked all the buckles and straps, reached the right altitude and are ready to jump.

FOCUS AND CONTROL

Of course when you do make that leap, you don't then simply flap around as you plummet to the ground below. You put into effect all your training and preparation, you adopt the correct position, you count down to when the parachute must be released, you pull the cord, steer your way down, and you make sure you roll into your landing without breaking both arms and both legs horribly.

I don't mean to scare you with this metaphor. But the writer's equi-valent of broken arms and legs is the complete incapacity to keep writing until the metaphorical bones have healed and you have learned to use the limbs again. So:

➤ Make sure you have everything you need to hand and know where you can find what you need.

➤ Make sure you demarcate a space and time as much as possible so that writing isn't scattergun but a dedicated effort.

➤ Make sure you ask yourself every time you sit down to write: what is the story and why am I writing it?

➤ Make sure you enjoy the writing, despite the difficulties.

➤ And make sure you enjoy your own company – otherwise it will be a lonely experience . . .

EXPECTATIONS

➤ Don't expect to get it right straight away.

➤ Don't expect the road ahead to be even and straight.

➤ Don't expect it to be easy.

➤ Don't necessarily expect to know whether or not it's going well.

➤ Don't presume that if the words are spilling out freely and fluently, then the script will necessarily be good.

➤ Don't worry if you get lost or stuck along the way – so long as you know where you are going, you can get back on track.

➤ Don't think you can go off on major tangents or make a fundamental change to the story on a whim – if they are necessary, you should think and work them through first.

QUESTIONS

Some questions should always be in your head, but especially at this stage:

➤ Is it the story I want to tell?

➤ Am I telling it in a way that suits the story?

➤ Is it the right form?

➤ Is it coherent and whole?

➤ Does it always feel like it's going somewhere?

➤ Am I using clichéd, familiar and predictable ingredients?

➤ Have the characters taken on a life of their own?

➤ Does it ever feel like the story is 'getting away from me'?

> ➤   Does it feel clear in my head even if it appears unclear on the page?
> ➤   If unclear, is it engaging intrigue? Or confusion and incoherence?

REALITIES

Writing a script can feel like a marathon – a monumental journey of endurance where you hit 'the wall' at some point but hopefully have the training, the preparation and the desire to get through it to the end. When you reach that finish line it can be a thrilling, relieving, satisfying moment.

But unfortunately it is just a fleeting moment. Writers are not one-off fun-runners. They are obsessive–compulsive and run every marathon there is to run. So enjoy the moment. But remember to wind down, train down, soak your tired muscles, eat well, sleep well and be prepared to have to go back to it before long.

Actually, it's not quite like a marathon – because in writing it's rather like running a marathon and then having to retrace parts of the route. And if you're really unlucky (or ill-prepared), you may have to run the whole damn thing again from beginning to end.

The chances of you writing a finished script first time round for *any* medium, no matter how well you prepare or how hard you work, are very slim. Paul Andrew Williams describes how writing the actual script of his film *London to Brighton* took more or less a weekend and that he didn't really rewrite it as such. But the story, characters, world, tone and ideas were writing themselves in his head long before. And in that time before, he also made a short film which was a literal precursor, creating the world, characters and tone and using actors that would go on to be cast in the feature-length film.

However you wish to frame it for yourself, the writing and rewriting will happen – no matter which you do before the other. I would argue that Paul did all his rewriting somewhere in his head and in his preparation, before writing the actual script very quickly. Also, he's a director and always planned to shoot it very low-budget so he wasn't writing a calling card script as such – he was preparing the blueprint to make a film. And although the script wasn't endlessly rewritten, the final film went through a kind of rewrite in production and editing. So there's different ways of skinning the proverbial cat. But it's still a cat and it still has skin.

REWRITING

TV and film writers like Paul Abbott have long asserted that 'writing is rewriting'. Yet in debunking contrast, theatre director Dominic Dromgoole has argued that great scripts aren't endlessly rewritten – they are just *written*.

So who is right? What is the real truth? Is 'development' and 'rewriting' necessarily a bad thing? Can writers really just write a play? There is no right answer and there is no real truth: there is what works for you and what doesn't work for you; there is what suits you and what doesn't suit you. And there is what other people ask and expect when they pay you money to write something. But when it's just you, the writer, telling a story you want to tell, and not under commission, then it's simply up to you.

It is true that over-developing things in rewrites can ruin them – just as under-developing them before they are written can ruin them. If only there were a simple truth, life would be a lot easier (and, it is true, many of us would be out of jobs). But there isn't.

Perhaps at the heart of Dromgoole's questioning the value of a bloated development industry is the fact that theatre never suffered without one before – and the bloatedness seems self-serving, capitalising on the vain aspirations of the many who want to be 'writers' rather than really helping great theatre or film or TV get made. When I had the 'literary' role with a regional new writing theatre company it wasn't my job to interfere with scripts, it was my job to find good writers with plays to showcase and help get them on. So I have much sympathy with his argument. Shakespeare and Chekhov and Beckett and many a great writer didn't need a script editor.

However, that doesn't mean they didn't rewrite. Although Shakespeare wrote fast, he did rewrite some of his most popular plays in repertory once they had been produced and he could see whether or not they worked. I think writing and rewriting happens in the head as much (if not more) than on the page (or under the supervision of a script guru). You may have rewritten your story any number of times before you commit it to paper.

Of course, there are some differences between theatre, radio, film and TV. I don't think ongoing development suits a lot of theatre and radio. Generally speaking, the narrative construction and the number and length of scenes are usually far less logistically complex in theatre and radio than in film and TV. In theatre you can try things out in the rehearsal room – in radio, film and TV you pretty much can't. Film and TV is so expensive to make that you have to feel absolutely sure and happy that what is written is worth scheduling and preparing and shooting. Get that wrong and it will be a costly mistake, whereas in theatre you can revisit the play and even lose whole scenes without great financial implications, while sound design and effects in radio mean that it generally costs no more to record any one scene than any other. The deciding factor is the numbers of actors and how long you need to get it the 'take' you want. There are no crane or aerial shots, night shoots, remote locations or massive crews to keep the whole thing going. You can do much on a bare stage or in a radio studio, but there are no blank cheques in film and TV.

REWRITING YOUR SIGNATURE

So what impact does any of this have on your signature calling card script? Well, less than if you're writing an episode of *Casualty*, which must be storylined, scheduled, budgeted and shot on time – all of which is an unavoidable logistical headache.

With signature scripts, however, that aren't written to tight briefs and commissions, you should rewrite as much or as little as you feel is needed. Nobody expects it to be perfect. In fact, I think the industry is slightly suspicious of perfection. They want a strong story and voice, and if that's rough round the edges and raw at its heart, fine – better, even. Producers like having something to work with rather than something cast in aspic.

TIME AND SPACE

Whatever you do, when you have finished what you think is a complete draft, you should put it to one side for a couple of weeks at the very least, do other things. Spend time with family, friends or all those neglected household chores. You need to give yourself the space to come back to the script as fresh as possible.

This is much harder than it sounds. Often writers are itching to take a look. I have asked writers to take a couple of weeks away, come back fresh, and see if the space has given them a useful new perspective. And often they come back within a couple of days having already done a rewrite they say they are totally satisfied with. And they have missed the point.

The point is: give yourself some time and space. It's not a race. It's not a sprint.

OBJECTIVE AND SUBJECTIVE

The near-impossible thing is putting aside our subjectivity – taking an objective look – in part because it is precisely their subjectivity that makes the best writers and their work stand out. But you can try fooling yourself into taking what you believe to be an objective look.

First, you should read your script as you think a random reader might. Print out a clean copy and read it at speed, without taking copious notes or making on-page edits. Do it as if it were a job. Get up, have breakfast, brew a coffee, get settled and read it straight through. This is the closest you'll get to a 'blind' read.

Second, ask yourself all the questions you think a reader might ask. What's is about? Who's it for? What's unique? Why tell this story now? Is it coherent? Does it feel distinct? Does it ring true? Is it clear? What does the story *feel* like? Make notes not on what you might tweak or change, but on what the script does and does not achieve as it stands. Ask yourself what existing work an objective reader might it compare it with – and how it might stand up to that comparison.

Third, know yourself and be honest with yourself. Some writers (for no necessarily bad reason) by default assume that what they have written is great and find it hard to accept what others see as problems and weaknesses. Other writers believe by default that what they have written is crap (even if it isn't) and find it hard to accept it might be good. In truth, the former can tend to be the unsuccessful writers who don't understand why their work isn't being accepted, while the latter may have an intrinsic critical eye and sense of dissatisfaction that stands them in good stead, because they always wish to better their work. But the point is that whatever your natural instinct, you need to consciously counter it and assume the opposite so that you can feel your way towards objectivity.

FEEDBACK

Tricky. If you have people you can trust to be honest, constructive, intelligent and helpful without it damaging your relationship, then use them.

If not, then don't. Friends, family and partners tend not to be useful because they can struggle to be objective about you – or honest with you.

Beware script feedback services unless one comes highly recommended. No feedback can be truly objective, we all carry personal tastes and opinions with us.

Writers' groups can be usefully supportive if you can find one close to home. But beware the failed, bitter rival among the members – the writer whose life is a sour invective against not only the industry that fails to recognise their genius, but also other writers who dare to compete for that industry's attention. Avoid these people. They can't help you.

If you're brave and have access to willing friends (or even professionals), the best thing you can have is a private reading. Get in some food and wine of an evening, read the script through, and talk it over. What you hear and don't hear in a reading can be worth reams of 'feedback'. But don't cast yourself in the lead role – you need to sit back and listen and hear and think and take notes rather than be wondering how to deliver a line.

It's true that although this can work brilliantly well for theatre and radio, it might work less well for film and TV simply because the formats don't lend themselves easily to a reading. So if you're doing a reading of a screenplay, you need someone really good to read the 'action' at pace.

THE RED PEN

You should learn to love the red pen. I reckon that for most great writers there is a moment where they come to realise, often after a struggle, how liberating it is to be able to wield the red pen and not be afraid to do whatever it takes to make their script work.

Only when you've done what you can to stand back and see the forest for the trees should you hunker back down and go through the script line by line, tree by tree. Make sure you have the time and space and concentration – if you don't, wait until you do. It's hard to do it in snatches. Ready yourself and do it properly.

Always print out a clean hard copy and use a coloured pen. Don't sit and read on a computer screen – because you will start tinkering straight away. Save making the on-screen edits for another day.

RECLAIM YOUR SUBJECTIVITY

The greatest danger is that you get so lost in rewriting and tinkering that you edit your voice and personality out of the script. This is fatal. You need to reclaim your subjectivity and reaffirm what it is that is *you* about this story and the way it's been told.

Nobody can tell you what is instinctively right: it's your story, and only you can do that. Whenever it's starting to feel like it's no longer your story, whatever the reason, then you need to put the script aside and ask yourself again what makes it yours – and then go back and see what it is that has thrown you off course.

IS IT REALLY FINISHED?

A script is never finished unless it has finished being made. Stage plays change over the course of a run and then again in new productions. Radio, TV and film changes in the edit right up until the final locked-off version. So it's not so much that the script is never finished, rather that your writing of it can come to a conclusion – whether or not it is made.

Unless your calling card is produced, then perhaps it will never be truly finished. But don't rewrite it and tinker with it interminably. Get yourself to the point where you've done what you can and then see how the world reacts to it. And if you get back a great note or piece of advice, then tinker away. But in the meantime – start something new.

HOW FINISHED DOES IT NEED TO BE?

As I've said, nobody expects perfection. We can embrace rawness, roughness, imperfection and even a right old mess so long as there are things in there that genuinely excite and engage us. You need to stop writing at some point but the script doesn't need to be 'finished'. As I once heard TV writer Tony Grounds say, it just needs to be 'ready to be read'. And if someone comes back excited about the possibilities of working with it and/or working with you, then your script has done its job with a flourish. It may never be made, but it will have been well worth the hard work of writing it.

A writer I know well who has some brilliant original calling card scripts for TV and film lives in eternal hope that they might one day be made. He fully appreciates and accepts that they probably won't. But those scripts have helped him get an agent, get on to a TV development scheme I put together, and consequently earned him some fantastic commissions for high-end, prime-time TV shows and more. They have helped him become a real, successful, proper writer.

It all started with a great calling card script.

CODA

So you've 'finished' a script. You've done all you can to get it right. It's ready to be read. You should feel satisfied and excited. You deserve to feel pleased with yourself.

But I'm afraid it doesn't end there. You've been through the beginning, middle and end, and arrived at the end of *this* journey as a writer. Yet it's only one script, one journey – one stage. The final word is that there are more marathons to come and although you need to rest and recover, you can't sit still for too long.

STARTING OVER

Just about every great ending is a beginning too, and that's no less the case for you. Great writers don't stand still, they keep moving. They write more. They can't help it. There are stories to tell and things to say and ideas to realise. The mark of a real writer is the next thing, and the next thing after that, and the next thing after that. They are always starting over.

Not every new script will be an original signature piece. If you're extremely lucky (and brilliant) then there will be commissions to briefs, or gigs on shows, or ideas to develop from scratch with a producer, or other and new mediums and formats to explore. But in a sense I think every new script is a statement of who you are at that point in your life and development as a writer. Every script is a kind of calling card script.

IT NEVER GETS ANY EASIER

At this point I should fill you with an inspirational hope, like a coach pushing his team to get that winning goal, no matter what the odds against it may be. ('Come on, you can do it! I believe in you! You can be a contender!') But in writing there is no full-time or winning goal as such. It's a game you just have to continue playing.

It never gets any easier. I heard Russell T. Davies say this at the absolute pinnacle of his spectacular roll with *Doctor Who* and its spin-offs. Looking back, he was able to say that every new script offers the same difficult challenge. At one time he thought success and experience would soon make writing easier. But it doesn't. It makes him more experienced and practised, more confident, resilient, understanding, knowing, insightful, ready and prepared. But that doesn't make the moment at which the writer must write, and the instinct and voice must speak, get any easier. It's always hard. It's meant to be hard. If it were easy, your script wouldn't be any good.

But if you're willing to embrace this, to keep writing, keep working, keep improving, keep thinking, keep developing, keep expressing, then you will have mastered the use of one of the most important tools in your toolbox: perseverance. Without it, all your talent and potential will never be expressed and realised. So make a virtue of 'difficult'. Relish it. Use it. Embrace it. It will help you be a better writer.

No short cuts. No tricks. No easy ways out.

Just the sheer difficult wonder of the act of telling a story that other people might want to hear.

Appendix

SCRIPT READING AND VIEWING

There are some works to which I refer regularly and which I recommend heartily. Many are available in script form; some you'll just have to watch and wonder what the script looks like . . .

A Number by Caryl Churchill (Nick Hern Books)
A Room for Romeo Brass by Paul Fraser, Shane Meadows (Screenpress)
Being Human by Toby Whithouse (BBC Writersroom website)
Betrayal by Harold Pinter (Faber)
Billy Elliot by Lee Hall (Faber)
Blue/Orange by Joe Penhall (Methuen Drama)
Bodies by Jed Mercurio (BBC)
Children of Men (dir. Alfonso Cuaron)
Chinatown by Robert Towne (Faber)
Closer by Patrick Marber (Methuen Drama)
Comedians by Trevor Griffiths (Faber)
Coriolanus by William Shakespeare
Criminal Justice II by Peter Moffat (BBC Writersroom website)
Dead Man's Shoes (dir. Shane Meadows)
EastEnders ('Pretty Baby') by Tony Jordan (BBC Writersroom website)
Eternal Sunshine of the Spotless Mind by Charlie Kaufman (Nick Hern)
Fargo by Joel Coen (Faber Reel Classics)
Hamlet by William Shakespeare
Hidden (dir. Michael Haneke)
Hustle by Tony Jordan (BBC Writersroom website)
Let the Right One In (dir. Tomas Alfredson)
Life on Mars by Matthew Graham (BBC Writersroom website)
Memento (dir. Chris Nolan)
Moon (dir. Duncan Jones)
My Summer of Love (dir. Pavel Pawlikovski)
Oh Brother Where Art Thou? (dir. Joel Coen)

Othello by William Shakespeare
Saved by Edward Bond (Methuen Drama)
Seven Streams of the River Ota by Robert Lepage, Eric Bernier (Methuen)
Shameless by Paul Abbott (Channel 4)
Spoonface Steinberg by Lee Hall (Methuen Drama)
Star Wars by George Lucas
State of Play by Paul Abbott (BBC)
Talking Heads by Alan Bennett (BBC Books)
The Birthday Party by Harold Pinter (Faber)
The Colony by Dennis Kelly (BBC Writersroom website)
The Crying Game by Neil Jordan (Vintage)
The Hitchhiker's Guide to the Galaxy by Douglas Adams (BBC)
The Incomplete Recorded Works of a Dead Body by Ed Hime
  (BBC Writersroom website)
The Lesson by Eugene Ionesco (Penguin)
The Rise and Fall of Little Voice by Jim Cartwright (Methuen Drama)
The Seagull by Anton Chekhov, trans. Christopher Hampton (Faber)
The Sopranos by David Chase (HBO)
The Station Agent (dir. Thomas McCarthy)
This is England (dir. Shane Meadows)
Twin Peaks by David Lynch (ABC)
When You Cure Me by Jack Thorne (Nick Hern)

BOOKS ABOUT WRITING

There are a million and one other books you might read and they all have
a worth and a use – even if just to confirm that you disagree with everything they say. But here are some that are either favourites of mine or ones
that have become common currency and therefore you ought to know about.

Alexander Mackendrick, *On Film-making: An Introduction to the Craft of
  the Director* (ed. Paul Cronin) – not on scriptwriting, but full of insight
  from a writer and maker of films who truly understood screenwriting.
Robert Towne, *Film Makers on Film Makers* (ed. Joseph McBride) – a
  brilliantly insightful interview-chapter on film with a master screenwriter.

William Goldman, *Adventures in the Screen Trade* – also not a book on scriptwriting, but one on what it was like to be a scriptwriter during a remarkable period in movie history.

Frederick Raphael, *Eyes Wide Open: A Memoir of Stanley Kubrick* – again not a book on scriptwriting, but on developing a script for a famous director.

Aristotle, *Poetics* – don't read this if you are hoping it might help you write your script, but do read it if you want to see the first extant piece of writing about drama.

Dominic Dromgoole, *The Full Room* – a brutally honest, devastatingly entertaining view of modern British playwrights.

Paul Schrader, *Schrader on Schrader* (ed. Kevin Jackson) – not just about writing, but a great insight into the man behind some great films.

Robert McKee, *Story* – love it or hate it, it is a Hollywood industry standard and an essential read.

Christopher Vogler, *The Writer's Journey* – an essential read for anyone with an interest in the power of story archetypes.

Syd Field – has written various books and is the master of handy, punchy, practical tips on developing a screenplay (for Hollywood).

Dara Marks, *Inside Story* – an intense book for anyone who wants to dig deeper and deeper into film characters' stories.

Adrian Mead, *Making it as a Screenwriter* – a brilliantly handy take on how to create a career out of scriptwriting from someone who did just that.

Julian Friedmann, *How to Make Money Scriptwriting* – it's no fun being a writer if you can't make a living out of it . . .

William Smethurst, *How to Write for Television: A Guide to Writing and Selling Successful TV Script* – a no-nonsense overview of writing for television.

Val Taylor, *Stage Writing: A Practical Guide* – full of sharply intelligent and practical insights.

Philip Parker, *The Art and Science of Screenwriting* – likewise full of sharply intelligent and practical insights.

RESOURCES

There are all kinds of resources, but the important ones are those where you can read produced scripts, get up-to-date information on how to get your work considered, find opportunities to apply for, or find writer networks. The BBC writersroom is a first point of call for all these things – explore the links section for other useful places to go.

BBC Writersroom: www.bbc.co.uk/writersroom
Writers' Guild: www.writersguild.org.uk
Twelve Point: www.twelvepoint.com
Simply Scripts: www.simplyscripts.com
Writers' and Artists' Yearbook: www.writersandartists.co.uk

Index